D1531714

Critical textwork

Critical textwork

**An introduction to varieties
of discourse and analysis**

**IAN PARKER AND THE
BOLTON DISCOURSE NETWORK**

Open University Press
Buckingham • Philadelphia

Open University Press
Celtic Court
22 Ballmoor
Buckingham
MK18 1XW

email: enquiries@openup.co.uk
World wide web: http://www.openup.co.uk

and
325 Chestnut Street
Philadelphia, PA 19106, USA

First Published 1999

Copyright © Ian Parker and the Bolton Discourse Network 1999

A catalogue record of this book is available from the British Library

ISBN 0 335 20204 7 (pbk) 0 335 20205 5 (hbk)

Library of Congress Cataloging-in-Publication Data
Critical textwork : an introduction to varieties of discourse and
    analysis / [edited by] Ian Parker and the Bolton Discourse Network.
        p.   cm.
    Includes bibliographical references and index.
    ISBN 0–335–20205–5. — ISBN 0–335–20204–7 (pbk.)
    1. Discourse analysis. I. Parker, Ian, 1956– . II. Bolton
Discourse Network.
    P302.C686 1999
    401'.41—dc21   98–39283
                                                              CIP

Typeset by Graphicraft Limited, Hong Kong
Printed in Great Britain by Biddles Limited, Guildford and Kings Lynn

Contents

Notes on contributing authors

The **Bolton Discourse Network** is an interdisciplinary forum for inter-disciplinary research into different forms of text, based at Bolton Institute. **John Allbutt** is a lecturer in psychology with research interests in deafness, sign language and human rights. **Kate Bevan** lectures in media studies, and is currently researching the implications of media for Asian youth. **Sam Bevan** was a Senior Lecturer in Education Studies and is now doing an MA in cultural studies. **Barbara Delafield** is conducting research on philosophy for children, and has presented papers to BPS conferences on this theme. **Hakan Durmaz** is carrying out research on the body, intimacy and the market. **Christine Noble** is a registered psychiatric nurse, and is currently conducting research on community support in mental health. **Susan Ford** is Senior Lecturer in Urban and Cultural Studies, and has published work on gardens in the field of cultural geography. **Dan Goodley** is a lecturer in psychology and a researcher and activist around issues of disability. **Sarah Gray** is a final year psychology student. **Dan Heggs** has an MA in psychoanalytic studies, and is conducting research on the contemporary graphic novel. **Heather Höpfl** is Professor of Organisational Psychology in the Business School, and publishes widely in management journals. **Mike Humphreys** is senior lecturer in education, teaches management in education and health settings, researches in organizational culture and has research links with Turkey. **Martine C. Middleton** is lecturer in cultural studies, and publishes in the field of urban geography. **David J. Nightingale** is lecturer in social psychology, and has published in the field of critical psychology. **Ian Parker** is Professor of Psychology, and writes on critical approaches in psychology and psychoanalytic social theory. **Richard Pearce** is a lecturer in marketing at the University of Central Lancashire. He writes on issues in business ethics, and social constructionism in the marketing context. **Tom Phillips** teaches in areas of community studies and health psychology and is Health and Social Studies Subject Leader. **David Rudd** works in Learning Support Services and is author of a number of publications on children's literature. **Helen Russell** lectures in psychology and is conducting research on the structure and function of the cultic subject. **Beverlea Schofield** is a tutor for the deaf and a sign language teacher.

Foreword

Recent years have seen a transformation in the social sciences and in the language that researchers use to make sense of action and experience. This transformation has also opened up a space in academic institutions for reflexive questioning about what that language does in the world. Critical research on discourse, text and the social construction of things that were once taken for granted has inspired work across the disciplines, including cultural studies, psychology, sociology and human geography. It is now time to take stock of what we have accomplished and where we are going with this work, and so these three books review social constructionist perspectives in order to explore new ground creatively.

We accomplish three things: produce a clear theoretical overview of social constructionist frameworks; move our understanding of textuality beyond language; and embed analysis of discourse in an account of practice. There is a different emphasis in each book: Nightingale and Cromby's *Social Constructionist Psychology* surveys existing work and gathers together critical reflections on the conditions and limits of research on language; Parker and the Bolton Discourse Network's *Critical Textwork* elaborates and extends the compass of research to many kinds of textual domain; and Willig's *Applied Discourse Analysis* consistently and provocatively asks through a range of examples how such research can be made useful.

There are fruitful overlaps, with examples of discourse analysis, discussions of types of text and theoretical reflections on the social construction of meaning in each. Together the books address different facets of a common task – they take forward critical social constructionist research on discursive practice.

Ian Parker
Professor of Psychology
Bolton Institute

1 Introduction: varieties of discourse and analysis

IAN PARKER

The study of discourse is usually confined to speech and writing, and it always eventually focuses on the *writing*, whether that is in interviews which are transcribed and then analysed or newspaper articles which are already neatly set out in written form. This book moves well beyond the scope of that kind of discourse analytic work to show how a wide range of texts can be opened up and read using different innovative methods. The early chapters do describe approaches to speech and writing, but then the book progressively extends the compass of discourse research to explore methodological issues of reading and representation applied to symbolic systems that are not usually thought of as textual. We provide critical descriptions of how we might analyse material from visual media and physical settings, and we also reflect on the role of the researcher in the texts he or she studies. The book illustrates ways in which discourse may be studied wherever there is meaning, and so it also includes an accessible introduction to the principles of discourse research across many kinds of texts.

This introduction provides an overview of the development of discourse analysis and textual research in the human sciences, and the underlying assumptions about representation, conceptualization of the research object and methodological principles which guide critical reading of cultural phenomena.

Reference points

The analyses of texts in this book are all grounded in certain shared assumptions about qualitative research, the role of interpretation, our objects of study as discourse and text, and problems that face researchers as they translate their analysis back into a written form.

Qualitative research

There is no quantitative analysis in these chapters, and we believe that approaches like 'content analysis' or attempts to use computer software to count and group words or phrases are likely to come to grief because they make a fundamental mistake about the nature of meaning. Words and phrases do not come ready packaged with a specific delimited meaning that a researcher can be sure to know as if they were fixed and self-contained. Rather, it is the interweaving of words and phrases in different contexts that gives them their sense, and when we attempt to grasp patterns in a text we always have to carry out that exercise against a cultural backdrop. The cultural backdrop is made up of many different social worlds (such as classrooms, families, clubs), subcultures (including age bands, classes and regions) and, in most societies, languages (and dialects). These provide shared systems of meaning that we selectively draw upon to communicate to each other. We share this complex contradictory backdrop as readers in the process of doing discursive research with those who read our analysis, and this activity of construction and assessment is a profoundly *qualitative* issue (Denzin and Lincoln 1994).

We would go as far as to say that any retreat to set 'methods' will end up restricting our understanding of the complexity and multiplicity of meaning, and you will find in the chapters a careful consideration of which particular approaches will help us best to illuminate a text, to help us to highlight nuances of meaning and patterns we all usually let pass by un-noticed. Instead of trying to construct a discourse analytic machine which we could then use to shred all varieties of text, we have presented 'ways of reading' that may be useful and which will have to be adapted and modified for other circumstances. When we show you these examples, we also want to make clear some of the interpretative activity that re-searchers have to engage in as they develop a 'method'. Every discourse analytic researcher has to go through that process of arriving at an appropriate method if he or she is to be true to the text. We see discourse analysis as being characterized by a sensitivity to language above any 'steps' to analysis, and, as with other forms of qualitative research, we see that sensitivity to language as being suffused with *interpretation* (Banister *et al.* 1994).

Discourse analysis

One of the difficulties students new to discourse research face is the be-wildering variety of approaches to the study of texts that go under the heading of 'discourse analysis' (e.g. Gilbert and Mulkay 1984; Stubbs 1993; Fairclough 1995). There are distinctive approaches in different disciplines, and in this book we have drawn upon methodological approaches which have offered something specific for the type of text in question. These approaches each have their own subtly different understanding of 'discourse' and 'text'.

Discourse

The term 'discourse' is sometimes used to refer to patterns of meaning which organize the various symbolic systems human beings inhabit, and which are necessary for us to make sense to each other. For example, a 'familial' discourse will describe relationships as revolving around a nuclear family structure as if it were natural and universal, and as if all the other ways we live in the world must be measured against it (Barrett and McIntosh 1982). It is important to emphasize here that the way we use the term discourse is not restricted to language, as it appears to be in some accounts of discourse analysis (e.g. Sinclair and Coulthard 1975; Brown and Yule 1983). Foucault's (1969: 49) maxim that discourses are 'prac-tices that systematically form the objects of which they speak' is useful here, for it draws attention to the way these 'practices' include patterns of meaning that may be visual or spatial, that may comprise face-to-face interaction or the organization of national boundaries. The 'objects' that such practices create (or 'form' in Foucault's words) will include all the things that we see, refer to and take for granted as actually existing 'out there'.

The kinds of analysis that have made use of Foucault's work (e.g. Fairclough 1990; Parker 1992) have tended to fracture texts into different discrete discourses which then hold positions for speakers and reproduce relations of power. Sometimes the term 'discourse' is used more broadly, to refer to the whole symbolic domain, and analysis is then of things that are done with discourse by speakers (e.g. Billig 1991) or of the distinct 'interpretative repertoires' they employ (e.g. Wetherell and Potter 1992).

Text

Sometimes the term 'text' is used in an all-encompassing way too, espe-cially in linguistics (e.g. Crystal 1987), and it is true that there is something artificial about abstracting an article or a piece of conversation from its context and studying it as 'the text'. Notwithstanding this, when we refer to the collections of sentences, figures or images that comprise our ex-amples in the chapters in this book as our 'texts', we are doing this in order to delimit an object of analysis. For *these* purposes, then, a text is any tissue of meaning which is symbolically significant for a reader (Parker 1992). As we read a text, of course, we produce something different, another text which is a *translation* and which we then subject to a discourse analysis. This translation is all the more dramatic when we try to move away from spoken and written texts which can easily be caught and pasted into a research study.

Translation

Much of the analysis conducted within the 'turn to discourse' in the human sciences and employing a variety of different frameworks for studying texts has still, in practice, confined itself to spoken or written texts (e.g. Potter and Wetherell 1987; van Dijk 1997). In the process of transcribing speech in interviews or group discussions, of course, the research always eventually reduces the spoken to the written. It is *writing* that is taken as the paradigmatic text, the model form for discourse analytic research. Conversation analysis in linguistics, psychology and sociology, for example, has rested on the assumption that 'discourse' is equivalent to speech or writing, whether in formal texts or in everyday conversation (e.g. Atkinson and Heritage 1984). Studies in the field of advertising (e.g. Williamson 1978), television (e.g. Fiske and Hartley 1978) and cultural studies (e.g. Hebdige 1979) have also often proceeded by way of a description, and so translation, of the text concerned into a written mode to permit analysis. In cultural studies and sociology, including feminist research and postcolonial work, the reflexive interrogation of the position of the reader has been through diary, ethnographic and fictional written representation of experience (Denzin and Lincoln 1994).

Of course, all the contributors to this book have had to engage in that process of translation so that you may now read their analyses as *written* chapters. It would be an unusual and bizarre book indeed that could actually include all the kinds of text we have analysed. In some cases we have been able to put pictures into the text box, but in most the best we could do was to reflect on that process of translation and show you aspects of analysis which tried to be true to the form of text while presenting it or, more precisely, *re-presenting* it to you.

Theoretical resources

A text cannot be read and represented in a piece of analysis without some theoretical work. Just as readers always approach a new book with certain assumptions which help them frame and interpret what they find, so a researcher always draws upon certain theoretical frames. The contributors in the different chapters explain which theoretical ideas they find most useful, and the variety of texts call upon a variety of theories. Some key theoretical ideas have guided us, even though we use these in different ways.

There has been a shift of attention across the human sciences in the past 25 years from a notion of representation as a direct or mediated reflection of reality to a conceptual and methodological account of representation as a form of *signification* which 'itself gives shape to the reality it implicates' (Henriques *et al.* 1984: 99). While a representation is *of* something which seems to lie outside, as if we just need to find the correct terms to capture and express its real nature, 'signification' draws our attention to the process of *forming* things. Instead of trying to tie things down, then, we are encouraged to trace the place of a word or phrase in the context of a symbolic system and to ask questions about its contradictions, how it is constructed and what it does.

Theories of meaning

The theoretical resources and pragmatic concerns of researchers studying signification have varied in the different disciplines. They have, for example, included a concern with ideology-critique drawing on structuralist and post-structuralist theory in cultural studies and literary theory (e.g. MacDonnell 1986), the analysis of action and cognition drawing on social constructionism and discourse analysis in psychology (e.g. Middleton and Edwards 1990) and the study of everyday and expert knowledge in conversation analysis and the sociology of scientific knowledge (e.g. Gilbert and Mulkay, 1984). In each case the focus has turned to how texts are structured and what functions they perform.

Structuralism

The broad range of structuralist theories of meaning – of 'semiology' and 'semiotics' – that derive from the work of the structural linguist Saussure (1974) are useful in drawing attention to the way that the meaning of any particular term is governed by its *relations* with other terms (Hawkes 1977). The study of these relations of 'difference' in networks of meaning underpins structuralism, post-structuralism and, more recently, postmodern approaches (Sarup 1988). Rather than looking for something underneath or behind a text (whether that is in a real world outside or in unconscious wishes hidden inside the head), these approaches stress the way language is structured independently of our intentions. It would not make sense to ask authors of texts what they 'really' meant.

Hermeneutics

At the same time, however, discourse analysis is trying to find its way through the patterns of signification, to make sense within what writers in the 'hermeneutic' tradition call the 'horizon of meaning' of a text (e.g. Gauld and Shotter 1977). Although there are objections in the realm of literary theory to some of the ways hermeneutics tries to uncover the real meaning of a text (e.g. Eagleton 1983), these ideas have been important in the social sciences through approaches like 'grounded theory' (e.g. Glaser and Strauss 1967).

Power

I wrote above that we draw upon different shared systems of meaning to communicate to others, but the process is a little more complicated than that, for as we use language we are also used by it. One of the important implications of structuralist and post-structuralist accounts of language is that we are not entirely in control of meaning. Words and phrases have meanings that are organized into systems and institutions, what Foucault (1969) called 'discursive practices' that *position* us in relations of power. The recent anxiety over 'political correctness' and the way language does things to us and to others regardless of our best intentions is an expression of a growing awareness of this, and more people than ever are doing little bits of discourse analysis in the real world as they notice what language is doing and try to correct it (Cameron 1997). Discourse analysis will not tell us what is 'correct' or not, but it does alert us to the intimate connections between meaning, power and knowledge (Foucault 1980). We are drawn into relations of power when we make meaning and it makes us who we are.

Reading and writing

As we read and write texts in discourse analysis we focus on three key aspects of language: contradiction, construction and practice. Social psychologists have usefully drawn attention to these aspects as variability, construction and function (Potter and Wetherell 1987). This means that we ask questions of the text as we read it.

Contradiction
What different meanings are at work in the text? Instead of trying to uncover an underlying theme which will explain the real meaning of the text, we look for the contradictions between different significations, and the way different pictures of the world are formed. We can go further than this, and it is often possible to identify dominant meanings, those that are part of cultural 'myth' or ideology (Barthes 1957). Some studies of discourse then attempt to recover subordinate meanings and highlight processes of resistance (e.g. Burman et al. 1996; Willig 1999).

Construction
How are these meanings constructed? Here we refuse to take anything for granted, and we try to trace how texts have been 'socially constructed' so that they make sense to readers (Burr 1995). Some researchers are concerned that this may lead us to abandon an account of the real conditions that make texts possible (e.g. Parker 1998), but we do need to suspend disbelief at this stage in discourse analysis to be able to unravel how the text works.

Practice
What are these contradictory systems of meaning doing? In some cultures, for some people, everything seems to fit into place and run smoothly. It is significant that cultures where there has been open contest over the nature of meaning and the organization of space have seen the development of forms of discourse analysis which are concerned with the political functions of texts (e.g. Levett *et al.* 1997).

Here we are concerned with issues of power, and we also want to open up a place for *agency*, as people struggle to make sense of texts. This is where people push at the limits of what is socially constructed and actively construct something different (Nightingale and Cromby 1999). We address this issue in discourse analysis when we include reflections on researcher subjectivity. Our attention to contradiction, construction and practice combined with an attention to the position of the researcher leads us to something we call 'critical textwork'.

Critical textwork

The original research reported in this book is designed to illustrate the value of discourse analytic readings of texts and to present ways of reading which respect the particular *form* of the text. Plenty could be said about the content in each case, and it would be possible to take any general model of discourse and apply it, but we see our task as exploring what is *specific* about the text and tackling the problems it raises for discourse analysis head on.

Organization of the book

The book is divided into four parts which bit by bit lead the reader into more and more unusual territory. Two trends will become increasingly apparent. The first is that discourse analytic research needs to be all the more interdisciplinary in order to be able to read texts that do not have the form of speech or writing that we usually take for granted as properties of 'text'. Work from literary theory is already used in the early chapters, but analyses of visual media also need to draw upon cultural studies. Likewise, the analyses of physical settings need to draw upon research in geography and urban studies. The second trend is the critical reflexive attention to the position of the researcher, the way *analysts* becomes part of the text and must be able to turn around, to take account of the way they represent a text to an academic audience and take responsibility for their activity in the construction of meaning. These issues are raised early on in the book, but we have devoted the last part of the book, on subjectivity in research, to exploring these concerns. In this way, we hope, we remain true not only to the reference points and theoretical resources we use in our research but also to an awareness of what we are doing in our rereading and rewriting.

Part I, which is devoted to spoken and written texts, describes the way concepts and methods from conversation analysis, discourse analysis and hermeneutics can be used to tackle textual material that always ends up being translated from speech and represented in written form before the analysis takes place. Here we have some illustrations of how discourse analysts make sense of interviews, letters, fiction and lessons. Even though each of these kinds of text can be reduced quite easily to written form, there are quite specific characteristics of the organization of speech and writing here that have to be respected. There is an attention in each chapter to the specific qualities of the text under consideration and an assessment of the theoretical framework adopted to read it.

Part II turns to visual texts, and explores modes of reading drawing on structuralism, semiotics, psychoanalysis and activity theory to re-present and analyse material that is primarily pictorial in form. These texts are comics, advertising, television and film. In some cases, as in the examples of comic texts and advertisements, the material is static and can be 'captured' by analysts even though it has to be wrenched out of shape as they try to redescribe their object of study to the reader. In other cases, in television and film, we do even more violence to the text as we stop its flow and present a snapshot, and different strategies are suggested in these chapters which may help us to address this problem. Here we focus on the varieties of transformation from the visual medium to written analysis that permit and obstruct a faithful rendition and interpretation of discourse.

Part III is concerned with physical texts, and the analyses in this part of the book include reference to studies of the architecture and microphysics of power in Foucauldian research. Here we move into the realm of studies of 'discursive practice' and a conception of textuality as a material force, with analyses of cities, organizations, gardens and sign language. These chapters are concerned with different kinds of physical embodiment that fabricate certain spaces and meanings for conduct. We 'move around' all kinds of text, metaphorically speaking, finding ways into the systems of meaning that comprise them so that they make sense and vantage points from which we can summarize themes and start to identify contradictions. In the case of the physical texts analysed in this third part of the book, we really can move around them and we must inhabit them, we must live them to be able to read them. This brings us to the position we take up in our research, and so to the last part of the book.

Part IV, on subjectivity in research, shifts attention from the 'written' – whether we are looking at actual written, at visual or at physical material as kinds of writing – to the researcher as *reader* of texts. These chapters elaborate ways of reflecting upon the position of the researcher, the ethics of translation and the imposition of expert narratives upon varieties of experience. The immediate topics include bodies, ethnography, silence and action, but each is an opportunity for us to focus on the possibilities of 'reading' the positions of researcher and researched and the relationships that are constructed between them within specific horizons of meaning. The settings which demand attention to these issues – working with the bodies we inhabit, interviewing in a different culture, caring for people diagnosed as schizophrenic and trying to change oppressive conditions faced by people with disabilities – are quite different and call for specific strategies to understand them as forms of text.

The issues raised towards the end of the book can also, of course, be turned back upon the analyses presented in the early chapters, and we are keen to see the development of forms of reading that would take these issues further with respect to all forms of discourse research. When we conduct interviews, for example, we are always participating in the account our co-researcher offers us and contributing to the sense that emerges. And every piece of text is both a medium for the communication of meaning and a physical thing, so that the material activity of leafing through transcripts is different from holding a book or discovering and deciphering long-lost love letters.

Organization of the chapters

All chapters have a common structure. We start with a *review of the methodological literature on the form of text* in question. The focus is on the particular *form* of text rather than on the topic, and with the specific issues raised by the *mode of representation*, and the ways in which a researcher might produce an illuminating reading of the text. The aim here is to provide a brief overview of existing approaches to this kind of text and so to arrive at a rationale for the approach that may be most useful for the particular example. This is followed by a *brief account of the characteristics of the specific text*. This serves to narrow down the focus, and to specify exactly which theoretical and methodological themes from the review so far will be employed to give a reading. The key task here is to explain why *these* themes are appropriate to *this* particular text.

We then present the *text example*, and this consists of pieces of transcript, images or, in some cases, a detailed description and reflection on the organization of the text. We have set ourselves the task of 'capturing' the text so that it can be displayed in a text box. For some of the chapters on physical texts and research subjectivity this material comprises detailed descriptions of material or an activity or a setting. Now we arrive at the *critical description and analytic reading*. This section brings the theoretical and methodological themes reviewed so far to bear on the text.

We have included an assessment in each chapter. First we consider the *disadvantages of the approach*, and this section anticipates critical responses to the analysis from within other relevant paradigms (those which have been reviewed in the first section of the chapter) and objections to the reading from practitioners of more 'traditional research approaches (within disciplines which have studied this kind of material). Then we review the *advantages of the approach*. This section responds to the possible objections raised earlier, and includes some observations on the value of the specific theoretical and methodological themes, showing how they add to our understanding of the form and functions of the text, and also comments on the value of a discursive framework generally in illuminating the text, compared with other more orthodox research strategies.

Here we move from the realm of the particular text to some more general issues about discourse analysis. There are, of course, a host of objections to discourse analysis from traditional researchers who imagine that only those things that can be measured are worth studying. This book does not address itself to the disputes between those who look to quantitative analysis as the mark of real science. We stand by our activity of interpretation, and invite the reader to assess whether the readings we have offered do justice to the bits of text. However, we have taken seriously concerns about the limits of discourse analysis which are constructive and are trying to find a better way to read the signs that make up human culture. Some general worries have been expressed about the model of the 'text' for analysing meaning (e.g. Parker and Burman 1993) and the 'esoteric' language that discourse researchers sometimes employ (van Dijk 1995). Each chapter concludes with two suggestions for further *key reading* that could take analysis and debate further.

Although the common chapter structure we have adopted here imposes some quite strict limitations, we expect that the book will be clearer and more useful as a result. We have wanted to challenge the ways a focus on written material as a model for analysis of the many varieties of text that we absorb and traverse in the course of our lives imposes limitations. And so we hope now that readers will be able to go beyond the limits of discourse and analysis in this book and engage in some even more critical textwork.

References

Atkinson, J. M. and Heritage, J. C. (eds) (1984) *Structures of Social Action: Studies in Conversation Analysis*. Cambridge: Cambridge University Press.
Banister, P., Burman, E., Parker, I., Taylor, M. and Tindall, C. (1994) *Qualitative Methods in Psychology: A Research Guide*. Buckingham: Open University Press.
Barrett, M. and McIntosh, M. (1982) *The Anti-social Family*. London: Verso.
Barthes, R. (1957/1973) *Mythologies*. London: Paladin.
Billig, M. (1991) *Ideology and Opinions*. London: Sage.
Brown, G. and Yule, G. (1983) *Discourse Analysis*. Cambridge: Cambridge University Press.
Burman, E., Aitken, G., Alldred, P., Allwood, R., Billington, T., Goldberg, B., Gordo-López, A. J., Heenan, C., Marks, D. and Warner, S. (1996) *Psychology Discourse Practice: From Regulation to Resistance*. London: Taylor and Francis.
Burr, V. (1995) *An Introduction to Social Constructionism*. London: Routledge.
Cameron, D. (1997) *Verbal Hygiene*. London: Routledge.
Crystal, D. (1987) *The Cambridge Encyclopaedia of Language*. Cambridge: Cambridge University Press.
Denzin, N. K. and Lincoln, Y. (eds) (1994) *Handbook of Qualitative Research*. London: Sage.
Eagleton, T. (1983) *Literary Theory: An Introduction*. Oxford: Blackwell.
Fairclough, N. (1990) *Discourse Analysis*. Cambridge: Polity Press.
Fairclough, N. (1995) *Critical Discourse Analysis*. London: Longman.
Fiske, J. and Hartley, J. (1978) *Reading Television*. London: Methuen.
Foucault, M. (1969/1972) *The Archaeology of Knowledge*. London: Tavistock.
Foucault, M. (1980) *Power/Knowledge: Selected Interviews and Other Writings 1972–1977*. Brighton: Harvester Wheatsheaf.
Gauld, A. O. and Shotter, J. (1977) *Human Action and Its Investigation*. London: Routledge and Kegan Paul.
Gilbert, N. and Mulkay, M. (1984) *Opening Pandora's Box: A Sociological Analysis of Scientists' Discourse*. Cambridge: Cambridge University Press.
Glaser, B. G. and Strauss, A. L. (1967) *The Discovery of Grounded Theory: Strategies for Qualitative Research*. Chicago: Aldine.
Hawkes, T. (1977) *Structuralism and Semiotics*. London: Methuen.
Hebdige, D. (1979) *Subculture: The Meaning of Style*. London: Methuen.
Henriques, J., Hollway, W., Urwin, C., Venn, C. and Walkerdine, V. (1984) *Changing the Subject: Psychology, Social Regulation and Subjectivity*. London: Methuen.
Levett, A., Kottler, A., Burman, E. and Parker, I. (eds) (1997) *Culture, Power and Difference: Discourse Analysis in South Africa*. London: Zed Books.
MacDonnell, D. (1986) *Theories of Discourse: An Introduction*. Oxford: Blackwell.
Middleton, D. and Edwards, D. (eds) (1990) *Collective Remembering*. London: Sage.
Nightingale, D. J. and Cromby, J. (eds) (1999) *Social Constructionist Psychology: A Critical Analysis of Theory and Practice*. Buckingham: Open University Press.
Parker, I. (1992) *Discourse Dynamics: Critical Analysis for Individual and Social Psychology*. London: Routledge.

Parker, I. (ed.) (1998) *Social Constructionism, Discourse and Realism*. London: Sage.

Parker, I. and Burman, E. (1993) Against discursive imperialism, empiricism and constructionism: thirty two problems with discourse analysis. In E. Burman and I. Parker (eds) *Discourse Analytic Research: Repertoires and Readings of Texts in Action*. London and New York: Routledge.

Potter, J. and Wetherell, M. (1987) *Discourse and Social Psychology: Beyond Attitudes and Behaviour*. London: Sage.

Sarup, M. (1988) *An Introductory Guide to Post-structuralism and Postmodernism*. Hemel Hempstead: Harvester Wheatsheaf.

Saussure, F. de (1974) *Course in General Linguistics*. London: Fontana.

Sinclair, J. and Coulthard, M. (1975) *Towards an Analysis of Discourse: The English Used by Pupils and Teachers*. Oxford: Oxford University Press.

Stubbs, M. (1983) *Discourse Analysis: The Sociolinguistic Analysis of Natural Language*. Oxford: Blackwell.

van Dijk, T. (1995) Esoteric discourse analysis. *Discourse & Society*, 6(1): 5–6.

van Dijk, T. (1997) The study of discourse. In T. van Dijk (ed.) *Discourse as Structure and Process (Discourse Studies: a Multidisciplinary Introduction, Volume 1)*. London: Sage.

Wetherell, M. and Potter, J. (1992) *Mapping the Language of Racism: Discourse and the Legitimation of Exploitation*. Hemel Hempstead: Harvester Wheatsheaf.

Williamson, J. (1978) *Decoding Advertisements: Ideology and Meaning in Advertising*. London: Marion Boyars.

Willig, C. (ed.) (1999) *Applied Discourse Analysis: Social and Psychological Interventions*. Buckingham: Open University Press.

PART I
Spoken and written texts

2 Interviews: meaning in groups

SAM BEVAN AND KATE BEVAN

Interviews are a central aspect of qualitative research methodology, usually dyadic when the interviewer talks to a single interviewee, with the former dependent on the self-disclosing language of the interviewee. The current literature shows that positivist methodologies are increasingly considered by critics to provide forms of interviewing which distort the representation of the views and needs of interviewees. Interviewees and interviewers are members of social groups, and of imaginary audiences, positioned within influential social contexts. These memberships are significant in understanding the discourse of interviewees and interviewers, and their respective constructions of interview texts. Feminist and other researchers have also problematized positivist research practices, seeing them as obstructing an adequate representation of women and other 'outsiders' in research. They contest the epistemological foundations of positivist interview designs, using constructionist, ethnomethodological, ethnographic and discourse analytic paradigms to emphasize local, experiential approaches.

Constructionists assume that individuals actively construe their own social realities, which are those that the interviewer then wishes to understand by interacting with the interviewee. Positivist methodology is seen as excluding the meanings arising from interviewees fashioning their daily realities, and this experiential view, of interviewee construction of their world, is viewed as performed within local contexts. Interviewees are understood to be performing to different audiences, real and imagined, and the forms of discourse they use are related to these specific intersubjective issues.

Interviewee disclosure is therefore viewed as being pragmatically and performatively constructed within a variety of local social contexts. Interpretivist critics seek to overcome positivist 'contextual stripping' (Guba and Lincoln 1998: 106) and its non-acceptance of the social 'contingencies of production' of discourse. Ethnomethodological and ethnographic attention to the 'sense-making' language processes of 'appropriate' local action have also led critics to use methodologies which do not 'exclude the meanings and purposes' of respondents, so that the work researchers finally present is more representative of the local worlds cited (Guba and Lincoln 1998: 107).

Interviewers are also socially contextualized by their relation to particular imaginary audiences. Academic membership groups with assessment and funding related expectations, for example, are influential in defining the research paradigm and the methodologies adopted. Guba and Lincoln (1998: 107), in their review of competing paradigms in qualitative research, comment that 'it now seems established beyond objection that theories and facts are quite interdependent, that is that facts are only facts within some theoretical framework'. The researcher's chosen paradigm and related interview methodology constructs 'facts' which will influence the representation of those interviewed. The interviewer's membership of these academic audiences thereby influences the epistemological beliefs which bear upon interview transcript editing and excerpting conventions, the 'authorial constructions' (Stacey 1988: 24) which interviewers engage in following the interview. Equally, they can be expected to shape the horizons of interviewer 'reflexivity'. This point will be expanded below, with group interviewing being referred to dyadic interviewing for these and other reasons.

In positivist paradigms, 'The investigator and the investigated "object" are assumed to be independent entities' (Guba and Lincoln 1998: 110), but we see inquiry as having to be interactive to respect the interviewee's own interpretations. Feminists also see an intersubjective or 'reciprocal' relationship with the interviewee as being necessary. They reject the idea that representations are 'discovered through objective observation as they really are' (ibid.), for this leads to searching for a social 'reality' which is assumed to be independent of respondents, and it excludes them from its construction. This has led feminist researchers to seek a more 'reciprocal' (Stacey 1988: 22) relationship with the interviewee, where an intersubjective relationship is the aim. The social distance of 'dualist' conventional designs undermines full self-disclosure by the interviewee and is viewed as 'neither possible nor desirable' (Oakley 1981).

A similar problematic social distancing also arises from cultural hierarchies defining 'academic' and 'mundane knowledge' (Sandywell 1996). The interviewer has the power to 'make public what is private' (Ribbens 1989: 581) about interviewee disclosures, or to 'establish the realities of respondents' (*ibid.*), and this is warranted by his or her cultural location within an academic institution. This establishes an asymmetrical relationship, of course, which feminist researchers have sought to overcome.

Most research occurs within institutions which have their own agendas. Interviewers have to negotiate and reassure the 'gatekeepers' that their work will not conflict with institutional goals. This can position them in relation to the institutional audiences they negotiate with on a daily basis, and interviewee disclosures can then be distorted. There is further complexity because institutional realities are not unified; interviewees will have different interviewers, and the researcher is a member of various groups which can influence his or her relationships with interviewees. The disclosures to the interviewer are potentially influenced by the existing interviewee agendas with gatekeepers. A reciprocal 'mutuality' (e.g. Devault 1990) of interest with the interviewee is sought, but many authors see this as having limited success at present (Ribbens 1989).

Critics are equally concerned about those interviewing methodological issues which societally disadvantage 'outsiders', such as gay, black or disabled people. Feminist constructionists, taking gender to be socially constructed, for example, contest research representations of women which are seen to limit their rights. These feminist researchers accept ethnographic and postmodernist 'linguistic turn' debates which see language as the major means by which realities are constructed and continued.

The language used by women is seen by some researchers (e.g. Devault 1990: 97) as different from that of men, such that women interviewees have to try to 'translate' their language into the categories which the researcher has devised. Some feminist researchers consider the local situated knowledges women use to be a source of 'linguistic incongruence' with male research categories: 'Such disjunctures between language and women's lives have been central to feminist scholarship . . . the lack of fit between women's lives and the words available for talking about experience, present real difficulties . . . then women must "translate", either saying things which are not quite right . . . or using the language in non-standard ways' (Devault 1990: 99). The 'recovery of unarticulated experience' is thus assumed to depend on the interviewer using the 'everyday language' categories which women use to construe their own realities.

This argument has led some feminist authors to argue that an adequate representation of women's perspectives requires interviewers of women to be other women, and to take a 'standpoint perspective' (Olesen 1998: 163): 'Any competent listening depends on various kinds of background knowledge. We have argued above that woman-to-woman listening can be based on a particular type of unspoken knowledge' (Devault 1990: 105). The location of women 'outside' male language categories is thus seen as a source of distortion of the representation of the 'voice' of women.

Similar representational issues are raised by black women and working-class women about the activities of white women researchers: 'What white feminists have been producing, it is argued, are generalizations based only upon white middle-class women's experiences. They are generalizations that do not take account of nor account for the experiences of working-class or Black women' (Edwards 1990: 477). Related to this point, 'there has been a growing emphasis on how racial and ethnic differences shape the relationships between the researcher and the researched, in the light of black criticisms that issues of "race" have been neglected by white researchers' (Song and Parker 1995: 242).

These different cultural issues complement questions raised earlier about the way academic institutions influence the construction of interview texts. Many 'outsider' researchers focus on the 'authorial constructions' and the 'recording, transcribing and excerpting from conversations of informants . . . Though these are usually thought of (if thought of at all) as mechanical or technical issues, researchers are increasingly aware of their substantive relevance' (Devault 1990: 105). These are important areas where interpretivist methodology needs to be more reflexive. There needs to be a greater methodological inclusion of these audiences within research designs to enhance the quality of the representations offered. The researcher can also already utilize these debates to produce a number of illuminating readings of interview texts. These arguments call for readings which emphasize the constructions of local social realities by respondents, the meanings which they ascribe to categories they value, what is considered competent and appropriate action and language, and how the interview text is influenced by the audiences the interviewees consider themselves to be a member of.

Text

The specific text here consists of conversations with young people in schools interviewed within their 'everyday language' contexts. The research topic was youth culture and was media-centred. The research took place in a number of schools, with white and Asian young people being interviewed. The excerpts here are taken from group interviews, where open questions were intended to facilitate reflections by group members among themselves. Questions were related to their choice of television programmes which they enjoyed and viewed regularly. The paradigm used is constructionist, and therefore localist, emphasizing the experiential shared realities of participants. Performative 'sense-making' is understood as being 'appropriate' local action, and this is examined through the language used by members.

Excerpt 1: Four Asian girls, discussing 'Friends'

1 *Dharti:*   Yeah, they're all different, but they get on. Their friendship is very strong.

2 *Waheeda:*   That's cool . . . that's what friendship is . . . even when
you're all different.

3 *Dharti:*   They survived through a lot.

4 *Asma:*   They rely and help each other . . . that's what it's about
I suppose . . . like when one needs help they are all
very cool . . . They're there for you.

5 *Dharti:*   Yeah, it's no sweat, they look for ways to help.

6 *Asma:*   It's a very funny programme too . . . like they have
their problems . . . sometimes it's serious matters . . . but
done in a funny way . . . I love all the situations they get
into and some of the stories you can really relate to.

7 *Dharti:*   Yeah, the ones about dating and marriage and
Valentines . . . like if my mum and dad thought I'd act
like that they'd give me the you don't date line.

8 *Waheeda:*   Yeah.

9 *Asma:*   That's right.

10 *Dipika:*   Me too.

11 *Asma:*   Yeah, but they do.

12 *Dharti:*   But no one talks about it, do they?

13 *Asma:*   No you know why?

14 *Waheeda:*   Reputations (said in whisper).

15 *All:*   Mmm. Yeah, that's right.

16 *Waheeda:*   But it's like it's not in the religion . . . dating . . . un-
chaperoned!

17 *All:*   (laughter)

Excerpt 2: Three Asian girls, discussing 'Friends'

1 *Dharti:*   I like all the Friends characters.

2 *Asma:*   Me too, they're so hilarious.

3 *Dharti:*   They're really funny . . . they make you laugh all the
time. They are all different.

4 *Asma:*   Yeah, each has their own personality. Phoebe is so
funny and she's so weird.

5 *Dharti:*   Why is she weird?

6 *Waheeda:*   She's a nutter, she likes witchcraft, voodoo . . . mystical.

7 *Asma:*   Rune stones . . . anything not usual.

8 *All:*   (laughter)

Excerpt 3: Four white boys and a girl, discussing 'Roseanne'

1	*Les:*	Roseanne is good.
2	*Ian:*	What? you cannot be serious?
3	*Les:*	Why not? It's quite realistic and it's funny?
4	*Ian:*	Realistic?
5	*Les:*	Yeah, it's how families are, the day to day things . . . but not glitzy.
6	*Richard:*	She's a big woman.
7	*Michael:*	Wouldn't mess with her.
8	*Ian:*	She'd flatten you (laughs).
9	*Les:*	I think it's good . . . she's a real person. OK it's a comedy . . . it deals with family things.
10	*Emma:*	Yeah, like I watch Friends because that's dealing with adult relationships, love, being together, getting on, falling out . . . Roseanne is the same but with family.

Excerpt 4: Gender mixed white group, discussing 'Baywatch'

1	*Michael:*	I watch Grandstand with my Dad on a Saturday, and then we watch Baywatch and . . .
2	*Emma:*	Babe-watch . . . bimbo-watch.
3	*All:*	(laughter)
4	*Michael:*	Come on . . . they're babes.
5	*Lisa:*	I suppose you drool over Pamela Anderson.
6	*Michael:*	Yeah . . . definitely.
7	*Emma:*	She's a dog.
8	*Michael:*	A . . . wh . . . you cannot be serious woman. She's seriously fit.
9	*Lisa:*	Yeah . . . we know what for.
10	*Emma:*	You're sad.
11	*Michael:*	No I'm not. I'm a perfectly normal lustful lad.
12	*Emma:*	Sad.
13	*Lisa:*	She's a blond bimbo with boobs.
14	*Michael:*	How do you know?
15	*Lisa:*	Well you can see for a start.
16	*Michael:*	No, if she's a bimbo . . .
17	*Lisa:*	Do you listen to what she says?
18	*Ian:*	No, he's too busy looking.
19	*All:*	(all laugh)
20	*Ian:*	He's just being lustful.

There is therefore a focus on the 'praxical reflexivity' (Sandywell 1996) of group respondents, where 'logics in action' are a part of the 'contingencies of production' of texts. The social groups these young people belong to are sites of intersubjective resources, and they are used to evaluate societal categorizations (Butler 1992: 9). Future adult identifications are also trans-acted through 'Sense-making activities as self making praxis in which human beings categorize, theorize and narrativize their experience' (Sandywell 1996: xi).

While group 'communicative competence' can entail 'referential cohesion' between members, these groups also provide opportunities for a contestation of opinion. Adversarial sites also arise from within different group affiliations, and subgroups contest the conclusions of other subgroups. Adler (1996: 111) argues that 'a hierarchy of friendship groups is stratified according to the dimensions of status and popularity', and group interview texts can be expected to include evidence of this.

Just as there are imaginary 'audiences' which are part of the intersubjective world of interviewer, so there are similar ones influencing anyone interviewed within an organization. These agendas can influence the text constructions of interviewees, because there is usually an awareness of the hierarchies they have to negotiate. This 'vertical intertextuality' (Kristeva 1986) was present in this text, as in when teachers decided to remain in the classroom while the interviewer was talking with the group.

The intersubjective resources of groups are drawn upon to defend group realities against those which outsiders use, and referential cohesion can therefore collectively express itself in the marginalization of the interviewer (Frey and Fontana 1991). There is an example of this in one of the early interview excerpts in the text box.

Reading

Excerpt 1

There are examples here of 'appropriate local action and competence', 'referential cohesion' and 'vertical intertextuality'. The easy flow of the turn-taking suggests that these shared realities are intersubjectively accepted between group members. The implied meanings, inscribed in the language used, are thus considered by us to be 'appropriate' and 'competent' to the local context. This is perhaps underlined by the signifiers of 'referential cohesion', in the 'yeahs' in lines 7 and 11. The excerpt is from an early interview, and Dharti's comment in line 12 was made with a sideways glance towards the interviewer, seeking to discourage Waheeda, Asma and Dipika from discussing this topic in front of the 'outsider'. This is also an example of where intersubjective resources are used for defending realities, and lines 7 and 11 are synonymously an instance of 'vertical intertextuality', where discourse is influenced by status differences. There is perhaps a triple audience effect in this example. The interviewees were perhaps unsure of the interviewer's relationship with the school 'gatekeepers', the teachers, and whether their disclosures would be disclosed by the interviewer to the teacher, who would disclose what they said to their parents.

Excerpt 2

Here intersubjective resources are used to define group categorical memberships. 'Weird' and 'nutter' are descriptors of group members who are on the boundaries of an insider–outsider dualism. The 'outsiders' mentioned here are not the larger groupings of gay people, the non-white, the poor, the disabled or women, but of what is thought to be the 'non-normal'. Butler (1993), among others, has shown that we define the groups we are happy to be thought members of by defining the qualities of those we do not want to be a part of, those who are different. These definitions of the different define 'us'. The qualities men construct of women and 'femininity' also define 'masculinity', for example, or the qualities constructed by heterosexual men about 'homosexual' men are an important part of defining 'heterosexuality'. These young Asian people entering 'adulthood' in a predominantly white culture can be expected to pay attention to understanding these boundaries as an important part of negotiating workable definitions of themselves.

Excerpt 3

This excerpt contains examples of performative 'sense-making' where there is an intersubjective evaluative reflection on categorical meanings. The connotative meanings of 'realistic' and 'real' are contested, with the opinion voiced by one participant that 'it's how families are' implying that all families are as represented in the 'Roseanne' script. Another comments that the physical size of Roseanne is relevant to reflecting on the meaning of what is 'realistic'. Two others in the group also consider this criterion as relevant (lines 6, 8). The reply, on line 9, is that Roseanne is a 'real' person because the programme deals with 'family' issues. There appear to be different 'logics in action', or frames of reference, at work here, where Roseanne's size as a woman is thought relevant by three members, but not by two other interviewees. One reading of this inconsistency is to accept that just as interviewers can be influenced by their membership of imaginary academic audiences, the meanings respondents construct are also culturally located in the same kind of way. This 'Roseanne' programme referred to was a part of the 'first series', the series which brought Roseanne a large audience. The 'first series' represented Roseanne without 'make-up', that which middle-income women usually wear, with the programme constructing representations of lower-income American family relationships. Roseanne's size also figured as part of her attempt to represent women differently, and the contrast with other representations was possibly seen as very relevant to deciding her 'realness' and the warrant of the programme to being 'realistic'.

Excerpt 4

Gendered clique stratification is present here, with referential cohesion present in turn-taking between members. The privileging of the visual appearance of 'Baywatch' actresses is understood by the young women group members to be the basis of male attraction to them. The young men contest the conflation of physical attractiveness with the 'bimbo' status of Pamela Anderson, resisting the category label of 'sad'. The contestation is more than one individual disagreeing with another, and men and women are consistently supportive of each side in this short extract from a longer sequence of the same nature.

Disadvantages

The principle disagreements with qualitative interpretivist readings of texts are reviewed by Olesen (1998) and Schwandt (1998). Hammersley (1992) provides useful comments on the disadvantages of ethnography. Important issues are involved in this case, because they relate to the representations and definitions of 'outsiders', and to those who are different from ourselves. These are unresolved methodological issues, and interpretivist paradigms do not appear to have all the answers. The key disadvantages here relate to the charges of 'subjectivism', 'relativism', 'interviewer bias' and 'ecological validity'.

'Subjectivism' is the view that the individual alone decides what his or her social realities are, without any constraints from social contexts. 'Relativism' here is the charge that one individual's opinion about what intersubjective realities are relevant is as valid as anyone else's. 'Bias' is the charge that the interviewer's values cause his or her voice to be given greater importance than that of respondents. 'Ecological validity' relates to the above and to the 'local' focus of interpretivist studies, the charge being that such studies provide results which can only be applied to the specific area of each study.

Interpretivists are sometimes seen as being 'subjectivist', as 'privileging the views of actors ... where constructions are resident in the minds of individuals' (Schwandt 1998: 130). Critics consider that this privileging decontextualizes interviewees and abstracts them from the social contexts they are members of. This approach is seen as leading to a 'descriptive' rather than analytical approach, with a 'lack of any . . . ability to critique the very accounts they produce' (*ibid.*). This criticism of subjectivism is expanded in the argument that interpretivist paradigms provide accounts which are 'relativist', where 'all accounts are equally bad, worthy or unworthy, true or false' (*ibid.*). Descriptivism and relativism are thought to make the assumption 'that voices are free of power relations' (Fine 1992), and that accounts are therefore part of a 'sociology of regulation' fostering the status quo, rather than a 'sociology of radical change' (Schwandt 1998: 122). Similarly, 'Critics hold that it is precisely because of this distancing of oneself as inquirer that interpretivists cannot engage in an explicitly critical evaluation of the social reality they seek to portray' (Schwandt 1998: 131).

This lack of acknowledgement of power-laden contexts is also seen as a source of interviewer bias. A 'concern with bias . . . has been a long-standing criticism of qualitative research' (Olesen 1998: 165), and the view is therefore that 'We cannot rid ourselves of the cultural self we bring with us into the field' (Scheper-Hughes 1992). The interviewer is a member of the culture seen to have values flowing from it, and is charged with placing his or her voice above that of the interviewees who are also cultural members. 'Bias' is considered to operate especially during the editing stage, and this is when powerful 'authorial constructions' can start to appear. These approaches position the interviewer as an interpreter of interviewee texts, where this second-order analysis can lead to the 'sociologist's voice and the . . . respondents' voices' being integrated (Olesen 1998: 166). The danger here is that an ' "overly sovereign" authoritative stance of the interpreter as inscriber' (Rabinow 1986: 131) is the result, and this 'authority and control . . . suppresses the dialogic dimension of constructing interpretations of human action' (*ibid.*).

These problems of subjectivism, relativism and 'bias', and the emphasis on the study of situation specific local contexts, has led other critics to consider the conclusions of these kinds of study as being of limited value. Their 'ecological validity' is considered to be lessened, and the results can be validly applied only to the local context of the specific study.

Advantages

Many interpretivist researchers are already seeking to address the objections raised in the previous section. These developments have focused on the value of an interpretivist framework in understanding the functions of intersubjectively mediated interview text. The analysis of the group interview excerpts sought to apply this approach to those texts, and the comments made there are extended here. The 'privileging' of the actor's views is an important part of interpretivist paradigms, and while early ethno-graphic work was open to the criticism of 'subjectivism', ethnomethodology and critical discourse analysis has fostered a greater contextualization of discourse. The comments made above, in respect of the need for awareness of the different audiences influencing textual construction and the exploration of group intersubjectivity, follow these contextualizing developments.

The comments by D'Amato (in Graue and Walsh 1998: 114) on the use of group interviewing are useful: 'They help each other with their answers. They also keep one another on track and truthful . . . when one would begin to embellish a tale, the other would respond, "You lie! you lie!".' This, however, also cautions us that individuals in groups are able to hold different constructions from others in the same group. Intersubjective in-fluences are seen as being, following Giddens (1990), 'rules and resources' for individual young people to utilize. Empirical work by Widdicombe and Wooffitt (1995), for example, has shown that young people do engage with groups in this way. The social contextualization of the interview text goes some way to replying to the charges of relativism and an ambivalence towards power differences. However, further methodological developments are needed in this area.

Feminist researchers are addressing important issues of asymmetrical discursive power relations. Their concern with overcoming the silencing of the 'everyday language' categories of women by exploring 'relational' interviewing are a part of this. Feminist research continues to move away from 'descriptivism' and feminists are more interested in 'radical change' than in fostering prevailing orders of the status quo. Ethnic modelling, reviewed by Stanfield (1998), goes in the same direction. Interviewer 'bias', which could be seen as a problem arising from membership of a specific culture, many now see as providing 'resources' and valuable 'background knowledge' for an in-depth understanding of respondent views. There is also the objection that the researcher's analysis leads to the 'sociologist's voice' or other theory-influencing 'authorial constructions' of the material (Edwards 1990; Song and Parker 1995). Guba and Lincoln (1998: 107) underline the difficulties for interviewers in this area: 'just as theories [or research paradigms] and facts are not independent, neither are values and facts. Indeed, it can be argued that theories are themselves value state-ments.' Many feminist interpretivists reply that with sufficient reflexivity this problem can be overcome.

The horizons of interviewer reflexivity are influenced by their academic and epistemological commitments. Enhancing the quality of reflexivity and representation appears to call for a greater contextualization of the inter-viewee when texts are elicited. Reducing the asymmetrical relationship, eliciting texts explicitly related to interviewee memberships and increasing triangulation should socially contextualize the given texts more. Group interviews investigate these memberships, seek to modify the asymmetrical bias present in dyads and contain more opportunities for triangulation to occur in the texts.

Interviewer reflexivity is, then, more culturally located. Interviewers' horizons are more influenced by the realities of respondents and made less dependent on academic assessment and funding audiences. This is not to suggest that academic audiences do not contribute valuably to the research process, but further steps are taken away from positivist designs towards more interviewer reflexivity with the 'logics of action' of non-academic cultural members.

The prevalence of the dyadic interview facilitates a positivist modernist theory of the 'rational' asocial individual. The group approach seems to offer fewer opportunities for a suppression of 'the dialogic dimension' (Schwandt 1998: 131), because dialogic intersubjectivity is emphasized and not avoided. Dyads imply the acceptance of the modernist theory of the 'unified subject' or respondent, but 'identities are never unified . . . increasingly fragmented, often intersecting and antagonistic across different positions, discourses and practices' (du Gay 1996: 4). The discourse individuals construct can therefore be seen as constituting the multi-identities they display, and multi-audiences are always present within interview discourses. Dyadic relations appear to emphasize one dimension and obscure another.

We can expect that there will be areas of group agreement on some issues, where internal sanctions are used against group members who act beyond commonly accepted limits, but it does not seem valid to assume that these always determine the language of the individual. These areas of group agreement are frequently made as a response to institutional social power, and dyadic interviewing appears to reduce our understanding of how individuals negotiate this aspect of culture.

Reflexive critical evaluation would be improved by interviewing a variety of the groups that the individual is culturally placed within. These multiple contexts reflect, and individuals can reflect upon, the micropolitical power present in them. Interpretivists, sharing a postmodern paradigm which opposes 'universal' rules, are often reluctant to accept that 'ecological validity' is desirable. This healthy caution not to repeat the elitest prescriptivism of positivism seems to be largely the right one.

Key reading

Guba, E. G. and Lincoln, Y. S. (1998) Competing paradigms in qualitative research. In N. K. Denzin and Y. S. Lincoln (eds) *Landscape of Qualitative Research*. London: Sage.

Schwandt, T. A. (1998) Constructivist, interpretivist approaches to human inquiry. In N. K. Denzin and Y. S. Lincoln (eds) *Landscape of Qualitative Research*. London: Sage.

References

Adler, P. A. (1996) Preadolescent clique stratification and the hierarchy of identity. *Sociological Inquiry*, 66(2): 111–42.

Butler, J. (1992) Contingent foundations. In J. Butler and J. W. Scott (eds) *Feminists Theorize the Political*. London: Routledge.

Butler, J. (1993) *Bodies that Matter*. London: Routledge.

Devault, M. L. (1990) Talking and listening from the women's standpoint: feminist strategies for interviewing and analysis. *Social Problems*, 37(1): 96–116.

Denzin, N. K. and Lincoln, Y. S. (eds) (1998) *Landscape of Qualitative Research*. London: Sage.

du Gay, P. (1996) Who needs identity? In S. Hall (ed.) *Questions of Cultural Identity*. London: Sage.

Edwards, R. (1990) Connecting method and epistemology. *Women's Studies International Forum*, 13(5): 477–90.

Fine, M. (1992) *Passions, Politics and Power: Feminist Research Possibilities, in Disruptive Voices*. Ann Arbor: University of Michigan Press.

Frey, J. H. and Fontana, A. (1991) The group interview in social research. *Social Science Journal*, 28(2): 175–87.

Frye, M. (1983) *The Politics of Reality: Essays in Feminist Theory*. Freedom, CA: Crossing Press.

Giddens, A. (1990) *Consequences of Modernity*. Cambridge: Polity Press.

Graue, M. E. and Walsh, D. J. (1998) *Studying Children in Context*. London: Sage.

Guba, E. G. and Lincoln, Y. S. (1998) Competing paradigms in qualitative research. In N. K. Denzin and Y. S. Lincoln (eds) *Landscape of Qualitative Research*. London: Sage.

Hammersley, M. (1992) *What's Wrong with Ethnography?* London: Routledge.

Kristeva, J. (1986) Word, dialogue and novel. In T. Moi (ed.) *The Kristeva Reader*. Oxford: Blackwell.

Oakley, A. (1981) Interviewing women: a contradiction in terms. In H. Roberts (ed.) *Doing Feminist Research*. London: Routledge.

Olesen, V. (1998) Feminisms and models of qualitative research. In N. K. Denzin and Y. S. Lincoln (eds) *Landscape of Qualitative Research*. London: Sage.

Rabinow, P. (1986) Representations are social facts: modernity and postmodernity in anthropology. In J. Clifford and G. E. Marcus (eds) *Writing Culture: The Poetics and Politics of Ethnography*. Berkeley: University of California Press.

Ribbens, J. (1989) Interviewing – 'an unnatural experience'? *Women's Studies International Forum*, 12(6): 579–92.

Sandywell, B. (1996) *Logological Investigations, Volume 1*. London: Routledge.

Scheper-Hughes, N. (1992) *Death without Weeping: The Violence of Everyday Life in Brazil*. Berkeley: University of California Press.

Schwandt, T. A. (1998) Constructivist, interpretivist approaches to human inquiry. In N. K. Denzin and Y. S. Lincoln (eds) *Landscape of Qualitative Research*. London: Sage.

Song, M. and Parker, D. (1995) Commonality, difference and the dynamics of disclosure in depth interviewing. *Sociology*, 29(2): 241–56.

Smith, D. E. (1987) *The Everyday World as Problematic*. Boston: Northeastern University Press.

Stacey, J. (1988) Can there be a feminist ethnography? *Women's Studies International Forum*, 11(1): 21–7.

Stanfield, J. H. (1998) Ethnic modelling in qualitative research. In N. K. Denzin and Y. S. Lincoln (eds) *Landscape of Qualitative Research*. London: Sage.

Widdicombe, S. and Wooffitt, R. (1995) *Language of Youth Subcultures: Social Identity in Action*. Hemel Hempstead: Harvester Wheatsheaf.

3 Letters: embracing letter writing within discourse analysis

TOM PHILLIPS

A favourite movie moment of mine is when events conspire in Steven Spielberg's *Back to the Future* to have the hero (Michael J. Fox) as a spectator at the High School Prom which brings his parents romantically together. Much of the drama is in the time travel and following an event through his eyes, whose existence is conditional on these people meeting. I seemed to live through the story as intensely as the hero, which may owe something to my appreciation of the delicacies of human destinies. Soon after seeing this, my own father died, and among the things that came my way was a collection of 32 letters, written by his mother to his father at the time of their courtship. An experience not unlike viewing this movie gripped me, as I first looked through these, empathizing with how their growing relationship could survive obstacles. We see both these couples embarking on what becomes an intimate relationship; or alternatively, in Buber's (1961) terms, a dialogic life constituting itself through words and involving a self and other. If taken in this second sense, a courtship is then a living discourse. Its letters are part of a process of warranting by this discourse (Gergen 1989) and, if given an appropriate reading, might allow us to share something of the vitality flowing from this life.

In my grandmother's suburban Dublin of the early 1900s, courtships were modelled on the ideal of a trial period before marriage, to allow the couple to widen and deepen acquaintance and confirm their commitment to each other. Awareness of this was shared with family and friends, and implied a change of status as regards availability to others. As a courtship progressed, it usually became increasingly exclusive and jointly constructed. Between the two people, it was what they said and did with each other that was critical: courtship being a discourse of interaction. Central to all these interactions was language as a medium for dialogue. The more the protagonists could exploit its resources for conveying meaning, communicating and influencing their own, and the other's, actions, the better a relationship could progress. In these ways a couple's interactions could involve, as Buber (1961) identifies, their thought, speech and action, and be all the richer for this. When apart, letters became relevant; and since maintaining interaction was paramount, letters could be fully exploited as a medium for dialogue. A courtship then could generate many interaction texts from music to dress to letter writing. Though often transient in nature, all text categories contributed in their own way to the diverse constructions making up a relationship, each reflecting its own processes of production.

To approach these letters, it is first suggested that they be *read* rather than analysed, where meanings, communications and pragmatics are sought in ways similar to how the writer intended. This is justified as more likely to lead to discovering and experiencing the coherencies of feeling and thought such writing helps the writer to formulate. Second, the emergent nature of a courtship needs to be conceptually embraced. As an episode in a life structure, consisting of an orderly sequence of meaningful actions, a courtship bears many resemblances to Harré's notion of informal social episodes, on whose understanding he makes some useful suggestions: 'To understand the less formal we can make use of three interrelated concepts of position (voice), illocutionary or act-force (or social significance) . . . together with the idea of local narrative conventions (or storylines)' (Harré 1993: 117).

If these generic discourse concepts help to describe something of the generative dynamics of a courtship in a life structure, then manifestations of this could be sought in the letters. Thus, reading the full correspondence might help to reveal story lines; examination of how the writer makes statements might reveal positioning, after which a more careful scrutiny of what was written might offer an informative scenario on its dialogue of actions. In this way an order can be introduced into how the writer exploited these texts. Third, as generative vitality is a feature of dialogue, and the letters reveal only one party's activities, account must be taken of what the letters suggest of the other's role. If this can be done then a fuller reading becomes possible.

Letters as data figure only faintly in traditional psychology. To a social psychology emphasizing the discursive construction of psychological phenomena (Harré 1993), letters written in a courtship are likely to be part of its processes of social construction. As such they fall within the scope of discourse analysis and its interest in linking categories of text with generative discourses (Henriques *et al*. 1984). With a discourse as powerful and intimate as that sustaining a courtship, it seems best to use it to approach the letters rather than use the letters to approach it. The letters will thus not be read to shed light on the discourse, but general notions of the discourse will be assumed to help shed light on constructive processes in the letters. This is what will be understood here as an appropriate reading. In this way the forces at work in the letters constructing new social and domestic realities will be explored. No other methodology will be invoked, and the reading will be done in an open way to allow you, the reader, to put my account into a fuller persepective.

Text: relating letters to their warranting discourse

To start with, some background on the two young people. Their involvement begins around 1900, with J, a young woman from the city (Dublin), meeting T, a local man, at the house of her aunt in the country (Co. Wicklow). Family legend suggests the meeting was arranged by her aunt, a match maker, a practice not uncommon among small propertied families at the time. From this a romantic attachment develops, which is to say a chaste involvement based on mutual liking, and a preparedness to explore, through further meetings and shared social activities, if they wished this to continue. For the greater part of the time they are apart, he working in the family corn mill, she living with her family in a city suburb, 40 miles away. Increasingly their families are treating them as autonomous adults. The time spent together is mostly arranged in conjunction with her visits to the country or his business trips to the city.

J comes over as an open minded, young, literate woman, whose interests seldom stray beyond the ordinary. The letters directly address T and read as written to a special friend to maintain contact between meetings. There are some elements which equate to love letters, some to deepening and extending her acquaintance with his world and most to immediate emotional, communicational and planning issues arising between them. As a correspondence, the surviving 32 letters from 1902 (when J was 19 and T 27) to 1906 have many gaps, suggesting that J must have written in excess of 60 letters within the courtship.

The contents of the letters will be treated as having continuity with the events of the couple's direct meetings and hence feature language being

Two text examples:

Letter 1

18 September 1903.

Dear T,

I sincerely trust your sister's finger is better by this and that you are quiet well too. I `ll tell you a great secret (I have been lonesome since you went back). It was a pity that stone suited so well as I hoped you might have to come for another one. We will have a big procession here on Sunday. I suppose you have heard of it, do you think you will come to see it.

How are all friends in Stratford have you seen Lizzie since. I hope you are not working too hard as I will not allow that even if I am not there to look after you. How did you enjoy the Croppy Boy or have you read it since. Do you take many rides on your bike, I hope you are not flirting now I am not there to see. Have you been to the Waterfall. I have made up my mind not to go as you say it is too late in the season. Did J Byrnes dance come off yet or did you go to it. I hope you enjoyed yourself. Does J Dwyer get the paper from you do you see him often. I cant tell what is wrong with me to-night I am making so many mistakes it is worse than the night you were here. You area very bad Boy for keeping me waiting for a letter. I hope you will make up for it now and let me have one soon. Mrs Murray desires to be remembered. I will now say, Good night hoping you will excuse all mistakes with love from J MM.

Letter 2

30 August 1906

My Dear T,

Received your very welcome letter, glad to hear you got back safe. Just think I am alive and had Father Byrne here yesterday he is very nice. All chat stayed just an hour and told me several nice places to spend our honeymoon. He seems to enjoy the talk about such things. I told him I was going to be very sensible and not think of such a thing. But he said there is no use in acting too sensible, to make sure and go to Killarney or Glendalough for a week or ten days and he could tell me what it would cost, so that looks like as if he had a couple of those honeymoons. He was very anxious to know what Fr. O Neill said to you or if he gave you any papers. I told him what you said was that true. Fr. Byrne is to marry us immediately after 8 oclock mass. I hope this hour will suit you and all. So sorry to hear your Father and Mother cannot be present but I can easily understand people like them do not feel always able for such excitement it might only knock them up. Dont be worrying about the place I know it is lovely and will be nicer soon. Have you been to Stratford since. I suppose my Aunt knows about the strange before this. How is Pat Doyle. Remember me to him tell him to takesome nerve tonic and be prepared for some shocks next week he will want to look alive and to learn all we say used to sustain and enrich interaction. As the linguistic units of analysis most appropriate to discourse as interactional speech are utterances (Herman 1995), the contents of the letters will be treated as utterances. This will allow our analysis to embrace the wider context of their relating as may be inferred from the writing.

Reading: critical description and analytic reading

A reading of two letters

Letter 1
The opening sentence illustrates one way of maintaining continuity, in its reference to an ongoing and vivid event. In the early part of a relationship there can be an artful spontaneity of feeling which readily translates into language, as this letter exemplifies. It reads as if written in a simple and happy frame of mind. Some drama is introduced in the contrast between her own small lonely self and such vast presences as the stone (a millstone) and the procession (an immense display of fireworks). Then she opens out to embrace the wider social world they are constructing, with three names being mentioned; Lizzie's inclusion is always significant, as she is perceived as a rival. It can be imagined how reading about items of pleasure like the bike, the waterfall, the book, the dance, the paper will have struck him in the middle of a hard working week. Finally she hints at his laddishness, her own tired state and how the next letter will serve to reassure her about him; continuity again.

Letter 2
Three years on and a much fuller person is projected, dealing with more complex issues. A great deal is now implicit: joint structures have been constructed, they are increasingly engaged in shared projects. Against the world of parents, sisters, aunts, priests, friends they are a partnership: they have come through, she is still alive. Continuity is now increasingly based on tasks to be done or decided upon. Immediately there is the honeymoon; will she be sensible? Some hard decisions have been made; his parents are not attending. She reassures him that the 'place' (his family dwelling that will be their new home) is lovely and will be nicer soon when she takes up residence. Events have moved quickly, there are no longer such close ties with her aunt, who may not be fully acquainted with 'the strange' (i.e. their latest news). There is also T's mate, Pat Doyle, who will be best man at the wedding: she reminds him of the emotional ordeal ahead for the three of them. This is the last letter of courtship, cueing in the next life episode whose texts will be found mainly in the family photograph album.

A reading of the correspondence

Harré's three discourse concepts will now help to frame the courtship as an episode in a life structure.

Reading for story line
The contrast between letters 1 and 2 reveal theirs to be a fairly conventional courtship. The correspondence verifies this with many examples of how they work at clarifying their notions of each other and their growing commitment to the relationship, where no great barriers are put in the way. These letters reveal a young city woman becoming romantically involved with a small businessman, resulting in increasing intimacy and orientation to his world, culminating in marriage and a future life together at his family house in the country.

Reading for positioning
In the letters, J takes up a number of very different positions and explores these through the voice or persona associated with each. As a young person, with her world opening out after the seclusion of childhood, many different vantage points are found from which her dialogue with T is conducted. The letters suggest she was quite adventurous in this, learning to exploit the resources of the language within the intimate space of the letters. Some caution is needed in generalizing from the letters to her wider social life, where similar positioning and repositioning was being experimented with as part of identity formation (Davies and Harré 1990). As these examples show, among the many vantage points are some which can be imagined as responses to T's own position-taking, or calculated to encourage him to respond in a complementary way. This also energizes and refreshes her letters:

> I must not say too much as you may want to watch for the eclipse it would not do to disappoint you this time. (Friend)

> Pity Miss Joyce is not going she might give you her necklace. (Entertaining companion)

> I wish you were here, I would tell you a good dream I had the other night about you it would make you laugh for a month. (Confidante)

> Dear T, I know you will pity me when I tell you I have not seen my darling sweetheart since and was so nice. (Lover)

> Did T Doyle give up his girl in B – I heard he was dead gone on her but some of those boys like every strange face they see. (Peer)

> You must excuse mistakes in this letter as there is a kid here all talk. (Family child minder [this niece grew up to be a published writer: Murphy 1994])

Received your welcome letter quite safe, very pleased to see by it your mother was getting on so well and that your cold was better a little petting would do a lot for you like all men. (Woman)

Reading for acts/actions
The vitality of a courtship is perhaps best judged by actions, and while these take their most real form when the couple are physically present to each other, letter writing can also achieve this. While J's utterances are mostly devoted to making meaning and communicating discrete bits of information, there are some which, in the terms of speech act theory (Austin 1963), are virtually discrete social actions, serving to occasion actual social actions in T. The following exemplify this in illocutionary terms, where just making the utterance has the force of an inducement to action, and in perlocutionary terms, when his utterances are revealed within some of her actions:

You must come along as soon as possible and let me see you once more. (illocutionary)

The Irish dancing was lovely it would make you wish to know how to dance. (illocutionary)

Did you learn your second step on Wednesday I will hope to have the pleasure of seeing you dancing in a few weeks. (illocutionary)

Have you been to the Waterfall. I have made up my mind not to go as you say it is too late in the season. (perlocutionary)

As to advising my sister it would make very little difference if I did when she makes up her mind. (perlocutionary)

Reading for processes of production

Iser (1978) suggests that part of the work of reading is to reproduce the codes generating an author's utterances, and use these to empathize with what the author is attempting. Such codes help us to understand the process of composition or production that underlie the text. The above reading offers some illumination of the production processes behind J's writing. If a representation of her utterances is now counterposed with those we assume T was writing to her, and these are further articulated in the position and action terms utilized above, it is possible to begin to show, as in Figure 3.1, how a deeper reading of the full correspondence is possible. Four kinds of evidence make this plausible. First, letter writing within a courtship is part of a dialogue of utterances underpinned by explorations of positioning and repositioning. Second, letter writing enhances the scope to engage in such explorations of voice and position. Third, as explicated

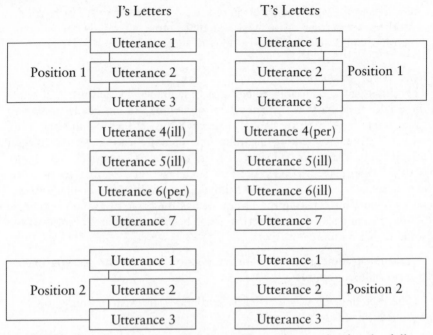

Figure 3.1 A representation of the possible reading codes for the full correspondence.

by speech act theory, many utterances can beget some social actions. Fourth, in her writing J seems to have been both mindful and deliberative in using utterances in these ways.

In this, utterances mediate the dialogue through being linked with a position or not. Where they are, the writer's scope to explore voice and persona, and prompt responses in like kind from the other, is enhanced. Where they are not, there is scope to induce social actions (illocutionary) or directly to reflect inducements from the interlocutor (perlocutionary). Such a sequence, when read across a courtship, summarizes its story line.

Stainton Rogers et al. (1995), in reviewing the critical agenda of social psychology, identify a reluctance among discourse analysts to follow an established methodology. Many wish to improvise an approach appropriate to whatever texts or data might present. The fact that a variety of texts can constitute valid data is one of the strengths of this research. A freedom has been exercised here, in both clarifying 'an appropriate reading' as the goal for this study and using a relatively novel investigative rationale to achieve this. With little extant literature linking discourse analysis to letters, it would be presumptuous to consider this approach as anything other than experimental, whose outcomes may apply to other studies of letters. Hence any evaluation of the study has to be tentative.

Disadvantages: some objections to this investigative rationale

A first objection is that this may not be the best way to utilize letters in studying common life events; and that an ethnographic approach, which aims to document a way of life (Fetterman 1998), would make more appropriate use of the data. Certainly, looking at these letters alongside other surviving items, such as a small box of shamrock he gave her on St Patrick's Day in 1905 or a postcard she sent him of a glamorous music hall singer, gives a glimpse of their wider cultural world. Letters also partake of the conventions of their time, and the gentility which letter writing imposed then may not fully reflect how they directly related as an ethnography might have.

Second, as discourse is about dialogue, data which do not contain a transcript of all voices may mean too much reconstruction. This is certainly a weakness of the present study, based on one set of letters: we never hear T's voice; it is at best what we reconstruct from J's reactions, ripostes and grounded assumptions. Transcripts as a full set of utterances would be particularly useful to pick up on processes of construction.

A third objection is that letters as texts do not figure much in contemporary courtships, replaced largely by telephone and now e-mail. Yet there is much to be learned from letters, as Barthes (1990) shows in his exquisite attempts to capture the discourse of lovers, and the variety of encounters such texts reveal. He also points to the disingenuousness within letter writing: however much the writer protests 'I am thinking of you', this can often mean 'I am forgetting you', and it is only the act of writing that can appease such guilt. There are moments towards the end of J's letters where you sense a similar phenomenon ('I am just commencing to wander, so will conclude'; 'can't think of anything else'). A fourth objection is treating courtship in such a simplified way. An alternative might have been to characterize the kind of relationship it was, and for this to illuminate the reading. If this courtship was seen as a project within her biography, J comes close to being disinterested in the relationship and 'marries, not in order to further an occupational career or to gain status, but in order to further the project of becoming a certain kind of person and successfully maintaining a certain "style of life"' (Berger et al. 1974: 71–2).

A final objection resides in the emphasis put on reading. That is, reading a set of writings drawn up within the privacy of a close relationship, where the researcher is at best an eavesdropper. With no participative structure to avail of, as exists for the person for whom they were written, the best the researcher can do is to seek to empathize with the addressee. This is an issue that needs discussing if 'found' letters like these are to be recognized as worthwhile data.

Advantages: promising features of the investigative rationale

The real test for this reading is how well the constructive processes are illuminated by what is known or can be assumed about the warranting discourse: in particular, how well the generative dynamics of this courtship are represented. A first test is in respect of Harré's three constructs, and how much they allow the reader to follow the influence of the discourse on what was being warranted as letter content. Certainly each has a useful developmental utility: position or voice serves to pick up the singularity of the young person's task of self-articulation; act-action identifies some of the forces the protagonists could invoke in a close relationship; and story line allows a shape to be sketched out as context in which to set the other two. The three proved most useful in embracing the correspondence, though much less with individual letters.

A second test arises in respect of the constructions which the discourse creates. While the notion of position helps to reflect an individual's power in a dialogue, its greater significance is in raising further questions about the interlocutions, and how language as performative acts can constitute actions taken and reacted to. If both T's and J's letters could be sequenced, they would shed interesting light on a number of J's utterances, or what Stainton Rogers *et al.* (1995) call 'perturbations' ('So I think it is better to give up this writing and acquaintance it seems to me you enjoy insulting some people') and deconstructions ('I am very sorry if I have wronged you, but really your letter did look like as if you did mean me to take it up as I did').

A third test arises in seeing the letters in the deeper context of everyday ordinariness. As articulations, they do begin to foreshadow likely domestic conversations they will later have as married partners, which, as Garfinkel (1967) intimates, is the kind of social glue that reconciles ordinary people. The ordinariness in these letters is at times striking:

Lucky for once on Sunday you had not to walk home.

I saw Chow Nolan yesterday he looks very well.

How did you enjoy the races, did you go the three days.

See how dangerous those old bikes are.

These comments could be read as evidence that J and T are already together constructing a household.

As many anthologies bear out (e.g. Pryor 1988; Kenyon 1997), letters have an infinite capacity to mirror different human experiences. Letters which extend across a life event as significant as a courtship, and involve a literate and involved young person, can provide a useful window on social constructionism. A final test is how well the letters show J clarifying aspects of identity. There are certainly places where the constructive utility of letter writing for J is fairly transparent, as in some patterns of self-articulation which look set to become part of her identity ('I am egcentric' [sic]; 'I do not want involvement with your sister without you'). Further, the sheer regularity of the letters suggests theirs is the momentum of the courtship itself, and can be read for signs of how the pressure of events impact and are being dealt with.

Key reading

Any chapter in O. Kenyon (1995) *Women's Voices*. London: Constable.
Chapter on 'The love letter' in R. Barthes (1990) *A Lover's Discourse*. Harmondsworth: Penguin.

References

Austin, J. L. (1962) *How to Do Things with Words*. Oxford: Clarendon Press.
Barthes, R. (1990) *A Lover's Discourse*. Harmondsworth: Penguin.
Berger, P., Berger, B. and Kellner, H. (1974) *The Homeless Mind*. Harmondsworth: Penguin.
Buber, M. (1961) *Between Man and Man*. London: Fontana.
Davies, B. and Harré, R. (1990) Positioning: the discursive production of selves. *Journal for the Theory of Social Behaviour*, 20(1): 43–63.
Fetterman, D. (1998) *Ethnography*, 2nd edn. London: Sage.
Garfinkel, H. (1984) *Studies in Ethnomethodology*. Cambridge: Polity Press.
Gergen, K. (1989) Warranting voice and the elaboration of self. In J. Shotter and K. Gergen (eds) *Texts of Identity*. London: Sage.
Harré, R. (1993) *Social Being*, 2nd edn. Oxford: Blackwell.
Henriques, J., Hollway, W., Urwin, C., Venn, C. and Walkerdine, V. (1984) *Changing the Subject*. London: Routledge.
Herman, V. (1995) *Dramatic Discourse*. London: Routledge.
Iser, W. (1978) *The Process of Reading*. Baltimore: Johns Hopkins Press.
Kenyon, O. (1995) *Women's Voices*. London: Constable.
Murphy, D. (1994) J'etais une jeune pale, mince, passionnee. In P. Rafroidi, P. Joannon and M. Goldring (eds) *Dublin, 1904–1924*. Paris: Editions Autrement.
Pryor, F. (1988) *The Faber Book of Letters*. London: Faber.
Stainton Rogers, R., Stenner, P., Gleeson, K. and Stainton Rogers, W. (1995) *Social Psychology: A Critical Agenda*. Cambridge: Polity Press.

4 Fiction: five run around together – clearing a discursive space for children's literature

DAVID RUDD

The very term 'children's literature' opens up the tensions in this backwater of literary studies. Unlike terms like 'children's art' or 'children's games', which express a sense of ownership on the part of children, 'children's literature' does not. To a far greater extent it is controlled by adults: they write, edit, publish, disseminate and often read the finished product on behalf of a child audience. Interestingly, if one goes back to the 1970s, it can be seen that 'women's literature' and 'black literature' were treated in a similarly ghettoized form – but these areas have now created their own space in the literary field. Children's literature, however, is still different.

Yet even among the adults who police this area, there are competing interests at work, which complicate the issue. They derive from separate discursive fields and, consequently, construct 'the child' and 'literature' in different ways. Broadly speaking, there are 'book' and 'child' approaches. The former comprises traditional literary theorists, for whom the child is very much secondary. For these it is Literature (with a capital L) which is the key term, and Leavis is their champion. F. R. Leavis saw Literature as the saviour of mankind. Across a narrow corpus of elevated texts – known as 'the Great Tradition' – he sought to outline the core values of a refined sensibility (Leavis 1948).

In children's literature, it has been argued, there is an even greater need to uphold and promote an ethical stance, in that children are the future citizens of 'the good society' (e.g. Inglis 1981; Rustin and Rustin 1987). Inglis is most explicit in this, nominating a 'Lesser Great Tradition' with its 'Promise of Happiness'. This approach has received substantial criticism in recent times; chiefly, that its notion of overarching, universal values is seriously compromised, for such values, in effect, turn out to be those of a middle-class, white, male – and adult – elite.

In contrast to the above, for whom certain books are good 'whether or not your child can make head or tail of them' (Inglis 1981: 7), 'child' critics argue that children are qualitatively different. This view is usually based on Piagetian notions of development, such that children of particular ages – or stages – will prefer certain books to others. Unfortunately, a similar critique can be made of this approach, for, although it presumes to start with the child, actual children tend to become mere abstractions. The stages that they represent, moreover, though supposedly universal, turn out to work backwards from the presumed culmination of development, which is based on a white, male, middle-class, rational *adult*, to which children should aspire. In this model children are always defined in terms of lack, i.e. what they cannot do or understand (e.g. McDowell 1976). Consequently, it is argued that children's books always need to leave out much of adult experience, and can, therefore, only ever be second class: 'no children's literature could ever be a work of art in the same league as, say, Tolstoy, George Eliot or Dickens' (Tucker 1976: 18). This is an interestingly phrased statement, for two of these writers also wrote for children – although the wording suggests that in their writing for this group these authors were not fully themselves.

Studies using this approach tend to look for elements in texts that are characteristic of children at a particular stage; hence 'Pooh' can be seen as a text for the 'concrete operations' child, inclined to think animistically (Singer 1972). However, the fact that these books are also read by many adults tends to undermine such a notion. Further, as all books for this particular age group are, *de facto*, concrete operational, the argument is tautological: what distinguishes certain texts from others? Other writers in this tradition have taken these notions even further, arguing that the texts themselves exhibit stages of development, often based on the protagonist's behaviour (e.g. Schlager 1978).

There is a third main approach to children's literature, which many see as an answer to the child–book divide. This is 'reader-response' criticism, which aims to start with the individual child's response to a text. Fictional works are seen to contain 'gaps' which readers fill in, based on their existing knowledge, yet guided by textual cues. The aim is laudable, but all too often children are not allowed to explore these gaps; rather, children are shown how to surmount them, in order to make the text cohere. So, once again, meaning is shut down around certain dominant cultural discourses, not opened up to a plurality of readings. It also needs to be said that the texts 'reader-response' criticism deems worthy of attention are largely those already canonized: 'A text with little indeterminacy is likely to bore the reader since it restricts his participation, a text with a large measure of indeterminacy . . . is likely to be exciting' (Benton 1978: 30). Blyton's texts, which I shall explicitly focus on, are usually seen to be determined to the point of cliché (e.g. Hunt 1978; Chambers 1985).

To sum up: I have argued that the first two approaches tend to ignore the child altogether; the 'book' approach quite vociferously, with Alderson (1969) explicitly commenting on the 'irrelevance of children to the children's book reviewer'; while the 'child' approach, presuming already to know the child – in fairly abstract, cognitive terms – usually considers it unnecessary to consult actual children. It is only the third approach that gives the child any space; yet even then only allowing tempered responses to established texts, ignoring children's own preferred reading material.

Text

From this point of view, Enid Blyton (1897–1968) is one of the most interesting children's writers to study. For the above critics, she is usually only talked about in order to be vilified and dismissed, being the perfect negative exemplar of what children's literature should be about. Further, almost uniquely, she manages to unite critics on both right and left, the latter objecting to her supposed sexism, racism and general middle-class cosiness. However, against this is the fact that Blyton is, for children, the most popular writer ever, with the 'Famous Five' being her most liked series. So unless we (i.e. adults) wish to appear like old-style imperialists (Speier 1976: 99), 'ideologically formulating only those research problems that pertain to native behaviours coming under the regulation of colonial authority', we need to revise our methods. Foucault's genealogical approach would seem an apposite starting point, entertaining 'the claims to attention of local, discontinuous, disqualified, illegitimate knowledges against the claims of a unitary body of theory which would filter, hierarchize and order them in the name of some true knowledge' (Foucault 1980: 83).

A discourse approach exploits the fact that all these 'knowledges' – whether given priority or filtered out – are textualized: by setting them alongside each other we can deconstruct the traditional hierarchy that pays attention only to certain voices and not others. We can begin to see how various discursive threads are interwoven; that is, how certain elements are picked up and teased out, how they are responded to, reworked, appropriated or dismissed, as befitting. In short, such an approach allows us to chart the dynamics of (inter)textuality.

But this requires us to look at the whole discursive field, to avoid the very partiality I have criticized above. A root meaning of discourse, 'to run around', effectively captures this notion. Hence I have given extracts from not only 'Five' texts, but those of its gatekeepers – texts which have shaped the hegemonic view of Blyton, drowning out the voice of that other group, children. This 'disqualified, illegitimate' group (because not fully grown, fully rational etc.) has, therefore, also been consulted in this approach, and their texts have been given space.

Behind these brief text extracts, then, lies the following 'textwork': a close reading of all 'Five' texts (21 novels, themselves 'edited' over the years); a reading of all references to Blyton in professional, academic, and more ephemeral literature; and, lastly, discussions (questionnaires and interviews) with child readers, both contemporary and past, across a number of cultures, classes and ethnicities (see Rudd 1997; forthcoming for more details).

For the benefit of those readers whose childhoods somehow managed to escape knowledge of the 'Famous Five', or whose parents forbade Blyton,

---

1(a) 'You'd never get your bunks made, or your meals cooked, or the caravans kept clean if it wasn't for me! . . . I love having two houses on wheels to look after.' (Blyton 1946: 40)

1(b) 'I'll just see what we've got in the larder, Julian,' said Anne, getting up. She knew perfectly well what there was in the larder – but it made her feel grown-up and important to go and look. It was nice to feel like that when she so often felt small and young, and the others were big and knew so much. (Blyton 1946: 61)

1(c) . . . Anne made them wash and tidy themselves first! . . . 'I'll give you five minutes – then you can come'. (Blyton 1946: 198)

1(d) 'You three girls must wash up for me afterwards' . . .
'Why can't the boys help?' said George at once.
'*I'll* do the washing-up,' said Anne . . .
Dick gave her a good-natured shove. 'You know we'll help, even if we're not good at it.' (Blyton 1954: 86)

1(e) 'But you're a *girl*,' said Toby. 'Girls don't understand the first thing about aeroplanes or motor-cars or ships – or spiders either, come to that! I really don't think you'd be interested, Georgina dear.'
'My name is *not* Georgina,' said George furiously. 'And don't call me "dear".' (Blyton 1957: 67)

1(f) 'Jolly girlish-looking boy you are, that's all I can say.'
George flared up at once. 'Don't be mean! I'm not girlish-looking.
I've far more freckles than you have, for one thing, and better eye-
brows. *And* I can make my voice go deep.' (Blyton 1947: 64)

1(g) 'I'm old enough to look after you all.' [Julian]
'Pooh!' said George. 'I don't want any looking after, thank you. And
anyway, if we want looking after, Timmy can do that.' . . .
    'You will be in complete charge, you understand, Julian,' said the
boy's father. 'You are old enough now to be really responsible. The
others must realize that you are in charge and they must do as you
say.' . . .
    'And Timmy will be in charge, too,' said George. 'He's just as
responsible as Julian' . . .
    'I bet we wouldn't be allowed to go without you, Timothy.' [said
Dick]
    . . . 'You certainly wouldn't be allowed to go without Timmy,' said
his mother. (Blyton 1946: 16–21)

2(a) [George] is a very bad case of that castration complex, or penis-
envy, first described by Freud . . . (Dixon 1974: 53)

2(b) . . . there is no suggestion that . . . [George's] fantasy of being a
boy is just as 'normal' as Anne's acceptance of a 'housewifely' rôle . . .
[rather] girls who 'pretend to be boys' . . . are pretentious and silly.
(Cadogan and Craig 1976: 342–3)

2(c) And then the girls tend to go straight from Enid Blyton to Mills
and Boon. (Librarian quoted in Ray 1982: 96)

2(d) . . . there is little . . . to suggest that the Famous Five . . . will carry
their readers to any future but the wonder world of pulp romance.
(Alderson *c.* 1982: n.p.)

2(e) I'm sorry that a new generation is to be encouraged to feed on
what I honestly believe to be slow poison. (Fisher 1973: 2231)

3(a) [Anne's] the oldest girl and you need a, like a girl because the
boys are a bit funny sometimes, silly . . . she tells them to wash and
stay clean when they're on adventures. (9-year-old girl respondent)

3(b) I liked George . . . because she refused to be patronized because
she was a girl or left out of the most exciting parts of the adventures. I also liked the way she often rebelled against adult authority.
(Adolescent girl respondent)

3(c) PS I would like to be called George. (8-year-old girl respondent) they comprise four children: three siblings (Julian, the eldest, Dick, and Anne, the youngest) and their feisty tomboy cousin George (more properly called Georgina), who is the same age as Dick (11 years old). The fifth member is George's mongrel dog, Timmy.

Reading

We start with some extracts from the books themselves. Extract 1(a) is a regularly quoted piece, indicating that Anne is a 'proper little housewife' – a phrase taken up with relish in the Comic Strip (1982) spoof; the quote is invariably used to indicate sexism. Indeed, many works by social critics list just such signifiers of this *ism*, often based on a crude content analysis.

What a closer analysis of the texts shows, however, is a different picture: the sexist signifiers are the tip of the iceberg, the rest of which reveals a more dynamic discourse about sex roles. For some girl readers, in fact, Anne actually emerges as a key figure (quote 3(a)) in the way that she uses the discourse of domesticity to elevate her status (quotes 1(a–c); see also Walkerdine 1990: 10–11).

This is not, then, an ideal, gender-equal society, but one that recognizes discrimination in favour of boys, of patriarchy, and engages with it. George, of course, is the key protagonist, and takes a different tack to Anne, always challenging the status quo (Anne's behaviour would seem a necessary norm against which George can rebel). Quote 1(d) shows this, where George manages to involve the boys, or 1(e), where she refuses to accept not only their pigeon-holing, but also their patronizing attitudes. Quote 1(f) shows a related issue; for whereas in earlier stories it has been established that George can outperform the boys in many activities, here it is not only behaviour, but physical attributes too, that are at issue: what exactly are the signifiers of a boy?

As should be becoming clear, there is no single sexist discourse (a list of signifiers that are intrinsically taboo); instead, there is a discourse about the relations between the sexes that is being explored and dramatized. To read it as sexist is to pull out quotations like 1(a) and isolate them from the discursive field. In Foucault's terms, this effects a sexist reading; that is, it undermines Anne's domestic power and reads George as an anomaly, an aberration (see quote 2(b)).

What gives sexism its bite – as with racism, colonialism and other 'isms' – is not the words *per se*, but the relations of power within which they operate. But, as Foucault also argues, these power relations are not 'set in concrete'; they are continually being renegotiated, argued out at the 'capillary level' – a flavour of which I have tried to convey. Quote 1(g) also demonstrates this, with Julian, the oldest, bidding for leadership, backed by his father. However, in retaliation, George, refusing obeisance, calls on

Timmy; eventually, as the quotation shows, she wins the support of the
other children, and of their mother – not that the battle is then won (itself
more of a fantasy!), but the struggle is foregrounded.

In my survey of Blyton readers, George proved Blyton's most popular
creation (Rudd 1997) – even outpointing Julian among boys; quite an
achievement given that most studies show that boys will usually only read
about male protagonists. However, part of Julian's problem, and another
key discourse, is also flagged up in this quotation (1(g)): for he is older, he
is responsible; but he is, therefore, also more like an adult. Sometimes this
works in the children's favour, as when they confront adult adversaries;
but, among the Five themselves, such signifiers of authority occasionally
work to distance him, and it is the more subversive activities of the under-
dogs – George and Timmy [*sic!*] – that court approval.

This brings me to the quotations from adult critics (2(a–e)). I felt it
necessary to include these, as it is the gatekeepers who have been largely
responsible for the 'moral panic' over Blyton's work (Ray 1982). As a consequence, there has been an added attractiveness of the books for children:
for it is precisely the adult world that is found unreliable, duplicitous and
dismissive in the Five series; a truth that adults can only underwrite in
their glib rejection of the books (another discursive effect).

To relate this to my earlier comments, it can be seen that it is the adult
critics who have closed the texts around a sexist reading which, effectively,
marginalizes and disempowers girl readers in particular: they are the ones
explicitly spoken for – not the boys. According to Dixon (2(a)), it is girls
who suffer the castration-complex, not the beleaguered Julians and Dicks
[*sic*]; it is George, the most popular character, whom adults position as
abnormal (2(b)); and it is the future of girls that is the main concern (2(c–
d)). In fact, another contemporary article is entitled, 'How does one wean
15-year-old girls from a diet of Enid Blyton?' (Anon 1966).

A discursive effect of this adult writing, then, is to see girls as being
particularly susceptible and, therefore, requiring more scrupulous regulation. So, while I am loath to perpetuate another *ism*, the books' overriding
crime, I would argue, is not sexism – which the books *explore* rather than
exploit – but ageism, with adult discourses seeking to maintain their control over texts that are troublesome precisely because they undermine this
adult world; by which I mean not only its representatives, but also what
they represent (i.e. a largely mythical, Piagetian, ratiocinative male with
refined Leavisite sensibilities). Blyton's works, it seems, explore another
space, one that celebrates sensuality and freedom: licence to roam, to feast,
to play and to challenge not only adult surveillance, but also its patriarchal
ascendancy.

The views of the primary readership support this (3(a–c)). To many
adult critics they must seem disappointing in their lack of sensibility and
precision. However, their directness has its own appeal. They also give an

interestingly *different* view. As I have quoted earlier, Anne was seen by some readers as an important figure, even being elevated to the oldest (3(a)). More typically, though, it was George's subversion of the gender norm that was celebrated (3(b–c)), in contrast to the adults' pathologizing of this (2(a–b)). For many, George was a 'proto-feminist', someone who first made them question the inequality of the sexes – to the extent that some even wanted to adopt her empowering identity (3(c))!

Disadvantages

The most obvious criticism of the above is that I seem to have repeated the very marginalization of children that I criticized in others: their voice appears only towards the end, and even then is given very little space. This certainly appears so in this chapter, and I can only say that the above ground-clearing (or discursive levelling of texts) has made this a necessary preliminary move.

This is one reason, but it also needs emphasizing that the children are not brought in at the end like some *deus ex machina*: as 'the answer', a site of truth from which we get a real insight into Blyton's or, indeed, any children's author's works. There is certainly no belief here in some Wordsworthian conception of the child as the fount of knowledge and wisdom. What I have tried to do is little different from what Foucault attempts when he seeks to recuperate any area of marginalized knowledge: such areas are not seen as in any way foundational, but are interesting precisely because of the attempts to marginalize, suppress or ignore them; I have simply tried to 'run around' them. Returning to the Speier quotation, I have sought to show how certain regimes of truth – promulgated by adult gatekeepers – have, in effect, framed discussion of children's literature in general, and of Blyton in particular, swamping other voices.

A second criticism of my approach might be the cavalier way I have mixed different types of material: extracts from the books are placed alongside critics' and fans' comments. I could be accused of merging very different sorts of data, eliding the text with its reception – often in the hands of relatively unsophisticated readers. However, I would see this as an advantage, arguing that what we have here is a far wider view of the total discursive field, not miscellaneous quotations out of context (in the way that 1(a) is often isolated); neither are they simply the voices of that minority, the often elitist gatekeepers who speak on the children's behalf.

A third, and related, criticism would be that I have not treated the fictional text as an artistic entity, with its own coherence. In other words, although there is a time of licence opened up in the Five stories, it is closed down at the end, when the existing cultural order is clearly reaffirmed. Traditional criticism would give far more weight to this closure. There are several responses to this matter. First, while this literary approach might be more suitable for certain single works, it is less so for series fiction, where characters and their brand name (the 'Five') become far better known than individual titles, and exceed any individual text. Relatedly, I would argue that the importance of endings is something that needs establishing, rather than accepting *a priori*. Though there is a rush to get to the denouement, there also seems a wish to defer its inevitability, and, once finished, to return to the adventure, or to become involved in another. In other words, as with other series fictions (soaps, especially), I would tend to reverse the normal order of things: it is being *in medias res* rather than 'at a loose end' that is the desired state, and one that readers strive to recreate – often by revisiting the same text.

Those who take a more 'child-centred' approach might voice another criticism, arising out of what I have just stated: for the books seem to do the very opposite of promoting any sort of growth (e.g. development of character, extension of vocabulary, increase in moral complexity); instead, there is escapism from these issues, indeed from physical development itself. George, especially, explicitly advocates resistance to growth – 'There can't be anything nicer in the world than this – being with the others, having fun with them. No – I don't want to grow up!' (Blyton 1957: 42) – and the rest of the Five generally endorse this, celebrating the joys of holiday, food and leisure.

The reader-response school is closer to my approach, though again, my choice of text would not normally be theirs, as Blyton's work supposedly offers little indeterminacy. However, I have argued that, in the 'Five' at least, spaces are opened up, just as the protagonists 'run around' together, probing the interstices of walls and crevices, frequently querying adult knowledge and behaviour (here, specifically, I have drawn attention to discourses about relations between the sexes, and between adults and children).

Moving towards more discursive approaches, the accusation of fragmentation might be made: I too have given a very selective representation of the material, with many 'gaps'. Has this not permitted me to construct, or privilege, an equally partial reading, albeit one different from those I attack? This criticism cannot be ducked, but I would simply argue that my empirical (i.e. discursive) base has been far wider than previous critics in the area. This approach does not rely on one, possibly unrepresentative, individual's reaction to the books, but demands that the whole discursive field be considered: to see how the discourses in the texts are constructed, and how they are then taken up and circulated; both among adults, whether in literary, educational or lay circles, and among the primary readership, of children, across generations and cultures.

This might suggest a final criticism: am I not mixing a qualitative approach with a quantitative, the two being incompatible? I would respond that the two are always intertwined, and that the charge of incompatibility itself perpetuates a false dichotomy. Were it not for the quantitative impact of Blyton's books over the years, in terms of sales and popularity, then doubtless this study would not have occurred; in the same way George emerged as the readers' favourite character (something that the qualitative, yet idiosyncratic, 2(b) gets wrong). It was these data that helped to focus a more qualitative investigation; one that could ask more searching questions, and attempt to grasp certain discursive regularities in the books. Quantitative research is not flawed *per se*; only when it is seen as the whole truth, rather than a particular regime of truth.

Advantages

Many of the advantages of this approach turn out to be the converse of the above. However, they are still worth expounding in some detail.

The primary advantage seems to be the way a discursive approach 'brackets' questions of value. As I have argued, all the main approaches discussed in the first section start with certain things being 'taken as read' before a text is ever engaged. However, the problems with this are that these critics' supposedly universal values turn out to be inveterately partial, and often linked to specific sites of power. Even the social critics, who rightly take issue with this partiality, prioritizing issues of sexism, racism and class bias, do so from a largely unproblematized, adult viewpoint.

A discourse approach works by recognizing the textuality of everything, seeing how and why certain discourses circulate, and among whom; it is interested in how discourses are appropriated, revised, distorted, criticized, silenced and negated. Thus existing hierarchical structures are dismantled. It is a healthily levelling activity.

But precisely because it lays its workings bare, it makes itself more open to criticism. Nevertheless, this provides a useful check on the approach, in that others can revisit the material and determine whether a particular analysis is or is not just; further, others can more readily see the partiality of the research (the specific historical and cultural location of the researcher, the timing and scope of the research and so on).

The approach also, I think, avoids the charge of *laissez-faire* relativism. For although it begins by 'levelling the playing field' – or, more appositely, the discursive field – it is only as a way of establishing the range of material in question (the corpus of texts, the requisite gatekeepers and more 'ordinary' readers), and of ascertaining the meanings ascribed to it. This seems to bring us back to a specifically Foucauldian conception of discourse, which certainly disavows any final truth, yet does attempt to show how certain truths come to be naturalized through particular discursive regimes – and, as a consequence, how other versions (readings) come to be silenced in the process.

A related advantage seems to be that a discourse approach remains committed to what other approaches espouse but do not practise. That is, it makes the text, in all its forms, central. The literary approach, while it gives close readings of certain works (especially poems), tends to dismiss other works as not worth close attention. In my analysis, I was surprised at how often characters' names, plot details and other basic information were misunderstood by critics; Fisher, for example, after a damning review (2(e)), goes on to misname two of the main characters. Children might well question the credentials of their adult gatekeepers. The child approach, too, often ignores the individual text in its hunt for signifiers of underlying cognitive processes, let alone ignoring the child.

A final advantage of the approach is that it steers between the idea of texts having one authoritative value (graded in terms of a Great Tradition, or, more recently, the National Curriculum), and another view which asserts that a text can mean anything you want (e.g. Fisher 1972). A discourse approach allows one not complete anarchy in a text, but 'to appreciate what *plural* constitutes it' (Barthes 1990: 5). In other words, it recognizes that meanings derive from social practices; therefore discourses always circulate within particular cultures – with the crucial caveat that, as noted above, these discourses are continually being renegotiated and reformulated every time someone speaks.

Let me now relate these advantages to three broader issues. First, with its close attention to textuality, to language, a discourse approach dovetails with other recent theoretical developments – for example, on the importance of 'intertextuality' in the generation and creativity of discourse – and with certain psychoanalytic approaches, which relate how words in texts can impact on questions of identity (as in quote 3(c)). Certainly, in my empirical work I found that Blyton's texts were not just *read*, but went deeper, being incorporated into games, fantasies, role-plays, story writing and so on; that is, into children's culture. This connects with a second point, which is that this approach breaks down disciplinary barriers, encouraging wider, cross-border cultural studies. Thus we can see the connections with work on soaps, comics, genre fiction, subcultures and the like (e.g. Willis 1977; Radway 1987; Barker 1989; Jenkins 1992; Harrington and Bielby 1995); in this paradigm, as the studies I have mentioned have shown, it is quite legitimate – if not normal practice – to bring in the views of the audience (to own their 'texts'). Finally, in its levelling function, a discourse analytic approach makes us look critically at the way that language is used to keep the categories 'child' and 'adult' in place, and discrete (Rose 1984; Rudd 1995). Children can be accused of naive reading, or plain misreading, but if enough of them read in a contrary way, it might be that they are reading against some adult-imposed grain: that these so-called invidiously divisive texts are, in fact, empowering children as a social category, against past adult-eration.

Key reading

Davies, B. (1989) *Frogs and Snails and Feminist Tales: Preschool Children and Gender*. Sydney: Allen and Unwin.
Stephens, J. (1992) *Language and Ideology in Children's Fiction*. London: Longman.

References

Alderson, B. W. (c. 1982) 'Knocking Noddy', unpublished transcript of talk given on BBC World Service.
Alderson, B. W. (1969) The irrelevance of children to the children's book reviewer. *Children's Book News*, 4(1): 10.
Anon (1966) How does one wean 15-year-old girls from a diet of Enid Blyton? *The Use of English*, 17(3): 199.
Barker, M. (1989) *Comics: Ideology, Power and the Critics*. Manchester: Manchester University Press.
Barthes, R. (1990) *S/Z*. Oxford: Blackwell.
Benton, M. (1978) *The First Two Rs: Essays on the Processes of Writing and Reading in Relation to the Teaching of Literature*. Southampton: University of Southampton, Dept. of Education.
Blyton, E. (1946) *Five Go off in a Caravan*. London: Hodder and Stoughton.
Blyton, E. (1947) *Five on Kirrin Island Again*. London: Hodder and Stoughton.
Blyton, E. (1948) *Five Go off to Camp*. London: Hodder and Stoughton.
Blyton, E. (1954) *Five Go to Mystery Moor*. London: Hodder and Stoughton.
Blyton, E. (1957) *Five Go to Billycock Hill*. London: Hodder and Stoughton.
Cadogan, M. and Craig, P. (1976) *You're a Brick, Angela!* London: Gollancz.
Chambers, A. (1985) *Booktalk: Occasional Writings on Literature and Children*. London: Bodley Head.
Comic Strip (1982) *Five Go Mad in Dorset*. Channel 4, 2 November.
Dixon, B. (1974) The nice, the naughty and the nasty: the tiny world of Enid Blyton. *Children's Literature in Education*, 15: 43–59.
Fisher, S. (1972) *Self-consuming Artifacts*. Berkeley: University of California Press.
Foucault, M. (1980) *Power/Knowledge: Selected Interviews and Other Writings 1972–1977*. Brighton: Harvester Wheatsheaf.
Harrington, C. L. and Bielby, D. D. (1995) *Soap Fans: Pursuing Pleasure and Making Meaning in Everyday Life*. Philadephia: Temple University Press.
Hunt, P. (1978) The cliché count: a practical aid for the selection of books for children. *Children's Literature in Education*, 9(3): 143–50.
Inglis, F. (1981) *The Promise of Happiness*. Cambridge: Cambridge University Press.
Jenkins, H. (1992) *Textual Poachers: Television Fans and Participatory Culture*. London: Routledge.
Leavis, F. R. (1948) *The Great Tradition*. Harmondsworth: Penguin.
McDowell, M. (1976) Fiction for children and adults: some essential differences. In G. Fox, G. Hammond, T. Jones, F. Smith and K. Sterk (eds) *Writers, Critics and Children: Articles from Children's Literature in Education*. London: Heinemann Educational.

Radway, J. A. (1987) *Reading the Romance: Women, Patriarchy and Popular Culture.* London: Verso.

Ray, S. G. (1982) *The Blyton Phenomenon: The Controversy Surrounding the World's Most Successful Children's Author.* London: André Deutsch.

Rose, J. (1984) *The Case of Peter Pan, or the Impossibility of Children's Fiction.* London: Macmillan.

Rudd, D. (1992). *A Communication Studies Approach to Children's Literature.* Sheffield: Sheffield Hallam University Press.

Rudd, D. (1995) Shirley, the bathwater, and definitions of children's literature. *Papers: Explorations into Children's Literature*, 5(2/3): 88–96.

Rudd, D. (1997) Enid Blyton and the mystery of children's literature. Unpublished PhD thesis, Sheffield Hallam University.

Rudd, D. (forthcoming) *Enid Blyton and the Mystery of Children's Literature.* Basingstoke: Macmillan.

Rustin, M. and Rustin, M. (1987) *Narratives of Love and Loss: Studies in Modern Children's Fiction.* London: Verso.

Schlager, N. (1978) Predicting children's choices in literature: a developmental approach. *Children's Literature in Education*, 30(4): 136–42.

Singer, D. G. (1972) Piglet, Pooh, and Piaget. *Psychology Today*, June: 71–4, 96.

Speier, M. (1976) The child as conversationalist: some culture contact features of conversational interactions between adults and children. In M. Hammersley and P. Woods (eds) *The Process of Schooling: A Sociological Reader.* London: Routledge and Kegan Paul/Milton Keynes: Open University Press.

Tucker, N. (ed.) (1976) *Suitable for Children? Controversies in Children's Literature.* Brighton: Sussex University Press.

Walkerdine, V. (1990) *Schoolgirl Fictions.* London: Verso.

Willis, P. (1977) *Learning to Labour: How Working Class Kids get Working Class Jobs.* Farmborough: Saxon House.

5 Lessons: philosophy for children

BARBARA DELAFIELD

Over the past twenty years classroom talk has become of increasing interest to researchers engaged in studying the process of teaching and learning. During the 1970s and 1980s research into cognitive development was motivated by a growing dissatisfaction with experimental studies (Donaldson 1978; Light and Butterworth 1992). This, together with an interest in Vygotskian theory, gave rise to a body of research that saw the process of education, rather than its outcome, as an appropriate focus of research. The elaboration of Vygotskian theory by developmental psychologists has led to research that is based on a socio-cultural perspective. This approach calls for the study of development by consideration of the linguistic, social and historical context of the phenomena under investigation (Cole 1991). With regard to classroom practice this means that in order to be meaningful any investigation must include not only an examination of what is happening in the classroom, but also an exploration of the institutional and cultural discourses that inform that situation. The investigation of classroom talk is seen as an important means of studying this process.

Much of the research into classroom talk has grown from an interest in socio-cognitive development, and has used a socio-linguistic framework to inform its methodology. A major influence in this area has been the work of Sinclair and Coultard (1975). This led to research that analysed and categorized the structure of classroom talk in order to explore how knowledge is presented in the classroom. However, the acquisition of classroom communicative competence was seen as an end in itself, and the meaning of exchange was of little consequence. Recent work from a socio-linguistic perspective has explored how the positioning of subjects within discourse determines what is seen as acceptable talk within that discourse situation. Deborah Hicks (1996) provides an overview of a number of studies that have used discourse analysis to investigate classroom talk.

One such study (O'Conner and Michaels 1996) proposes that the construct of a 'participant framework' is a useful unit of analysis for the study of classroom discourse. They describe the participant framework as 'encompassing (a) the ways that speech event participants are aligned with or against each other and (b) the ways they are positioned relative to topics and even specific utterances' (O'Conner and Michaels 1996: 69). In a socio-linguistic study of literacy, James Gee (1990) looked at how conflicts can arise between the teacher's traditional educational discourse and the child's traditional cultural discourse. He described how the early school experiences of a black working-class girl acted to devalue her dominant creative story telling discourse. This had the effect of alienating the girl from the idea of schooling, with the result that by the time her skills as a story teller would have been valued in educational terms, she was uninterested and had switched off from schooling. A proposed solution to the problem of alienation is the introduction and acceptance of multiple discourses in the classroom. If, however, we accept this solution it becomes of even more importance to investigate the *meaning* of the discourse rather than its structure.

Dissatisfied with methodologies that did not consider the meaning of classroom utterances, Edwards and Mercer (1987) carried out research that explored the language of teaching and learning. This research illustrated the way that knowledge is constructed and shared in the classroom. Mercer (1995) proposed that in order to investigate the process of teaching and learning it is necessary to investigate the linguistic, psychological and cultural aspects of classroom interaction. He demonstrated how such an investigation can help to uncover the type of talk that is successful in helping children to achieve an 'educated' discourse. Mercer first of all identified three analytic categories of talk that typify classroom talk: disputational talk, cumulative talk and exploratory talk. He describes these categories as models of 'three *distinctive social modes of thinking*' (Mercer 1995: 104), which can then be used to help us understand how talk is used in the joint construction of knowledge. He then took these analytic categories and investigated them from linguistic, psychological and cultural perspectives. At the linguistic level examination is of the talk as spoken text: what kind of speech acts do the students perform? (Do they assert, challenge, explain, request?). The psychological level focuses on the type of ground rules that the speakers seem to be following: how does the way they interact mirror their interests and concerns? The third level, the cultural level, Mercer (1995: 106) saw as a 'consideration of the nature of "educated" discourse and of the kinds of reasoning that are valued and encouraged in the cultural institutions of formal education'. He concluded that exploratory talk provided the context best suited to the development of the type of reasoning valued in an educated society.

Implicit in much of the research into classroom discourse is the assumption of the privileged position of this discourse. Research that has focused on ways of encouraging 'educated discourse' has failed to investigate the effect of privileging educated discourse on those whose dominant discourses are devalued by this approach. Research that has looked at these issues has pointed out that the privileging of educated discourse acts to advantage middle-class children, and to alienate those whose dominant discourse not only differs from this accepted norm, but is also considered inferior (Gee 1990). It is perhaps because research has tended to focus on ways of enculturing children into an educated discourse that there has been little research on classroom discourse from a Foucauldian perspective (see Walkerdine and Lucey 1989). This would involve an investigation of the discourses produced in the classroom in order to uncover the power relationships embedded in discourse (Parker 1992). Work that has studied educational practice from this perspective has demonstrated that educational practice is influenced by Piagetian theory (Burman 1994). This perspective sees the child as a 'psychological individual' rather than a 'cultural participant' (Edwards and Mercer 1987).

Text: 'P4C'

The research reported here is taken from an ongoing research programme investigating the introduction of innovation into the classroom from a socio-cultural perspective. The particular innovation being investigated is Lipman's (1988) 'Philosophy for Children' (P4C), a discussion-based programme designed to enhance children's reasoning skills. The programme originated in the United States, but has been introduced to the UK under the umbrella of an organization called SAPERE. Teachers are trained to use Socratic dialogue as a means of encouraging discussion on a number of philosophical questions. The use of Socratic dialogue requires the teacher to encourage the type of talk described by Mercer (1995) as 'exploratory talk': talk that requires the children to reflect critically upon their contributions, and provide reasons and justifications for their ideas. I do not make any evaluation here as to the validity of the philosophical nature of the questioning. What I am concerned with in this chapter is the participants' construction of the session.

Sequence 1: What was the reason?

T: The teddy wanted the girl to buy him, and how how would kicking the crayons off the shelf, how would that make that happen.

Bill: Because she might, I'm not sure.

T: You're not sure let's choose somebody else who can help us. John?

John: Loud noises attract people, loud noises especially near them attract people, they turn round to see what it is.

T: Loud noises near people attract people who turn round to see what it is.

John: Yes or just to make sure it's nothing dangerous or just because they want to see what it is.

T: Or because.

John: Because they want to see what it is [ ]

T: So you're saying that's why the teddy kicked the crayons off the shelf.

John: Yea because he thought if he did it might attract the girl.

T: He thought it might attract the girl. What are other people's ideas about this?

Sequence 2: Another question

Jill: Maybe the girl found the button for the girl.

T: Well that's another question isn't it.

Jill: Yea.

T: And that's a question that we've got up there.

Jill: That's right.

T: That we'll answer later on let's try and answer the one that we're trying to answer at the minute about kicking the button off erm Stephen.

Sequence 3: This could be the story

Jill: Where wherever the girl found the button she could have took it home and looked after it and maybe her mum gave her the money to go and buy the teddy bear and er took it home and could have found the button again wherever it was and sew it back on and sew it on the teddy.

T: It could possibly have happened go on Simon what did you want to say to that.

Sequence 4: This is how it was

Simon: When [ ] he didn't know what that button was for so he just
pressed the button [ ] he wanted to get out but the managers
kept looking in [ ] so he couldn't get out.

T: And you're telling us a bit about when the teddy looked for
the button and he couldn't find it yes he got mixed up with
the train button didn't he. Robin what have you got to say
about all this?

Sequence 5: I have nothing to say

T: Jill.

Jill: I didn't put my hand up.

T: That's OK.

Theoretically, my research is informed by the socio-cultural perspective
outlined by Cole (1991, 1995) and Mercer (1995). Because this calls for
research that takes into consideration the multifaceted nature of classroom
interaction, I have chosen a methodology based on that proposed by Mercer (1995). I have, however, attempted to extend Mercer's ideas on the
cultural focus of the analysis. Rather than seeing this as one level of focus,
I see it as a number of interconnecting facets, each deserving consideration
as part of the overall investigation. To demonstrate how exploration of
these facets can add to our understanding of the teaching and learning
situation, I focus my analysis on the discourse themes used in this session
from a number of different perspectives. By using discourse analysis I am
able to explore the discourses drawn on by both the teachers and the
pupils, and examine how these may be mediated by the context into which
they are being introduced.

The text is taken from a P4C session held with a class of 6- and 7-year-old children. There were 25 children, 12 boys and 13 girls, in the class.
The session was run by the school's headteacher, who has trained in the
use of P4C, and the class teacher was also present. I recorded the session
on audiotape. The participants knew that they were being recorded, and I
was introduced by the teacher as someone 'who was interested in finding
out how they did philosophy'.

Reading

Exploration of the text at the 'linguistic' level indicated that the talk was characteristic of 'exploratory talk'. Sequence 1 illustrates how the teacher prompted the children to clarify their answers and provide explanations and justifications for their ideas.

Analysis focusing on the psychological level revealed the following ground rules: (a) one person should speak at a time, the teacher choosing who is to speak next; (b) everyone will be given a chance to speak; (c) what is being looked for is a number of different ideas, not one right answer; (d) ideas must be backed by reasons, and must relate to the question being explored; and (e) all contributions are to be valued.

Investigating the text from the cultural level, as outlined by Mercer (1995), I found that the session as a whole was characterized by the use of exploratory talk. Section 1 of the transcript in the text box typifies the kind of talk that was encouraged in this session. In previous sessions the children had watched a video of the story and collected a number of questions about things in the story that interested them. The question that was being discussed in this session was 'Why did Corduroy [a teddy bear] kick the crayons off the shelf?' The sequence reported here occurred after another child had suggested that the crayons might have been kicked off in order to make a loud noise. The teacher asks for other contributions, and then, by repeating John's remark, or focusing on certain aspects ('or because'), prompts him to give a reason for his answer, before offering the discussion back to the group. During the discussion the children are invited to agree or disagree with each other's statements, and give reasons for their responses. Now, by expanding the analysis I shall demonstrate how the privileging of one discourse acted to repress attempts to introduce other discourses into the session.

Analysis of the text concentrating on the children's discourse focuses on four discourse themes. These I have labelled 'explanatory', 'questioning', 'story telling' and 'recall'. Of these themes, 'explanatory', as exemplified by sequence 1, was, as I have illustrated above, the one that was encouraged by the teacher. The point being made here is that in this particular session the discourse that is being privileged is an 'explanatory' discourse, and that the privileging of this discourse is achieved by the repression of the attempts by the children to introduce other discourses into the discussion. Although in each instance the teacher closes the child's move by inviting another child to speak, there are differences in the way other discourse moves are repressed. We will take first of all Jill's initial attempt at entering the discussion, using a 'questioning' discourse, in sequence 2. The teacher acknowledges this question as suitable for discussion, at the same time pointing out that it is not relevant to the question being discussed: 'That we'll answer later on let's try and answer the one that we're trying to answer at the minute.' Simon's contribution, sequence 4, is acknowledged as something he could add to the discussion, 'you're telling us', and correct recall, 'yes he got mixed up with the train button didn't he', even though the teacher does not encourage Simon to expand further. When Jill, sequence 3, attempts to enter the discussion using a 'story telling' discourse, the teacher's response, 'It could possibly have happened', is more dismissive, neither offering promise of later discussion, as in 2, nor acknowledging its use to the group, as in 4. Having explored the differences in the way the children's attempts to enter the discussion were repressed, my analysis goes on to focus on the ideology underpinning the session.

My analysis so far has indicated that this session was characterized by the teacher's use of an 'exploratory' discourse. This discourse could also be described as a 'Socratic' discourse as advocated by Lipman (1988), as a means of enhancing children's reasoning skills. In order to illustrate how an investigation of the discourses that inform the session could increase our understanding of the teaching and learning process, I will look briefly at how the acceptance of a Socratic discourse could account for the differences in the way the children's other discourses were repressed. We have already looked at how, in sequences 2 and 4, the teacher, while closing the child's turn, does acknowledge the discourse as being legitimate. These discourses, although not appropriate to the current session, are legitimate discourses to use at other stages of Socratic inquiry as proposed by Lipton, when the children would need to 'recall' the story in order to gather 'questions'. The offering at 3, however, a 'story telling' discourse, would not be seen as appropriate to this process, and can therefore be dismissed without encouragement.

Having proposed that Socratic discourse was the theoretical basis influencing this session, I now turn to some of the implications of accepting this model as a basis for educational practice. Socrates, as the 'master', is seen as the authority on the way his pupils should express their ideas. He prompts them to search for the 'truth', which is seen as something within their heads. This view is consistent with the Piagetian view of the child as a 'psychological individual', and therefore also consistent with institutional views of the aims of educational practice (Edwards and Mercer 1987; Burman 1994).

Another focal point for the analysis relates to the proposal by Gee (1991) that repression of a child's own discourse could alienate him or her from schooling. While the analysis reported in this chapter has not explored the discourses used from this perspective, it is interesting to note that there was a possible association between the repression of a child's discourse and his or her subsequent involvement in the session. For example, in sequences 2 and 3, Jill's attempts to enter the discussion were unsuccessful. If we now look at sequence 5, which was taken from the end of the session, there are two points worthy of further investigation. The first is that when invited to do so by the teacher, Jill declines to speak. The second is that in doing so she makes specific reference to the ground rules, something the teacher did in sequence 2, when she rejected Jill's contribution.

The analysis reported here is necessarily brief and incomplete. The aim has been to illustrate how discourse analysis can be used to investigate the multi-layered nature of classroom interaction, and thus to provide a framework for research, rather than to present an in-depth analysis of the text presented.

I will now look at the disadvantages or problems that arise first of all as a result of my choice of methodology, then from the viewpoint of other researchers who use a discursive approach to investigate classroom talk, and finally from the viewpoint of researchers who advocate an empirical approach. I will then conclude by investigating how these problems can be tackled, and outlining some of the advantages to be gained by using the discourse approach I am advocating here.

Disadvantages

Research of this kind is time-consuming on a number of levels. In order to research classroom talk, I need transcripts of classroom sessions, and not only is transcription itself a lengthy business, but gaining permission to tape sessions and spending time in schools to collect data also take time. The length of the report itself can appear prohibitive. The approach advocated here requires the reporting of each layer (or stage) of analysis in full. This is in order to provide a socio-cultural reading of the processes being explored. This is not only a problem for the researcher, of the time needed to complete such a report, but the report itself can appear long-winded and difficult to read. A related difficulty is that in trying to give a brief overview there is the risk of presenting what may appear to be a banal or sanitized version of the research, which does not do justice to the complexities and contradictions present in the text.

The next set of problems is connected with the position of the researcher in the research. In presenting *my* way of reading the text, there is a danger that this could be perceived as *the* way of doing discourse analysis. Not only do different texts require different readings, as can be seen in the diversity of approaches presented in this book, but one text can also be read in different ways. The interests and concerns of the person reading the text will, for instance, affect the way a text is read. This leads us to the danger of reporting the reading in such a way that its reflexive aspects are concealed, and tends to close the reading to alternative interpretations. It could also lead to the view that the discourse is something already in the text waiting to be found, rather than something that emerges through our reading of the text. A related difficulty is that of the power of the researcher, for the researcher's interpretation of the text is one reading of the text that can, if we are not careful, become seen as the 'expert' analysis of the text, one that describes what is actually happening. This produces a dilemma for the researcher, who, while wishing to carry out research that empowers others, can at the same time be accused of wielding power over the words of the very people he or she hopes to help.

This leads me to a criticism that I have encountered with regard to the research I am carrying out. This comes from a view which has been put to me by other researchers carrying out research into classroom interaction. This is that teachers have to teach within the education system as it stands, and that research into classroom practice that might be seen to question that system might also be seen as a criticism of the teachers who carry out that practice. In this view, classroom practice should be studied from the viewpoint of current educational aims, and theoretical studies of the implications of those aims should be a separate issue.

It is not difficult to find objections to this approach from an empirical standpoint, many of which have been dealt with elsewhere (see Parker and Burman 1993). It is worth looking here at one criticism that is aimed at the use of discursive methodology in developmental and educational research in particular. This is that in order to ascertain that development has occurred we need to be able to measure the degree of that development. Education is above all about outcomes, about becoming 'educated', and the only way we can see if this is happening is by having empirical measurements of children's abilities.

Advantages

There is little that can be done about the workload and length of time it takes to carry out this type of research, except to be aware of this from the outset. The problem connected with the length of the report can, however, be viewed from another perspective. One of the advantages of applying different levels of analysis to the same situation is that although the completed report will be a lengthy document, each level of analysis will also be a mini-report in its own right. For example, teachers participating in the study have found the analysis of the type of talk reported at the linguistic level a useful indication of whether or not the discussion was fulfilling criteria they had in mind.

The problems connected with the position of the researcher in the research are best addressed by ensuring that the report carries an adequate discussion of these issues. In doing this I would make clear that the reading of the text that I am presenting is *my* interpretation of the text. The discourses presented have arisen from my work on the text, rather than being something inherent in the text waiting to be discovered. The advantage of discourse analysis is that it makes public the sources used in the reading. By making clear the subjective influences that help to inform the reading, discourse analysis allows the reader to evaluate the work from a position of understanding.

My answer to the criticism that this approach could be seen as a criticism of the teachers involved is to work with the teachers as joint participants in the research. This has the added advantage of gaining another perspective on the text, which is helpful as part of the process of analysis. With regard to the point that theoretical studies of the aims should be looked at as a separate issue, my response is that in order to make a full study of these aims we need to explore the effect they have on classroom practice, and one way of doing this is to carry out discourse analysis on classroom interaction.

When looking at the objection, from an empirical viewpoint, that education should be measured by statistical measures, I would say that I am not maintaining that such measures have no place in research. There may well be times when it is valid and useful to have numerical data that can inform us of children's individual progress. These measures will not, however, inform us about the *processes* involved in such progress. The advantage of taking a discourse approach is that it allows us not only to explore how teachers and children work together to develop an 'educated' discourse, but also to look at how children become aware, or fail to become aware, of the appropriateness of different discourses to different situations. Moreover, education does not happen in a social or historical vacuum. Using discourse analysis to carry out a socio-cultural exploration of the teaching and learning situation can help us to develop a critical awareness of the underlying assumptions informing classroom practice. This knowledge will enable us to evaluate the practice from an informed position.

Key reading

Hicks, D. (1996) Introduction. In D. Hicks (ed.) *Discourse, Learning and Schooling*. Cambridge: Cambridge University Press.
Mercer, N. (1995) Talking and working together. In N. Mercer, *The Guided Construction of Knowledge: Talk among Teachers and Learners*. Clevedon: Multilingual Matters.

References

Burman, E. (1994) *Deconstructing Developmental Psychology*. London: Routledge.
Cole, M. (1991) Conclusion. In L. Resnick and S. Teasley (eds) *Perspectives on Socially Shared Cognition*. Washington, DC: American Psychological Association.

Cole, M. (1995) Socio-cultural-historical psychology. In J. V. Wertsch, P. DelRio and A. Alverez (eds) *Sociocultural Studies of Mind*. Cambridge: Cambridge University Press.

Donaldson, M. (1978) *Children's Minds*. London: Fontana.

Edwards, D. and Mercer, N. (1987) *Common Knowledge: The Development of Understanding in the Classroom*. London: Methuen.

Gee, J. (1990) *Social Linguistics and Literacy: Ideology in Discourses*. London, Falmer Press.

Hicks, D. (ed.) (1996) Introduction. In D. Hicks (ed.) *Discourse, Learning and Schooling*. Cambridge: Cambridge University Press.

Light, P. and Butterworth, G. (eds) (1992) *Context and Cognition: Ways of Learning and Knowing*. London: Harvester Wheatsheaf.

Lipman, M. (1988) *Philosophy Goes to School*. Philadelphia: Temple University Press.

Mercer, N. (1995) *The Guided Construction of Knowledge: Talk among Teachers and Learners*. Clevedon: Multilingual Matters.

O'Conner, M. C. and Michaels, S. (1996) Shifting participant frameworks: orchestrating thinking practices in group discussion. In D. Hicks (ed.) *Discourse, Learning and Schooling*. Cambridge: Cambridge University Press.

Parker, I. (1992) *Discourse Dynamics: Critical Analysis for Social and Individual Psychology*. London: Routledge.

Parker, I. and Burman, E. (1993) Against discursive imperialism, empiricism and constructionism: thirty two problems with discourse analysis. In E. Burman and I. Parker (eds) *Discourse Analytic Research: Repertoires and Readings of Texts in Action*. London and New York: Routledge.

Sinclair, J. and Coultard, R. (1975) *Towards an Analysis of Discourse*. London: Oxford University Press.

Walkerdine, V. and Lucey, H. (1989) *Democracy in the Kitchen: Regulating Mothers and Socialising Daughters*. London, Virago.

PART II

Visual texts

6 | **Comics:** strip semiotics

DAN HEGGS

The surprisingly long and contentious history of comic books and strips can be viewed as doing the medium an undeserved disservice. Frequently it has served to focus attention on such emotive topics as suitable reading material for children and the effects of violent images on (impressionable) minds. In fact, for a period in the 1950s, comics occupied a similar position in the public imagination to that of violent film and video today. Public campaigns were fought in Britain and America that, successfully, sought to restrict the content and variety of comics available (for further detail concerning the ideological underpinnings of these campaigns see Barker 1984, 1989). However, almost constantly overlooked was the *form*, the perception being that comics were 'at best a marginal, silly medium, suitable only for children' (Barker 1984: 6). If the medium was the message, then it hardly deserved serious attention. It has been said, however, that 'Though American comic books and comic strips have often been unsophisticated in their subject matter, in form they display a highly developed narrative grammer and vocabulary based on an inextricable combination of verbal and visual elements' (Witek 1989: 3). These verbal and visual elements are commonly known as the *conventions* and are the standard set of pieces which enable comics to be read.

There have been a number of attempts to examine the relationship between word and image, but these have usually relied on more conventional texts, such as magazines and newspapers, where written texts have been accompanied by illustrations (see, for example, Barthes 1957; Kress and Van Leeuwen 1996; Kress *et al.* 1997). Unfortunately, comics tend to mix word and image to convey information, and are therefore a hybrid medium that has rarely been scrutinized. However, with greater visual literacy and, in particular, the rapid growth of the World Wide Web, there is an increasing need to understand, and advance, methods that critically engage with the heady cocktail of words and images. Comics, with their well established conventions, 'provide a fertile half-way zone for those seeking to couple the visual and the literary' (Nericcio 1995: 83). Comics remain, in this formulation, a marginalized medium, positioned unnoticed in the opposition between word and image, but they do offer consolation for those seeking to explain what Nericcio describes as a process of ' "contamination" of word *by* image' (Nericcio 1995: 79).

The beguilingly simple mix of words and pictures in comics can be problematic. Caution needs to be exercised so that one register is not emphasized to the detriment of the other; especially, as I will argue, considering that the verbal register is held under the sway of the visual. The issue of translation is therefore a central concern, often stressed when the focus is placed on how images may 'communicate' and be 'used' by readers. As a result, a semiotic approach is often favoured. Kress and Van Leeuwen, in their book *Reading Images: a Grammar of Visual Design* (1996), are critical of approaches that emphasize the formal or aesthetic description of images. They prefer to consider how a 'grammar of visual design' is involved in the production of meaning. This is, for them, an attempt to describe 'the way in which depicted people, places and things combine in visual "statements" of greater or lesser complexity and extension' (p. 1). This is to say that they are concerned with the way in which these statements 'are combined into a meaningful whole' (*ibid.*). This is an important project, but it still maintains an opposition between word and image, as 'language and visual communication realize the same more fundamental and far-reaching systems of communication that constitute our cultures, but that each does so by means of its own specific forms, and independently' (p. 17).

This problematic break, albeit useful on their terms, does not take into consideration *hybrid* texts like comics. In a discussion of Barthes (1957), reference is made to comic strips as an example of an *image–text* relation. The inclusion of verbal information in *speech balloons* (see below) is thought of as *extending* the meaning of the image, or vice versa. This relation is called *relay*, and is where new and different meanings are added to the image (as opposed to *elaboration*, where a restating of the information is put into more precise terms). Indicated here is a limit to Barthes's theory which suggests that images have meaning related to, or dependent on, verbal texts, and that 'visual meaning is too indefinite' (Kress and Van Leeuwen 1996: 17). When one is considering a hybrid form, like comics, the inclusion of verbal elements must be treated with caution, especially as the word and image relationship is reciprocal; elements from each register affect the way that the other can be read. This idea is centrally placed within Barker's (1989: 1) *dialogical* approach to comics, where the stated intention was to test theories of ideology and how these discuss 'persuasive forms of communication in our society'.

The method adopted by Barker was part of a move away from arbitrary interpretations that result in a 'confusion of possible "meanings"' (Barker 1989: 13). He wanted, rightly, to 'show that a methodical, checkable account can be given' (*ibid.*). At the centre of this account was the 'contract' between reader and text as the point where 'meaning' arises. This relies on the formulaic nature of comics, where certain situations and styles can be expected, and so a dialogue between reader and text can be initiated. Barker (1989: 261) contends that an approach to one (reader or text) implicitly starts to define the other. This is evident early on when Barker describes the form of the comic text. He suggests that the conventions turn 'out to be involved in much more than the simple transmission of meanings' (p. 11). Rather, the use of conventions functions to condition the meaning of the text and, also, to 'condense social relationships' and 'help to determine the type of reader we become', and 'make reading a social relationship between us and the text' (*ibid.*). In other words, comic books cannot be approached critically without some understanding of their form.

One of the chief problems with comic analysis is the need to be cautious about translation from one register to another. Through a descriptive reading of the example text, I will show how the conventions work to represent a wide range of actions and situations. I will use a style similar to that of Eco's (1987) semiotic approach. However, in place of a search for the meaning of the text through the identification of the various semiotic elements, I wish to illustrate how narrative and discourse might signify within a comic text.

Text: Einstein's Last Case

The chosen text is taken from a compilation comic called *Negative Burn*, which appears bi-monthly from the American publisher Caliber Press. The example is the opening page of a six-page short story. It relates how Albert Einstein, having been invited to speak at the Groves Institute by a graduate student, successfully uncovers the true identity of the killer of a physics researcher and in so doing clears the name of the graduate student who, we are told later, had been framed for the murder. The text was chosen

partly for copyright reasons, but a number of points have informed its use: (a) it is from an independent publisher and so stereotypical expectations might be avoided; (b) there is clear page layout and use of conventions; (c) there is use of caricature of well known figures.

At a glance, the use of half-tones to colour the page, the obvious caricature of Einstein and the inclusion of gothic script would seem to give the page an unusual appearance that does not fit the stereotype of American big-footed heroes in garish colours or stylized characters from British children's comics. However, while this example is clearly not part of mainstream comic book production, the use of conventions remains the same. A comparison of the uses of the conventions within mainstream and alternative comics demonstrated that the major difference between the two was in subject matter rather than differences of form (Huxley 1990). This is important, in this instance, as the signifying qualities of the text will be emphasized over and above the different genres. This would appear to support the tautological dictum that, 'a comic is what has been produced under the definition of a "comic"' (Barker 1989: 8). Of course, Barker also argues that prevailing definitions can serve to constrain the subject matter. To stray from what is considered suitable is to court controversy.

The approach to be taken will be similar to that of Eco's (1987) semiotic reading of the Steve Canyon comic strip. This will enable the interaction of the verbal and visual elements to be highlighted and will consider the manner in which visual elements condition the way in which verbal elements might be read (Barker 1989). In other words, the different parts of a comic page and panel will be examined with a view to showing how speech balloons, separate panels and dialogue boxes function visually and semantically to carry narratives meaningfully. Barker also stresses the importance of the conventions in the formation of a 'contract' between reader and text. The disruption of the relationship between word and image enables a consideration of the ways in which readers may be positioned with regard to a text.

Eco saw the critic's task as identifying the mode used by the author as part of a process that allows the message of the story to be decoded. Here the point is merely to demonstrate the signifying properties of comics and the difficulties in approaching a hybrid verbal/visual medium with a view to analysis. This necessitates the identification of themes and discourses immanent to the text and any intertextual connections to other comic or film texts.

Reading

A critical reading of the opening page serves a twofold purpose in this context. First, it allows the separate parts of the comic page to be distinguished and the relationships between the conventions to be indicated. Second, it offers an example analysis of a comic text. This double exercise will illustrate how the conventions work to signify and represent meaning through word and image, and also how the reader might be positioned with respect to the page and narratives.

The first thing to be noted is the basic layout of the page, as it functions as a hard edge or a panel that cannot be altered in the way that individual panels can. The opening page here is a *splash* page, where the five panels of increasing height function as an introduction to the story, and it 'prepares [the reader's] attitude for the events that follow. It sets a climate' (Eisner 1985: 62). Such pages may also appear in the middle of a story as a single panel, which break up the narrative sequence. At a glance, however, little sense can be made of the page, as each panel contains particular information. The panel is the smallest syntactical unit of a comic page (although not the smallest meaningful unit), and panels are usually read from left to right, down the page and in sequence, where the eye follows both verbal and visual elements in order to follow the narrative (see Sabin 1993: 6). The size and shape of a panel, as well as the panel frame, can be altered to achieve certain effects. This is to say that the panel and frame can function as a 'narrative device' (Eisner 1985: 46). The frame, according to Barker (1989: 11), 'establishes our relation to the world being presented'. Changes to the frame affect the way in which the panel's contents may be read. Finally, the gaps between panels, known as *gutters*, are central to the way in which comics are read. McCloud (1993) suggests that this is associated with *closure*, which forms the grammar of comics. Transitions from panel to panel are therefore central to reading and understanding comics.

Panel 1

The first panel is very wide but short and the people shown are in the middle distance. The sign indicating 'town trains' tells us that the location we are looking at is a station in a large town. The speech balloon points in the direction of the central character, Einstein, and also brings the 'man in black' to our attention. The typeface within the balloon is slightly gothic, or Germanic. It indicates how the text ought to be read, or heard. As Barker (1989: 11) says, 'it is as if, in fact, we don't *read* the words at all. We Hear them.' The characters represented are caricatures, which McCloud suggests makes identification simpler. However, the background is far more detailed. This can be thought of as what Barthes (1957) called a 'reality effect' that functions 'to confirm the mimetic contract and assure the reader that he or she can interpret the text as about a real world' (Radford 1989: 31).

Panel 2

The focus is now drawn closer to the figure of the 'agent' impatiently looking at his watch. Einstein sneakily moves away as an old woman innocently wanders past. The panel is slightly taller and less extraneous information is given. However, a *dialogue box* is included, which introduces the story and the reason for Einstein's presence in a station. These boxes, in a sense, are similar to Barthes's idea of *relay*: the image is being extended by the information. It is a snapshot allowing the dialogue box to introduce the narrative and also giving more information about the central character.

Panel 3

In the two prior panels a sense of movement was achieved 'between panels': from Einstein in the phone box to his avoidance of the agent. The third panel continues this between-panel movement – what McCloud (1993: 70) calls an *action-to-action* movement – but also introduces *within*-panel movement. We can deduce that Einstein is moving away from his sprinting guard through the taunting gesture, the lines implying the blurring of speed and also the speech. The balloon measures the distance between Einstein and the guard, but what is said, and the time required to read it, only increases this distance. In other words, the panel is using space and dialogue to give the impression of the passing of time. Finally, the dialogue box follows on from the previous panel and is integrally connected to the title, designed as part of the page. This can, then, be read from the second panel and the content of the third panel is read next, where the title functions as a full stop indicating the start of the main section of the narrative.

The first three panels introduce the story and set the scene of the narrative, which takes off in the following panel. This is what Eco (1987: 23) calls a *crescendo effect*.

Panel 4

Again, the width of the page is important, but with the fifth panel breaking up the frame as an inset so that focus is drawn to the close-up of Einstein in repose and can be thought of as a *scene-to-scene* (*ibid.*) transition from the third panel. Shown with pen and book in hand, Einstein is deep in thought preparing his talk. This impression is reinforced by the included dialogue, which uses the same typeface as Einstein's speech. However, quotation marks mark the dialogue as written, as in a notebook. It is as if the dialogue comes after the image and helps to make sense of it. It introduces a central theme of the narrative, responsibility.

Panel 5

The final panel is a small inset and proportionally much taller and narrower than the others. As can be seen, changes in panel size and shape allow different perspectives to be stressed, and the artist can alter the position of the reader with regard to the content of the panel. In this instance, a twofold movement is achieved. First, the reader is distanced from Einstein. He is shown in the distance to be out of breath, which juxtaposes with the naughty professor escaping from his guard, emphasizing the age of the character. Second, the dialogue continues from the previous panel, so the reader is still privy to Einstein's thoughts and preoccupations.

There is a film-like quality to the opening sequence, where the focus tracks the movements of Einstein, emphasized by the wide (letterbox) panels. However, the transitions are not the equivalent of film shots. There is a jumping between different shots that are made understandable through the process of reading. In other words, meaning is retroactively conferred to each panel. The use of word and image combines information that supplements each for the other. For instance, Einstein appears to be a slightly frivolous figure enjoying his ability to outwit the guard. At the same time, the thought dialogue (in panel 4) shows a more serious side to his nature. Further, the 1950s setting is emphasized through the use of half-tone colouring and Einstein's ominous guard functions as a reminder of Cold War paranoia. The overall effect is similar to a thriller film, and film noir in particular. In conclusion, then, the verbal and visual elements function in tandem to provide a complex overall representation, with the juxtaposition of the two adding to the drama. As Sabin (1993: 9) states, a 'strip does not "happen" in the words, or the pictures, but somewhere in-between'.

Disadvantages

The reading of this example page examined the interactions between the verbal and visual elements and demonstrated how a reciprocal relationship exists between such elements that influences the production of meaning in the explication of the narrative. In other words, a symbiosis between word and image is in place; each affects how the other is read. However, there are a number of issues pertaining to this kind of reading that can be problematic. I will identify four main areas of concern. These are all interconnected, with the central focus on the close reading of the text as a common theme.

The first problem concerns the example text. Using only the first page might be seen as limiting the effectiveness of the analysis. This is because only a segment of the narrative is included and, obviously, the story unfolds over several pages. The analysis might have reached different conclusions given the full text. The other issue associated with this is the complexity of the comic page. First, the different parts of the panel require greater elaboration and, second, the complete range of comic conventions was barely touched upon.

The second problem concerns the particularity of the example. Such a close 'reading' cannot easily be used for large-scale studies. The approach adopted by Barker (1989) for the analysis of British children's comics relied upon the formulaic nature of comics, whereby situations and characters could be expected to behave within certain limits. However, we have been examining compendium comics where one-off stories and strips quickly have to forge a connection with the reader. One might argue that the strips need to reference other genres using iconographic hints to enable the reader to orientate himself or herself to the text.

The third problem is the reliance on description to enable an analysis of the page. This is an important issue, as it involves the cleavage of word and image. I have argued that comics are a hybrid form. The descriptive style of analysis is not just long-winded, therefore, but also entails a process of translation. As such it might be thought of as doing violence to the text, as complex hybrid representations are thus circumscribed and reinscribed in a single register. The process of translation is also an impoverishment of the text, and the particular form of the information is altered so that it now signifies in different ways. This translation also relies on the subjective interpretation of different aspects of the images where various connotations were available for the images. Inclusion of the text enables the description to be checked and differences to be registered. It was this confusion of meanings that Barker wished to avoid. The problem of the descriptive nature of the analysis is closely connected with the final disadvantage of the approach, that of the place of the reader.

This final problem concerns the nature and position of the 'reader'. Barker's dialogical approach attempts to account for the relationship that is forged between reader and text. The contract that he proposes, as the point where meaning arises, links both sides of this equation. The disadvantage here is that the 'reader' functions as a concept that is required to make sense of the particular reading. This is to say that the reader is constructed and positioned through the process of critical reading as an ideal reader. A close reading should open up the ways in which the text might be read, but it does not necessarily thereby engage with alternative readings that might arise in different contexts.

Advantages

Having identified and outlined four key disadvantages to the approach used here, the task remains to respond and examine how some of these methodological weaknesses also offer strengths and advantages over other methods. This is not in order to invalidate or negate the problems already mentioned, but rather to show how such aspects can be useful in developing critical readings. Again, these four advantages are interconnected.

The problem associated with the use of a single example page is not easily overcome. However, the intention of the chapter was to examine how comic conventions function as a hybrid form of verbal and visual text. To try to analyse and describe them *in situ* would be to treat them as pieces of a jigsaw, where the jigsaw is not shown. Further, the number and variety of conventions cannot be adequately or easily covered. McCloud (1993) shows how different genres and authors use the conventions and transitions in radically differing ways.

The particularity of the close reading presented here allows the text to be opened up and examined in ways that large-scale studies would miss. While the manner in which comics can be treated may seem formulaic, the distinct signifying properties of individual texts can be examined for different purposes. There is also a problem for large-scale studies, as the representational qualities of comics do not easily give way to large-scale analyses without the need to translate from the hybrid register of word and image to that of word alone. This approach does not take the comic form for granted in ways that large-scale studies usually do (see Friedburg 1990).

The descriptive style of analysis also helps us to open up the text in unexpected ways. The process of translation that occurs through careful description can enable it to be examined from different perspectives. The function and complexity of the text is highlighted through the critical reading, and this allows the signifying processes to be contained and examined. In other words, the functioning of discourse through the text becomes clearer. The text is annotated and the subsequent reading facilitates the restating of information as relay and elaboration.

Finally, the place of the reader is still open to interpretation. A critical description aids the identification of constructed subject positions within the text. This enables such positions to be read critically for their possible effects. This does not mean that readers will necessarily occupy such positions while the comic is read. In this manner, the functioning of discourse and subjectivity within the text comes to the fore. This is not to fall into the trap of reifying the conclusions of the analysis or to deny the possible material consequences of the identified discourses and positions.

The reading of the comic text has focused on the relationship between word and image in comic books. It has tried to show how the conventions are implicated in much more than the simple transmission or communication of information, but also how they influence how the information is read and represented. However, in opposition to Barker and Eco I have not tried to identify modes of texts or tried to get to the meaning of the text. Rather, I have left the text open to further interpretation in order to place the emphasis on the functioning of the conventions, avoiding their reduction to simple semiotic elements.

Key reading

Barker, M. (1989) *Comics: Power, Ideology and the Critics*. Manchester: Manchester University Press. Chapter 1: Thinking about ideology and comics.
Nericcio, W. A. (1995) Artif[r]acture: virulent pictures, graphic narrative and the ideology of the visual. *Mosaic* 28(4): 79–109.

References

Barker, M. (1984) *A Haunt of Fears: The Strange History of the British Horror Comics Campaign*. London: Pluto Press.
Barker, M. (1989) *Comics: Ideology, Power and the Critics*. Manchester: Manchester University Press.
Barthes, R. (1957/1973) *Mythologies*. London: Paladin.
Eco, U. (1987) A reading of Steve Canyon. In S. Wagstaff (ed.) *Comic Iconoclasm*. London: Institute of Contemporary Arts.
Eisner, W. (1985) *Comics and Sequential Art*. Florida: Poorhouse Press.
Eisner, W. (1995) *Graphic Storytelling*. Florida: Poorhouse Press.
Freidberg, A. (1990) A denial of difference: theories of cinematic identification. In E. A. Kaplan (ed.) *Psychoanalysis and Cinema*. London: Routledge.
Huxley, D. (1990) The growth and development of British underground and alternative comics 1966–1986. Unpublished thesis, University of Loughborough.
Jackson, D. and Wagstaff, P. (1994) *Einstein's Last Case*. In C. Moore and J. Pruett (eds) *Negative Burn*, 1(15).
Kaplan, E. A. (ed.) (1990) *Psychoanalysis and Cinema*. London: Routledge.
Kress, G. and van Leeuwen, T. (1996) *Reading Images: A Grammar of Visual Design*. London: Routledge.
Kress, G., Leite-García, R. and van Leeuwen, T. (1997) Discourse semiotics. In T. A. van Dijk (ed.) *Discourse as Structure and Process. Discourse Studies: A Multidisciplinary Introduction, Volume 1*. London: Sage.
McCloud, S. (1993) *Understanding Comics: The Invisible Art*. Northampton: Kitchen Sink Press.
Moore, C. and Pruett, J. (1994) *Negative Burn*, 1(15).
Nericcio, W. A. (1995) Artif[r]acture: virulent pictures, graphic narrative and the ideology of the visual. *Mosaic* 28(4): 79–109.
Radford, J. (1989) Coming to terms: Dorothy Williams, modernism and women. *News from Nowhere*, 7: 25–36.
Reynolds, R (1992) *Superheroes*. London: Batsford.
Sabin, R. (1993) *Adult Comics: An Introduction*. London: Routledge.
Wagstaff, S. (1987) *Comic Iconoclasm*. London: Institute of Contemporary Arts.
Witek, J. (1989) *Comic Books as History: The Narrative Art of Jack Jackson, Art Spiegelman and Harvey Pekar*. Mississippi: University Press of Mississippi.

7 Advertising: critical analysis of images

RICHARD PEARCE

Depictions of 'psycho-salesmen' by Packard (1960) recur throughout critical literature on advertising (see Meyers 1984), an example being Lasch's (1991: 164) description of psychiatry as 'the handmaiden of advertising'. There are evident historical (and discursive) links, therefore, between psychology and marketing 'cultures'.

Barthes (1972) employs quasi-psychoanalytic techniques to analyse advertisements, looking to implication, connotation, legend, correlatives, comparison, imagery and signification to extract meaning. Davidson (1992: 105) sees a tradition in Barthes that explores 'patterns of belief whose individual components rarely ever get probed or justified'. On the theme of culture and implicit mythology, Inglis (1972: 75) notes that 'we take in their [advertisements] exceptionally dense meanings only by reference to the culture which produces them.' He does not specify discourse, but discusses (pp. 101–3) 'ideas in society' that advertisements refer to. Useful material can be found in Goffman's (1976) work, which chronicles meaning generation through various dynamics associated with 'gender relations', as expressed in advertising imagery. A number of his observations are utilized in the analytic section of this chapter.

Williamson (1978) provides demonstration of what Leiss *et al.* (1990: 202) describe as the 'transference of meaning' between 'signs' (e.g. 'persons', 'objects', 'feelings' and 'social situations'). However, Leiss *et al*. (1990: 213) are suspicious of Williamson's lapse into 'anthropological notions', suggesting that her frame of reference is too broad to say much about how advertisements, as a distinct textual form, make meaning. They argue that 'All of modern culture crawls with references to archaic impulses' (*ibid*.). Cook (1992) criticizes Williamson's 'haste' in regarding meaning making as a simple process of encoding and decoding. Pearce (1997: 181) similarly expresses caution that Williamson (1978: 11) is not 'simply analysing what can be *seen* in advertisements' (original emphasis).

Seeing particular significance in imagery, Dyer (1982: 86) feels that analysis 'involves . . . regarding the pictures to be as, if not more, important than the written or spoken material'. She argues that analysis must contemplate constituent parts of the image (objects, people, social class, colour and so forth) – the denotative – and their relevance to the social ('how these objects relate to our culture') – the connotative – and the complete package of meaning ('underlying principles and attitudes') – the ideological (Dyer 1982: 94–5). For Leiss *et al*. (1990: 5), advertising is a phenomenon that 'appropriates and transforms symbols and ideas'. Culture is 'recycled' and directed back towards the audience, who utilize it to constitute part of their own identities. Their main approach is to link 'semiotics' (analyses of systems of signs) to 'content analysis' (counting pre-specified 'elements' of content), attempting to make meaningful comparisons between advertisements. They comment too upon 'market segments', an advertisement being meaningful in terms of 'who' it might appeal to, relevant to beliefs seemingly held by marketeers about qualities of distinct categories of audiences. Goldman's (1995) evidence supports notions of the subjectification of the viewer. The audience is 'hailed' by an advertisement, and responds through its socio-cultural frame of reference (Leiss *et al*. 1990: 283). Dyer's (1982: 115) explanation, 'We come to adverts as social readers,' illustrates the nature of this process, as a form of 'interpellation'. Dru (1996: 196) feels that 'only apt, intelligent, appealing, or funny images that speak to them [consumers] and say something new will be worthy in their eyes.' This implies regular redefinition of various boundaries (e.g. technology, taste, humour and taboos).

One influential methodology is 'deconstruction', which includes 'attempts to take apart texts and see how they are constructed in such a way as to present particular images of people and their actions' (Burr 1995: 164). This can assist identification of discourses, and their resultant effects within 'power relations, ideology and institutions' (Parker 1992: 17–20), thus tying into Morgan's (1992: 147) assertion that 'it is necessary to go further than simply uncovering meanings . . . it is necessary to understand how meanings are constituted and . . . how power is implicated in that process.' Davidson (1992: 195) comments that consumerism outdistances deconstruction, making 'it seem intellectually top heavy', sometimes achieved through 'postmodern' appeals to humour, rendering it seemingly ridiculous (and humourless) to analyse them. He talks too of 'making resistance to it [consumerism] appear so drab, boring and wrong' (Davidson 1992: 191).

Burr (1995: 176) directs attention towards 'metaphors, grammatical constructions, figures of speech and so on'. This can be extended to the analysis of imagery, a rhetorical device like 'antithesis' existing visually as well as in writing/speech. From a 'meta-perspective', an advertisement can also be analysed in terms of what its content and connotations might be a metaphor for (Leiss *et al.* 1990). Similarly, Dyer (1982), in stressing the need for an analytic framework, describes numerous rhetorical devices which emphasize 'the constructed nature of advertisements and avoid some of the weaknesses associated with intuitive analysis'. However, texts might display features that fall outside a particular framework, and tyranny may pervade an overly prescriptive model, leading researchers to ignore intuition.

From a wider, discourse perspective, Cook (1992: 1–2) stresses a number of research considerations: physical context of the text, non-verbal communication, qualities of lettering, 'properties and relations of objects and people', other texts that use similar discourse (interviews/newspaper articles) and 'associated' texts with different discourses (other advertising texts), the people involved in 'sending and receiving' the advertisement and 'function'.

This chapter presumes that there is no 'right' way to interpret an advertising image and cautions against ideas about 'proper' readings. The structure of the analytic section below is loosely based on a methodology advanced by the author (Pearce 1997: 179–85), which primarily advocates: (a) description; (b) exploration of connotation; (c) identification of discourse; (d) definition of subjectification; (e) search for similar discourses in other texts; (f) appreciation of historical dimensions; and (g) summary of overall structures of meaning.

Text

The focus of this work is on what Game (1991: 5) describes as 'the how of meaning', how advertisements mean as well as what they mean. This is useful because to focus on *what* advertising images mean does not automatically allow objectification of the 'insane cultures' that facilitate 'unthinking juxtaposition' between a signifier (see below) of an eating disorder and an image of a consumer good (Davidson 1992: 190). Williamson (1978), Dyer (1982) and Leiss *et al.* (1990) all advocate the practical application of semiotics to the critical analysis of advertising, a significant theme throughout the literature. Although overdependence upon 'analysis of signs' can be criticized, it remains a potent tool in the examination of meaning making. By way of example, Inglis (1972: 92) claims that some cigarette advertising uses 'signs' of 'freshness', creating associations beyond the 'reality' of the product.

In brief, a 'sign' is part of a specific text that 'points' to something else ('the referent') existing outside the specific text. Signs have two functional dimensions, the signifier and the signified. The former is the image (or 'objectification') used in the text (e.g. a very thin woman in a fashion context). The latter is what it potentially means (e.g. anorexia). Williamson (1978) describes the method for encoding and decoding signs as a 'referent system', here that which the viewer uses to interpret that 'a very thin woman' can mean 'anorexic' (or does not use, when he or she fails to complete the association). The 'transference of meaning' works in at least two ways. The weight of the watch (a product characteristic) is made meaningful by contrast with the fragility of the model. Second, jokes and puns about a taboo subject are meaningful by being slightly 'shocking', and hence signify 'cool', suggesting that the product has similar qualities.

Dyer (1982) argues that signs in advertisements point both inwardly and outwardly. The 'put some weight on–thin woman–heavy object' juxtaposition can be understood a priori of the social world. However, 'very thin women in fashion are anorexic' and 'Omega Watches are hypocrites' (explained below) associations only make sense *a posteriori*. In addition, Dru (1996) suggests, advertising 'over-codes' its messages. Audience interest can be obtained through subverting this process (referring to the expectation that an inevitably thin model would promote a reasonably fashionable watch, but not one as 'distinctively thin' as this).

Cook (1992) argues that the power to create a version of reality can be analysed in advertising images. Similarly, Davidson (1992: 113) states 'Images are . . . constructions designed to communicate, and consolidate, ideological "truths".' He describes how image deconstruction of a sportswear advertisement reveals a covert 'nuclear family' discourse. Parallel to this, Dyer (1982: 82) argues that images are 'made to seem true' (here the watch is 'fixed' to the model's arm), and are potentially more persuasive than accompanying prose. She makes the point that there is special ease of access to pictorial meaning, images being well suited to communicating 'excitement, mood and imagination' (Dyer 1982: 86). She maps a method to analyse the imagery of an advertisement for a stove, stressing dynamics of perception (and, implicitly, interpellation), implying people do not view 'free of value' and focus on different elements of content. Importantly Dyer (1982: 97–104) cites 'non-verbal communication', including appearance (age, gender, race, hair, body size, looks), manner (expression, eye contact, pose, clothes) and activity (touch, body movement, position). The following analysis (as the image depicts a person) draws upon this approach.

Game (1991: 139) writes of how photographic representations of people 'objectify' them, freezing space and time. Their depiction as 'means to promote a product' emphasizes their status as object, and this is echoed by Inglis (1972), who feels the humanity of persons in photographs is removed (although the illusion remains) by this commodification process. More specifically, Dyer (1982) emphasizes the rhetorical power of photographic techniques: lighting, colour, angle and 'cropping'. In one example, Davidson (1992: 8–11) analyses the imagery of a simple Persil advertisement, looking to 'associations' of colour and 'unity of effects'.

A photographic image can be viewed as 'an element of the past', existing in the present (Game 1991). Advertising imagery, often striking and memorable and despite being limited to a campaign, can sometimes endure, being analysed by advertising regulators (ASA 1998: 6), newspapers (the Omega/ Vogue case, discussed by Fowler (1996), the Accurist case, covered by McCann (1997) and Frankel (1997)) and books like this. A few advertising images have a 'second life' as cultural artefact, becoming involved with another set of discourses. As Cook (1992) notes, advertisements often contain visual jokes, puns and metaphors. Humour is sometimes used to diffuse a potential controversy 'where "straight" descriptions would not do' (Leiss *et al.* 1990: 294).

The implication that something is 'only a bit of fun' deflects attention from the original text, inviting the audience to partake of the joke or display a lack of humour (Burr 1995: 147–8). This also reinforces the idea that any perceived politico-ideological 'problem' does not originate in the text. Fowles (1996: 8) comments that 'Anything that exists in culture . . . is a candidate for parody', stressing the significance of who will respond to the humour and who will not. Likewise, Inglis (1972: 125) highlights how resistance to, and criticism of, an advertisement can 'declare oneself a backward-looking old fuddy-duddy'. This is allied to Dru's (1996: 55–7) comment that 'great campaigns' subvert the boundaries of both style and content in advertisements.

The text considered here perhaps appeals to the 'postmodern ironic young'. Dru (1996: 127–8) notes that younger people 'hate being labeled'. This implied rejection of segmentation points towards the appeal of the postmodern (a categorization for those who resist categorization). Davidson (1992: 157) comments on the aspirational dynamics of advertising texts, not discernibly advocating 'thinness', as the regulator suspects (Smith 1998), but being 'cool enough to be in on the joke'. Similarly, Fiske (1991: 59) stresses the way 'sensuality of the surface' and 'denial of depth' legitimate any issue's potentially lighthearted treatment, and Davidson (1992: 199) sees a symbiosis between the postmodern and advertising texts, citing 'pastiche' and 'irony' as commonalities. This casts a variety of new perspectives on Tuchman's (1978: 3–38) notion of 'the symbolic annihilation of women'.

The text example for this chapter is an advertisement produced by the advertising agency TBWA Simons Palmer for Accurist Watches. It was published in the national press and on poster sites in November 1997. A copy is available, attached to Frankel's (1997) article in the original edition of *The Guardian* G2.

The advertisement, which is in landscape orientation, contains a photograph, from the waist up, of a young woman wearing a skintight, sleeveless garment. She is almost sideways on to the camera, twisting her upper body, with her face looking down her right shoulder at the audience. Her right hand is placed on the rear of her hip. She wears a metallic watch on her right upper arm. No other jewellery can be seen.

The model could be described as unusually thin. (Here the phrases 'abnormally' or 'even for a fashion model' almost creep in, and the difficulty in providing an uncontroversial description of this dimension illustrates the value of the inclusion of a reproduction of the text.) The outlines of her ribs, cheekbones and collarbones are visible. Her hair is backcombed and piled on her head with strands hanging down at the sides. Her head is inclined backwards and to her right. She looks somewhat expressionlessly at the audience. Her eyes are darkly made up.

This image is to the right hand side of the advertisement. On the left are the headline words: Put some weight on. The writing is unusually styled, tall with long down strokes, and seemingly untidy yet paradoxically regular, employing a number of elongated letters. The 'p' of 'put' on the extreme left is especially long, running the height of the page. The 'i' of 'weight' is wider at its top and base than in the middle. The 'o' of 'on' encircles the model's upper arm and the product she wears there. 'Weight' seems underlined with a series of scribbles. This analysis is not especially concerned with the writing in the text, but the headline here has both a literal ('weight'/thinness) and a physical (the 'o' forms part of the image) relationship with the image, so it seems unnecessarily restrictive to separate image and prose.

The headline and image dominate the text, occupying seven eighths of the space. There is another, smaller photograph of the product to the right of the advertisement with some other words: 'New from Accurist, a range of hallmarked solid silver watches for men and women. Prices start at a not so hefty £79.90.' The words 'solid silver' appear below, as if engraved. Below this is the Accurist brand signature, with 'mean time' written underneath.

Reading

On an overt level (the denotative), the advertisement in the text box promotes a solid silver watch through juxtaposition and by employing an
imaginative typeface, physically linked to an unusually thin model wearing
the product in an unexpected place. But the advertisement is not meaningful merely if taken on face value.

A valuable resource in the exploration of connotation is Dyer's (1982:
97–104) analysis of non-written communication. The model is young. If
she were older it would be difficult to see her as a fashion model. She is
white, avoiding immediate explicit associations, were she black, of a stereotypical starving African woman. Her hair is untidily styled, appearing
unkempt, unhealthy even, the backcombing making it seem dry or matted.
Hair has traditionally represented a person's 'spiritual or social status'
(Chevalier and Gheerbrant 1996: 459).

The model is of extremely slight build, the main force for meaning
generation. This works through 'antithesis', two contrasting elements used
together. The watch is relatively heavy, the woman is ostensibly light. As
Dyer (1982: 98) suggests, 'Size is an important signifier of meaning.' She
states that 'iconic signs' depend on 'likeness' (Dyer 1982: 124). The woman
'looks like' she is anorexic (which is denied: Frankel 1997), and thus
'points' to anorexia stereotypes. The nature of the image (Potter 1996)
assigns the model to a 'group' with certain characteristics, and the limited
content reduces perceptual ambiguity (Dyer 1982).

Interestingly, Leiss *et al.* (1990: 290) comment on an 'incongruity of
elements', 'reversing our normal associational fields'. The anorexic model
fails to radiate the glamour normalized in this context, found in 'similar'
texts. Ewen (1988: 183) feels that because 'the ideal body is one that no
longer materially exists', anorexia can be regarded as a 'logical extension of
the norm'. It is a reaction to 'constructed thinness'. In taking her beyond
'thin but beautifully so' and thus making it difficult not to connote anorexia, the text may thus act as 'social critique'. Dru (1996: 69) identifies
'defamiliarization' as a common tactic for attracting attention.

Advertisements typically do not have 'rough edges' (Fowles 1996), but
here this 'rough' look constitutes meaning, reflecting the concept of a
'highly stylised paragon' (Fowles 1996: 153), strongly dependent on the
presence of an 'anorexia' discourse. The paragon is echoed by the model's
expression: blank, apathetic or lethargic. Her eyes are heavily made up,
partially closed and appearing sunken. Her face seems pale. The model's
gaze is focused on the middle distance, suggestive of psychological withdrawal (Goffman 1976), and is not really engaged with the viewer. There
is connotation of both physical and mental frailty. Goffman (1976: 57)
argues that psychological withdrawal creates dependence on the 'protec-
tiveness and goodwill of others', linking to the entreaty in the headline.

The text specifically depicts a woman (though the product is styled for both sexes), an interesting choice as there is evidence to suggest anorexia has been 'gendered' as a 'women's illness' (Hepworth and Griffin 1995). This relates to assertions that 'women are defined as the problematic sex' (Ang and Hermes 1991: 308).

The model's twisted pose emphasizes her skeleton, detaching the product away from her torso towards the centre of the advertisement. The hand on the hip adds support to her body, ironically relating to the stereotypical pose of the heavily pregnant woman. Self-touching itself can connote 'delicacy' (Goffman 1976: 31). Turning to the model's clothing, her lack of sleeves facilitates an unobstructed view of the product. The tightness and low neckline highlight her prominent bones and small breasts. The lack of other jewellery emphasizes the product's importance.

Williamson (1978: 77–84) refers to 'types of absence', and Potter (1996) talks of making sense of content through what is not included. There is a lack of narrative, leaving space for readers to provide their own. There is a 'desirable context' (Dyer 1982: 96), provided by the attractive appeals to deconstructive and ironic humour, in turn drawing upon societal narratives (that Omega Watches threatened Vogue, that fashion models are often anorexic).

Moving to the headline, the elongated 'p' mirrors the model. The thinly nipped waist of the 'i' is also an 'objective correlative' (Dyer 1982: 120), creating connection between the headline and the model. The 'o' that encircles the model's arm is an 'accent', highlighting the product as the headline is scanned. Cook (1992: 78–9) discusses 'Iconicity by letter shape', suggesting that associations can be drawn between qualities of lettering and products or other elements of imagery. The scribbled underscoring of 'weight' emphasizes significance, acts as a visual pun (under 'weight', thus 'underweight') and is an objective correlative to her backcombed hair. 'Anacoluthon' (impossibility) operates subtextually, through where the watch is worn. This is revealed as 'hyperbole', the watch not being fastened but fixed to appear so, thus exaggerating the model's thinness (Frankel 1997).

The text says nothing about anorexia but implies a great deal, with meaning deriving from other, external texts. It is through 'consensual notions of normality' (Potter 1996: 194) that the audience plots and makes meaning through the model's relation to the 'normal'. If the text is seen as a commentary on a relationship between anorexia and fashion, and implicitly on notions of 'heroin chic', it supports Gamman and Marshment's (1988) assertion that advertising often appropriates feminist discourse.

There are at least three 'jokes' in the text: the visual pun of 'weight' being underlined; the 'put some weight on' marks the heavy watch/thin woman antithesis; and an obscure humourous reference is to Omega Watches' temporary withdrawal (and perceived hypocrisy) from advertising in Vogue, protesting at the use of extremely thin models (Fowler 1996).

Moving on, the audience themselves are subjectified by the humour, defined by how they relate to it. Parker (1992: 9–10) talks of texts 'making us listen as a certain type of person'. Advertisements that depict people often implicate the viewer as 'voyeur'. This text hails people who identify with ironic humour and arresting images, with the implied rejection of overt conservatism. Williamson (1978) argues that advertisements thus provide audiences with means for personal identity construction, which includes people who identify themselves by *resisting* the advertisement.

Disadvantages

The analysis of imagery in television and cinema advertising is problematic. It is difficult to represent effectively in print form, thus limiting reader exposure to still images and the commentary on form and content that the researcher supplies. Cook (1992) suggests that most researchers (including this one) sidestep this intractable difficulty. This 'tension' can be seen in his analyses of advertisements from Sprite and Wrigley's, where the reader cannot fully engage with an original text (whose meaning generation involves movement and sound), risking texts being closed to alternative readings (Parker and Burman 1993: 156), not to mention being altogether ignored/neglected or inadequately investigated.

Another concern involves moving beyond relativism. Nothing from the analysis above provides the 'objective conclusion' that 'this advertisement is intended to be offensive to anorexic people'. Cook (1992) cautions against feeling one has freed the viewer from the 'oppression' of the advertiser. Discourse analysis is a capable descriptive tool, but its normative powers are limited by paradigm. Further, analyses that 'take sides' tend to 'say more about their creators than about the ads they assault' (Cook 1992: 200).

Advertisements can be criticized (Cook 1992: 229) for their 'unsolicited intrusiveness', here in that anorexic people, their friends and families may not want to see 'this sort of image' used to sell a watch (Frankel 1997), regardless of whether the model has a 'real' eating disorder or society increasingly sanctions postmodern humour. When one is analysing advertising imagery, a decision must be made as to 'how far a researcher should go beyond the particular text they are analysing to arrive at an interpretation of what is happening' (Burman and Parker 1993: 11). One objective of the above analysis has been to map the breadth of other texts that can be consulted. Burr (1995: 180) suggests that reflexive activity creates two types of problem for the analyst: first, one asks 'how can my account of the image be especially valid?'; second, 'why have I decided to research this particular image' and 'is discourse analysis similarly fruitful for all advertisements?'

Potter and Wetherell (1987: 170–2) argue that discourse research validity can be confirmed by four characteristics. First is 'coherence', here reinforcing the need to 'go beyond the specific text'. The above analysis would have been less productive without this. Second is 'participant's orientation', exposing an omission, as this work does not directly analyse, for reasons of spatial economy (Parker and Burman 1993: 156), the 'talk' of consumers, advertisers and regulators. Third is the identification of 'new problems' created by the discourses. Here this relates to how tapping into 'anorexia discourses' solves the problem of 'being noticed', by being 'slightly shocking', but creates a new problem in attracting censure. Fourth is 'fruitfulness', which 'make[s] sense of new kinds of discourse and generate[s] novel explanations'. The reader is perhaps in the best position to judge whether this has been achieved. Parker and Burman (1993: 168–9) go on to analyse some pitfalls of 'confessing subjectivity'.

Regarding the second question, this image was selected as one of the most striking, complex and ambiguous at the time. However, discourse analysis of any advertising image should produce a valuable perspective on the social world. All advertisements tap into discourses; otherwise they would not be meaningful. An additional point to make is that researchers require 'cultural competence' to produce a reasonable analysis (Parker and Burman 1993: 158).

Inglis (1972: 78) talks of 'detail which can look ludicrous when written down'. A common criticism is that 'people do not look at advertisements like this'. But how could anyone view them 'in the same way' as someone else? Analysis needs to withdraw from confusing taxonomies like 'phoney' and 'authentic', and set about discovering how people account for the world in a particular way, not least as though some things are 'real' and others not. Davidson (1992: 10) talks of 'stylistic panache', something which is hard to express and analyse, although discourse analysis exposes how talk of 'need' for aesthetic and intellectual stimulation is utilized and reinforced, by mapping jokes and distinctive imagery as part of the meaning-making process.

One final problem concerns the temporally bound nature of analyses. Accurist has recently produced a new version of the text, which uses very similar lettering, depicting a mannequin's hand wearing the product around its wrist, which lies detached on a broken glass surface at the dummy's feet. This text, in many ways, refers to the one examined here. The incompleteness of analyses is a function of method, but it is sometimes hard to judge where to end a study.

Advantages

A recurring debate in advertising concerns whether the medium reflects society, or plays a part in constructing it (Pearce 1997: 182). More specifically, 'does this advertisement contribute to making ironic jokes about anorexia legitimate, or does it reflect the growing legitimacy of this type of humour in society (which advertising might have a responsibility to accurately reproduce)?' These questions are rendered unanswerable, and an examination of 'how meaning is constructed' provides a more convincing and less generalized diagnosis of 'ideology, institution and power relations'. Dru (1996: 12) reflects this confusion, claiming simultaneously that advertisements are 'mirrors of society', and that they reduce difference to stereotype. Advertising is 'symptomatic of the society that produced it' (Davidson 1992: 61), although, as Leiss *et al.* (1990: 200) suggest, it adopts elements of the social world and 'reconstitutes' them, implying the existence of 'constructive input', adding its 'accounts' to those of other texts. Further as Fairclough (1995) implies, the prevalence of 'marketing' discourse legitimates both marketing 'talk' and consumer society, thus framing the way people talk. Parker and Burman (1993: 156) suggest that there are moral issues to be considered when one 'has power over the words of another'. The analysis of promotional text avoids these dilemmas. Advertising images are expressly produced to be analysed for meaning.

Suspicion surrounds approaches that rely on semiotics alone (e.g. Leiss *et al.* 1990), but to widen the methodology to include semiotic analysis (with elements like non-written communication and rhetorical devices) as a tool for unearthing discourses avoids some of the problems raised. First, there is the concern that interpretation depends on the experience of the researcher. Because discourse analysis relies on wider reference beyond the text and the input of other people (Parker 1992), it potentially avoids making trite or arcane observations. Second, meaning extracted from an individual text by semiotic analysis cannot be universalized. Discourse analysis examines 'ways of talking', moving from the original text to texts that use similar associations to make meaning, or that tap the same discourses. In this way, meaningful research can be taken beyond a single text, the text being (temporarily) viewed as a 'vehicle for discourse'. This is not to say that conclusions formed about one text can be generalized, but they can be traced to other texts and, with discretion, the scope can be broadened. Finally, there are suspicions that only 'semiotically rich' advertisements are researched, and many that are not analysed would not prove fruitful anyway. This is a valid comment, and to limit one's research to exploration of signification would often not provide interest and depth. But, as suggested above, all advertisements mean something (even one that 'appears' meaningless has meaning in virtue of this), and thus they all relate to particular discourses.

Game (1991: 17) notes how cultural analyses that isolate elements of text can ignore 'chains of association', something which discourse analysis is well suited to. Davidson (1992) argues that locating the origin of a 'social' problem in the mass media is difficult, with the wealth of discursive activity that proliferates around it.

Qualitative researchers sometimes adopt a position of power regarding their accounts of meaning (Burr 1995), an issue relevant to Cook's (1992) comments regarding the 'heroic and patriarchal' actions of the researcher. The discourse analysis of advertising imagery partly evades this charge, as the original text can usually be reasonably faithfully represented (within copyright limitations), facilitating reader participation and empowering alternative interpretations. This point can deflect another criticism (Burr 1995), that the methods of the analyst typically remain obscure. Regarding advertising images, the text can be reproduced and the analysis can become a participative exercise, readers, it is hoped, agreeing or disagreeing as they see fit.

The dispassionate methodologies of discourse analysis also serve to answer Dyer's (1982: 114) concern that analysts can become critically entrapped in the 'falseness of ads'. The discourse analyst is primarily concerned with the text in front of him or her, and from this looks beyond into the social world. Discourse analysis in many ways answers the critique of meaninglessness directed at Williamson's (1978) 'anthropological notions'. The search for discursive activity gives purpose and focus to interpreting psycho-social chains of association. In doing so it says something valid about how advertising makes meaning from the social reference points around it.

Key reading

Cook, G. (1992) *The Discourse of Advertising*. London: Routledge (pp. 38–44 and 48–53).
Dyer, G. (1982) *Advertising as Communication*. London: Routledge (pp. 86–112 and 161–82).

References

Ang, I. and Hermes, J. (1991) Gender and/in media consumption. In J. Curran and M. Gurevitch (eds) *Mass Media and Society*. London: Edward Arnold.
ASA (Advertising Standards Authority) (1998) *Monthly Report – May 1998*. London: ASA.
Barthes, R. (1972) *Mythologies*. London: Vintage.
Burman, E. and Parker, I. (1993) Introduction – discourse analysis: the turn to the text. In E. Burman and I. Parker (eds) *Discourse Analytic Research*. London: Routledge.
Burr, V. (1995) *An Introduction to Social Constructionism*. London: Routledge.
Chevalier, J. and Gheerbrant, A. (1996) *Penguin Dictionary of Signs*. Harmondsworth: Penguin.

Cook, G. (1992) *The Discourse of Advertising*. London: Routledge.

Davidson, M. (1992) *The Consumerist Manifesto: Advertising in Postmodern Times*. London: Routledge.

Dru, J.-M. (1996) *Disruption: Overturning Conventions and Shaking up the Marketplace*. New York: Wiley.

Dyer, G. (1982) *Advertising as Communication*. London: Routledge.

Ewen, S. (1988) *All Consuming Images: The Politics of Style in Contemporary Culture*. New York: Basic Books.

Fairclough, N. (1995) *Critical Discourse Analysis*, 2nd edn. London: Longman.

Fiske, J. (1991) Postmodernism and television. In J. Curran and M. Gurevitch (eds) *Mass Media and Society*. London: Edward Arnold.

Fowler, R. (1996) How to end the fashion famine. *Independent*, 1 June, 17.

Fowles, J. (1996) *Advertising and Popular Culture*. Thousand Oaks, CA: Sage.

Frankel, S. (1997) Do you find this ad offensive? *Guardian G2*, 26 November, 15.

Game, A. (1991) *Undoing the Social: Towards a Deconstructive Sociology*. Buckingham: Open University Press.

Gamman, L. and Marshment, M. (eds) (1988) *The Female Gaze: Women as Viewers of Popular Culture*. London: The Women's Press.

Goffman, E. (1976) *Gender Advertisements*. London: Macmillan.

Goldman, R. (1995) Constructing and addressing the audience as commodity. In G. Dines and J. Humez (eds) *Gender, Race and Class in Media*. Thousand Oaks, CA: Sage.

Hepworth, J. and Griffin, C. (1995) Conflicting opinions? 'Anorexia nervosa', medicine and feminism. In S. Wilkinson and C. Kitzinger (eds) *Feminism and Discourse*. London: Sage.

Inglis, F. (1972) *The Imagery of Power*. London: Heinemann.

Lasch, C. (1991) *The Culture of Narcissism*. London: Norton.

Leiss, W., Kline, S. and Jhally, S. (1990) *Social Communication in Advertising*. London: Routledge.

McCann, P. (1997) The very thin line between glamour and starvation. *Independent*, 8 November, 1.

Meyers, W. (1984) *The Image Makers: Secrets of Successful Advertising*. London: Orbis.

Morgan, G. (1992) Marketing discourse and practice: towards a critical analysis. In M. Alvesson and H. Wilmott (eds) *Critical Management Studies*. London: Sage.

Packard, V. (1960) *The Hidden Persuaders*. Harmondsworth: Pelican.

Parker, I. (1992) *Discourse Dynamics*. London: Routledge.

Parker, I. and Burman, E. (1993) Against discursive imperialism, empiricism and constructionism: thirty-two problems with discourse analysis. In E. Burman and I. Parker (eds) *Discourse Analytic Research*. London: Routledge.

Pearce, R. (1997) Discourse, ethics and advertising. In G. Moore (ed.) *Business Ethics: Principles and Practice*. Sunderland: Business Education Publishers.

Potter, J. (1996) *Representing Reality: Discourse, Rhetoric and Social Construction*. Thousand Oaks, CA: Sage.

Potter, J. and Wetherell, M. (1987) *Discourse and Social Psychology*. London: Sage.

Smith, C. (1998) Watchdog on adverts weighs in on use of thin model. *Scotsman*, 31 March.

Tuchman, G. (1978) Introduction: the symbolic annihilation of women by the mass media. In G. Tuchman, A. Kaplan Daniels and J. Benet (eds) *Hearth and Home: Images of Women in the Mass Media.* New York: Oxford University Press.

Williamson, J. (1978) *Decoding Advertisements.* London: Marion Boyars.

8 Television: signs on the box

HELEN RUSSELL

Television is a powerful form of mass communication in Western society. This form of mass media has the power to assist the re-election of corrupt governments and to transform the suffering of others into entertainment for us, as, for example, in charity appeal programmes where we switch between film of suffering, and song, dance and jokes. The way in which television represents the world can influence beliefs and values which in turn can change the way we think about ourselves and our relationships with others. Television is both a part and a product of modern, everyday living, influenced by and influencing society. It is precisely because of the way in which it reflects society that television analysis can contribute to our understanding of society, culture and the shifts, contradictions and changes within it (Fiske and Hartley 1978). However, traditional methods within the discipline of psychology – the context for my research – have tended to use quantitative methodologies that reduce complex human behaviour to simplistic states using 'experimental' laboratory techniques and making generalizable laws or universalistic assumptions that appear to be based on the 'truth' (Fox and Prilleltensky 1997). The turn to language within the discipline, however, has provided 'postmodern' researchers with different methodological resources that can help us to see and understand the world a little differently. These resources are well suited to the analysis

of television because the chaos that calls itself television is constituted
through an intertwined mass of signs and symbols.

Emerging analytic methods – including versions of discourse analysis –
have looked at the linguistic content of television programmes, examining
the way in which males, females, ethnic minorities and violence are represented. Early studies utilizing content analysis suggest that on television
the world is represented more as we would like it to be than as it is, with
women and black people portrayed as having more advantages in television 'workplaces' than occurs in society (de Fleur 1964). Content analysis
can also tell us something about the way television contributes to and
reinforces constructions of gender and racial hierarchies. For example,
Messner *et al.* (1993) illustrate the way that certain sports commentaries
categorize women and black people in stereotypical terms, and then represent these categories to the viewer.

When one is using conversation analysis, attention is paid to the way
that people maintain, interpret and understand conversation and the
methods by which this is achieved. Although they mainly focus on everyday
conversations or conversation between equals, some conversation analysts
have taken an interest in forms of institutional discourse, including media
discourse. Heritage (1985), for example, was interested in understanding
how the structure and constraints of television affect the televised interview process. It appeared to him that interviewers on television 'managed'
their interviewees' discourse by using 'formulations', or summaries of what
interviewees had said. He argued that this was due to the form of television (its symbolic, ephemeral nature) and the constant necessity of interviewers having to clarify situations for viewers. Research such as content
or conversation analysis, however, does not help us to focus directly on
social, ideological or political concerns.

Research concerned with analysing the ideological functions of television can inform us how the mechanics of commercial advertising addresses
potential consumers of products and how those products are presented for
consumption in such a way as to appeal to viewers. Ideological analyses of
television can assist in the revelation of how issues of legitimacy, inequality
and exploitation are embedded in and constructed through language (e.g.
White 1995). This kind of work takes that position that 'discursive practices' on television 'work to "settle" the population into the acceptance of
particular social arrangements or to treat inequalities as a necessary part of
modern living' (Potter 1997: 59). For this type of analysis, television can
be considered as a form of 'cultural discourse' (Dahlgren 1986) through
which dominant values, ideas and beliefs are expressed, received and
understood by those on the 'outside' of the screen. Ideology, however, is
not found only by carrying out an ideological analysis, informative, useful 'readings' of television and its politics can also be achieved using a
semiotic/structuralist approach that takes into account the unconscious.

Often associated with Ferdinand de Saussure (1974), semiotics (the study of sign systems and the rules that govern their use) has been used in television analysis to attend to the codes and conventions of television illustrating various ways in which signs can be encoded and combined to produce particular meanings. These meanings are then understood or interpreted by viewers in particular ways. Fiske and Hartley (1978) and Hartley (1982), for example, draw on semiotics to describe how different ways of presenting televised material (in terms of colour, sound effects, shot framing, camera angle, camera shots and sequence of shots shown) can produce different effects. A semiotic 'reading' of television reveals some of the ways in which television is structured or organized and assists our understanding of how television functions as an influential oral and visual mass medium. This analysis of ideological functions can be extended to link discursive practices to socio-cultural practices.

A detailed study of television carried out by Hodge and Tripp (1983), drawing on post-structuralist ideas, stressed the necessity of taking into consideration the subjectivity of the researcher. The interest of the analysts in this study was focused on how children make their own analyses of cartoons, in order to understand them. Hodge and Tripp acknowledge the value of the children's own ideas with regard to the television they watched, and asked them to explain their experiences. They also acknowledged the role of the unconscious in the children's (and their own) interpretations of the text, here drawing on psychoanalytic notions of the unconscious. Including psychoanalysis in this kind of study involves Lacan's claim that the unconscious is structured like a language. Any text is always simultaneously representing, setting up social identities and social relations and influencing the way we think about the world. Thus the 'messages' transmitted through these texts reach the viewers whether they want them to or not (Parker 1996). Thus, psychoanalytic notions, semiotics and structuralism can be drawn on when one is carrying out particular forms of discourse analysis. In this particular case, discourse analysis is applied to television to open it up and enable other ways of interpreting the images, sounds, signs and symbols. Discourse analysis can also reveal particular ideologies, forms of knowledge and power within television.

A Foucauldian discourse analysis understands 'discourse' as sets of statements or multilayered texts. These sets of statements in effect construct the 'object' of which they are speaking, in the process of their being spoken about. Foucault draws our attention to questions of power and knowledge in society and in doing so has deepened our understanding of 'products' of society, often taken for granted (for example, human sexuality and mental illness). A Foucauldian approach to television analysis involves recognizing that discursive practices and social practices are linked, and that connections can be made between language and the exercise of power.

Text

The example text to be analysed in this chapter derives its form from different combinations of images, sounds, effects and 'special effects' used to produce meaning. Analysing television in this way can help us to understand *how* signs are combined to produce meaning and how that meaning may be received and understood.

Semiotic analysis concerns itself with two levels of signification, the sign and its constituents. The signified and the signifier represent a denotative level of significance, the first level. The signifier (the word) is attached to the signified (the concept) to produce a 'sign'. For example, Fiske and Hartley use the sign 'rain' to illustrate the way that the signifier (the word 'rain') represents the signified (the idea of water falling from the sky) and so gains its social meaning. In this case, the concept or object, the signified, is a 'cult' and the signifier(s) are the words and images that are used and combined in such a way that they produce meaning of what a 'cult' is. A second level of significance, however, is perhaps more relevant to studies of knowledge and power in contemporary society. This level of understanding is concerned with 'myth'.

Associated with Roland Barthes (1957), the concept of 'myth' is useful to help us understand how second, 'deeper' meanings, 'connotations', become attached to signs. Like television, myth functions in society in such a way as to reify culture while at the same time contributing to its social construction. The notion of myth can be applied to contemporary media in such a way that the relationship between culture and communication becomes clearer. On television, myths attached to signs often make sense to us because they form part of the perceptual system of a culture. Unfamiliar situations are interpreted through the cultural perceptual system and fitted into known symbolic situations in order for them to make sense. Myth also creates models for people to imitate, and these are constantly changing in relation to changes in culture (Breen and Corcoran 1982). Myth also gives us a way of handling conflict within a culture.

Claus (1976), for example, applied the idea of myth to a *Star Trek* programme that, he argued, revolved around moral problems, stated in the form of conflict between opposites. Claus saw Captain Kirk and his crew as rational men devoted to order and democracy. The *Enterprise* crew oppose the ways of the Klingon Empire, who are thought to be exploiting the weak and innocent. The conflicts of life presented and resolved in *Star Trek* result in an ethnocentric view of American life, the pure 'we' opposing the evil 'they'. In this instance, myth functions to reify the 'cult' image that the television programme portrays. In recent times the signifier 'cult' has had meanings attached to it that lead us to interpret non-conventional groups as dangerous entities that lure victims in order to exploit them in some way.

The first shot opens with a view of an empty room. The camera is placed at the doorway to the room giving an open view of the inside. The room is empty but for a large window bathed in sunlight. The window is covered with soft white curtains that move gently in the breeze. From its position at the doorway, the camera moves forwards, taking us with it to the window, where it fixes at the top of the right curtain. Slowly the camera moves down the curtain until its gaze rests on the floor. As we reach the floor with *our* gaze, the camera picks out a patch of a red substance that could be taken for blood. After lingering for a second on the patch of 'blood', the shot fades to black.

The next shot, the second of the analysis, is a head-and-shoulders shot of a man talking. Dressed in white, the man speaks slowly and quietly, saying 'Why can't it be an option to go to your creator the way you feel . . . like you want to go? Why do you have to wait? Here's all these people that I . . . love that are now gone and I . . . you know . . . just want them to know that I . . . I love them and I miss them.' No reporter is visible, the man alone is speaking into the camera.

Semiotics and structuralism can tell us something of the way that signs are juxtaposed to produce powerful non-verbal statements that are made sense of by the viewer. How these statements are understood can be illustrated by drawing on psychoanalytic theory. This is not because psychoanalysis is somehow 'true', however, but because psychoanalytic notions 'work' in Western culture to determine how people understand themselves and the world around them (Parker 1997). Psychoanalytic theory can be used as a cultural resource to assist our understanding of how people see themselves in relation to the television programme and also to understand how people understand the world in relation to the group of people being described as a 'cult'.

The text chosen for analysis consists of two shots taken from a 'Network First' BBC (1996) television documentary concerned with the group now known as the 'Heaven's Gate Cult'. These two particular shots have been chosen for analysis partly because they represent the way in which 'messages' often conflict and contradict each other and partly because the modes of representation are different in each.

Reading

The documentary or public affairs programme that these shots came from operates at the border between information and entertainment. In today's market, the television viewer is courted by programme makers in order to achieve good ratings. It is this push to gain audiences, perhaps, that causes television makers to sensationalize or dramatize events so as to catch viewers' attention as they glance at the screen. The informative function of television, in this instance, is performed by an authoritative voice-over. A male reporter relates the events, supposedly 'as they happened', reconstructing the suicides and representing them to viewers. The reporter is portrayed as merely relating the 'facts' of what happened in the days that led 39 group members to die in a house in California. The audience, on the other hand, is situated as unknowing, waiting, wanting to know, receptive to the 'facts' imparted by the authoritative reporter. With this context in mind, we can turn to the first shot to be considered as 'text'.

In this first shot, we can 'see' into a room, the camera angle positioned possibly at the doorway. The room is empty and is bathed in the sunlight that pours through an open window covered by white muslin curtains that drift gently. We have the impression we are standing at the doorway, on a peaceful summer's afternoon, looking at the emptiness. The camera angle, the sunlight, the window and the empty room are signs frequently combined in television to produce a perception of tranquillity and peace (Fiske and Hartley 1978), and that is taken on board by the viewer. This peaceful scene is interrupted by background music, the sound of a musical instrument, a triangle, making single-note sounds that add connotative meaning to the shot. Background music is often added to a shot to produce suspense or anxiety, eerieness or peace (see Berger 1972). In this shot, however, the sound seems to have a dual nature, supportive of the peace but an eerie intrusion nevertheless. The sense of anxiety produced by the juxtaposition of the music is exaggerated as the camera moves into the room, across to the window and down the curtain, coming to rest on a patch of red fluid, similar to the image of spilled blood.

This shot pulls in the viewer by first combining signs to produce a sense of peace and then disrupting that emotion by introducing other signs that encode in a different way, in a way that produces eeriness and a sense of anxiety. The addition of the 'blood' patch draws on the high value people in the West place on blood or, better, on what blood represents – life, and death. Despite an earlier shot of the bodies after death – a video taken by one group member who remained to carry out this task – lying intact, peacefully, on beds in the house, this shot indicates the spilling of blood, of violence perhaps. The shot initially lulls the audience into a sense of security then replaces this with feelings of anxiety. It is possible that audiences may perceive these feelings as anxiety about the object signified – the 'cult' – producing mythical second-order meanings which enter the unconscious. The voices that speak here are those of the film makers rather than those of the group members. The effect is entertaining and sensational. The scene fades to black and the second shot is presented to us.

The second shot involves the head-and-shoulders image of a man speaking. The head-and-shoulders shot suggests intimacy, denoting a conversation between equals. In contrast to the first shot, the iconic nature of this one makes the denotative meaning clear. Here is a friend of the group calmly attempting to make sense of events as they had happened. In order to do this, he draws on a traditional Christian discourse that presupposes knowledge of the concepts of emotion, choice, love, a Creator and life after death. 'Why can't it be an option to go to your creator the way you feel . . . like you want to go? Why do you have to wait? Here's all these people that I . . . love that are now gone and I . . . you know . . . just want them to know that I . . . I love them and I miss them.'

These two shots conflict and contradict each other in various ways. In the first shot, the images and sounds are presented to the viewer in such a way as to be anxious and uneasy about 'cults', their members and death. The second shot, however, suggests that group members were merely wishing to go early to life after death; those looking for a 'better' way of being are themselves being prevented from doing so. The first shot gets its meaning from the way that images and sounds are combined to situate the viewer in an anxious state by indicating violent death. The second shot, however, implies that the group members, by committing suicide, had found peace, a 'better' way of dying and the end of a quest.

Disadvantages

Using discourse analysis in relation to media communication allows (at least at first glance) the freedom to open texts and 'read' and interpret them in different ways that illuminate the 'messages' television both reflects and reinforces. Postmodern ideas that now underpin discourse analytic approaches are often quite complex and difficult to access. The approach is cross-disciplinary in that it draws on philosophy, sociology and anthropology, calling for a deep understanding of the issues concerned and some knowledge of the way other disciplines 'work'. As each discipline usually has its own closely guarded borders, this can appear challenging in the first instance. Criticisms can be made of postmodern approaches in relation to their non-scientific, non-objective content, but postmodern ideas challenge the validity of the scientific approach and question the objectivity of scientists who tend toward experiments intended to 'explain' human behaviour rather than understand it. Discourse analysis pays no attention to the *number* of messages contained within television, and content analysis would draw our attention to the frequency of media representations.

While content analysis is useful in terms of revealing how and how many times media programmes represent the world in particular ways, it does not make a link between the images communicated by and through the language of television, and social or cultural practices. We therefore have no idea of the effects this 'symbolic reality' may have on viewing audiences. There is also no way of knowing how people act on these messages.

Similarly, conversation analysis makes no connections between talk, culture and society. While it is interesting for the way it shows how discursive practices are embedded in the structures and practices of cultural institutions such as the media, illustrated by instances of 'turn-taking' and topic control in the media interview, the links between language, ideology and power are ignored. While analysing conversations in this way can tell us something about the way in which media language is organized, there is no link made between talk, society and culture. This omission causes us to ignore any possible relationship there might be between language, socio-cultural changes, power and ideology.

With its roots in Marxist theory, ideological analysis gives us a detailed reading of the assumptions and implications of television programmes. Ideological analysis helps us to understand how particular forms of knowledge and positions for actors and viewers are set up within television discourse, in a similar way to the way spoken or written language can represent identities and social relations. However, ideological analysis pays no attention to the way texts 'work' or are interpreted and understood by others or to the effects this may have on specific groups. Unlike discourse analysis, ideological analysis does not make heard the voices of minority groups (including researchers) who will produce different readings of texts.

A multiplicity of meanings can occur in different contexts. While using signs to describe other signs (as these words on this page do), I am in some way reconstructing and representing combinations of signs to tell this story, and this is accounted for in the reading. Semiotic analysis tends to edit texts, with some elements given more significance than others. Some elements are excluded altogether, repressed. Further, the 'rules' of semiotic inquiry are often very much like grammar. Texts do function ideologically but sometimes they also entertain. The tension between information and entertainment is not always apparent in semiotic analysis as it is here. Sometimes semiotic analysis understands texts as if their meanings are pre-given, translatable and predictable, and can be discovered by a sufficiently skilled semiotician.

While discursively analysing texts reveals to us something of the nature of socially constructed reality and the multiplicity of 'truth', it is wise to remember that each reading, each analysis, is itself another representation or construct of a text. The problem of power relations between the researcher and the researched must also be taken into consideration, along with any prejudices or bias which may be evident. In order to do this, it is necessary that a researcher be aware of social and political conditions around him or her. It is necessary to know something of that to which you

are referring, but also to remember that any analysis reproduces or transforms the text (Burman and Parker 1993) and reflects the researchers'
ideas. Analyses are but one way of interpreting and making sense of the
world.

Advantages

The two key ideas in the example text – violent death or peaceful passing
to another plane – form part of the mythologies that surround groups of
non-conventional believers in Western society. The myths that circulate in
society about such groups are reflected in television presentations such as
this one. The discourses that contribute to the idea of dangerous groups
enticing vulnerable people in society are reconstructed and represented to
the viewer of television in the form of signs, symbols and sounds that
produce 'messages' that flood into a person's unconscious whether he or
she wants them to or not. Analysing television's output in this way gives us
some idea of the socio-cultural notions, the connotations, denotations and
messages, that are attached to the label 'cult'.

Carrying out a semiotically oriented discourse analysis, however, allows
a reading of television text that focuses on the way signs, convention and
codes can be combined and understood in various ways, producing representations, identities and social relations that mediate reality and giving
them some social first-order significance (denotation), as suggested by analysts such as Eco, Barthes, Fiske and Hartley and Hodge and Tripp. The
notion of myth in such accounts is a particularly useful concept of second-
order 'connotative' or ideological significance, which implies an 'extra'
second meaning that 'fixes' the first into place. For example, myth in this
text operates through the sign made by focusing on a window left symbolically open in the first shot. Various meanings can be projected using an
open window and an empty room, but a secondary meaning was 'fixed'
into place by the camera slowly moving down the length of the window to
focus on a patch of red 'blood'. This combination of a house, an open
window, silence and 'blood' produces an image that carries particular
social meanings: fear or violence or both. Fiske and Hartley's (1978) research into the language of television assists our understanding of socio-
cultural changes in society by analysing their reflection within television
programmes and revealing the social meanings that combinations of signs
produce.

A semiotic form of inquiry can be open to the fact that the researcher
forms part of the analysis and does not take the objective and neutral
stance of the semiotician. Stress is placed on the idea that meanings found
are partly a product of the researcher's own subjective interaction with the
text. This approach does not repress elements but draws attention to the

relations between signs themselves and signs in different contexts. With a focus on language as medium through which to understand television, we know of the practices of television by talking about them in other discourses. Foucault, for example, refers to this type of understanding as seeing discourses as multi-layered complex texts that produce forms of knowledge that limit what can be said and by whom. This approach points to the way that discourses serve particular interests in relations of power, amplifying some voices while silencing others. Theories of psychoanalysis and ideology, influenced by post-structuralism, focus on the gaps and fissures, the absences in a text, in terms of why one thing is included and not another.

Analysing language or 'text' using ideas taken from Foucault has the advantage of making power relations within culture more visible. Those with 'scientific' knowledge, for example, because of its supposed objectivity, are very powerful. Science is said to transcend everyday or 'common-sense' beliefs and as such tends to be seen as the 'truth'. So when scientific psychologists speak in scientific terms about 'cults' and 'cult members', they tend to be believed. Are *all* groups of people who hold different beliefs *really* the dangerous entities that particular psychologists would have us think? Do they have the power to control minds?

Cult monitoring groups have sprang up in response to their hypothetical dangers. Journals like the *The Cultic Studies Journal* are dedicated to writing about cults, the people who join them, why they join them and how to escape and recover from them. Challenging the validity of scientific notions and explanations draws our attention to their social construction. Understanding that entities such as 'cults' are socially constructed and interpreted gives us a chance to choose or change what we say about them, and how we read them when they appear on television.

Key reading

Fiske, J. and Hartley, J. (1978) *Reading Television*. London: Routledge (Chapter 3: The signs of television).
Fox, D and Prilleltensky, I. (eds) (1997) *Critical Psychology: An Introduction*. London: Sage.

References

Barthes, R. (1957/1973) *Mythologies*. London: Paladin.
Berger, J. (1972) *Ways of Seeing*. London: Penguin.
Breen, M. and Corcoran F. (1982) Myth in the television discourse. *Communication Monographs*, 49: 127–36.

Burman, E. and Parker, I. (1993) *Discourse Analytic Research. Repertoires and Readings of Texts in Action.* London: Routledge.

Claus, P. J. (1976) A structural appreciation of 'Star Trek'. In W. Erens and S. P. Montague (eds) *The American Dimension.* New York: Alfred.

Dahlgren, P. (1986) Beyond information: TV news as a cultural discussion. *Communications,* 12: 125–36.

de Fleur, M. (1964) Occupational roles as portrayed on television. *Public Opinion Quarterly,* 28: 57–74.

Fairclough, N. (1995) *Media Discourse.* London: Edward Arnold.

Fiske, J. and Hartley, J. (1978) *Reading Television.* London: Routledge.

Fox, D and Prilleltensky, I. (eds) (1997) *Critical Psychology: An Introduction.* London: Sage.

Hartley, J. (1982) *Understanding News.* London: Routledge.

Heritage, J. (1985) Analysing news interviews. In T. van Dijk (ed.) *Handbook of Discourse Analysis.* London: Academic Press.

Messner, M. A., Duncan, M. C. and Jensen, K. (1993) Separating the men from the girls: the gendered language of televised sport. *Gender and Society,* 7(1): 121–37.

Parker, I. (1996) Discursive complexes in material culture. In J. Howarth (ed.) *Psychological Research – Innovative Methods and Strategies.* London: Routledge.

Parker, I. (1997) *Psychoanalytic Culture: Psychoanalytic Discourse in Western Society.* London: Sage.

Potter, J. (1997) Discourse and critical social psychology. In T. Ibanez and L. Iniguez (eds) *Critical Social Psychology.* London: Sage.

Saussure, F. de (1974) *Course in General Linguistics.* London: Fontana.

Singer, M. T. (1995) *Cults in Our Midst.* New York: Jossey-Bass.

White, M. (1995) Ideological analysis. In R. C. Allen (ed.) *Channels of Discourse Re-assembled: Television and Contemporary Criticism,* 2nd edn. London: Routledge.

9 Film: a surface for writing social life

HAKAN DURMAZ

If the late 1940s, after the Second World War, was the period of distribution of the world between the winners of the war (the USA, the UK and the USSR), the late 1980s and 1990s witnessed the collapse of that status quo and a time of redistribution. Europe has recently witnessed long forgotten ethnic cruelty, violence and massacre on its soil, with the Balkans at centre stage. While one set of causes for the rise of ultra-nationalist tendencies leading to actual genocide and ethnic cleansing in the region could be traced to the collapse of the Eastern bloc, where a multitude of repressed ethnic identities have re-emerged, one should not close one's eyes to the effects of an economic-political struggle for the region by Western European countries and the United States.

This social turmoil has also had a crucial impact on artistic production in the Balkans. The 1995 Cannes Film Festival best film awards were shared by two Balkan films: *Underground*, a film by Emir Kusturica, took the Palme d'Or, and the Grand Prix was awarded to Theo Angelopoulos's *Ulysses' Gaze*. Both films emphasized the tragedy and the pain in the Balkans and the roles of film and film making are also included in these stories as important aspects of a specific period of their countries' history. While *Underground* ridicules the exaggerated propaganda film production in former Yugoslavia, in *Ulysses's Gaze* film has a central place in the script. The latter film tells the story of a Greek-born American director's (Harvey Keitel) struggle to find the lost three reels of undeveloped film shot by a documentary film making team, the Greek Manakis brothers, set in different places in the Balkans at the turn of the century. Keitel travels to Albania, Macedonia, Bulgaria, Romania and finally Sarajevo to find the films, and as he gets involved in the recent and past histories of those countries, he gains a 'multiple personality' through which Balkan history flows. But what is the significance of these films, why is he trying to find them? Is it just an archival pursuit? He is trying to find the *lives* captured in those films, which are mostly documentary-type films about the social life of the region. Everything is there in those films, the reason and probably the solution of the Balkan conflict. It is like the struggle for finding the cure of an awful illness. He is looking for a cure in the film. But is there any cure of any sort anywhere, or was the *journey* itself the key subject matter?

Film is a form of text where social life is produced and reproduced. For cinema fans it is often a weekend ritual, a breakaway from everyday problems, a condensed period of excitement, fun, romance and entertainment. For some cinema producers it is a huge market operation, supported by products such as soundtracks, books and toys, for earning massive amounts of money, and a couple of Oscars if they are lucky (Turner 1993). For some social researchers, on the other hand, it is an invaluable field for producing insights into changing social relations. Here I want to draw attention to critical work on the significance of film as a discursive medium, and I argue that film analysis has an important role in social studies in observing the dynamic structure of society. I do not go as far as searching for a 'cure' in film, but nevertheless see it as a precious textual form of life. Thus it may seem that film is to be understood, in this context, as a representation of social life which the researcher can use as a form of data. To a certain extent this is true, film is a form of representation showing such qualities, but this is not the only way a film can be perceived and certainly this is not the only way it can become an important component of discourse research.

Film is not (only) a mirror reflecting social life but it is a genuine semiotic system, a communication medium where meaning is created and displayed in a certain way (Lotman 1976; Turner 1993). Any social research willing to utilize film has to work on and try to understand what kind of a semiotic system film is. Psychoanalysis, for example, is one of the most influential theoretical frameworks in film studies, drawing upon commonalities between psychoanalysis's and cinema's 'processes of constructing the subject and of the circulation of desire' (Kaplan 1990: 10). Likewise, some postmodernist approaches emphasize the fragmented nature of social life in late capitalism by referring to film as a key medium (Giroux 1996).

Donna Haraway (1991: 153) in her article 'A manifesto for cyborgs' emphasizes the relation between technology, text, and power:

Modern machines are quintessentially microelectronic devices: They are everywhere and they are invisible. Modern machinery is an irreverent upstart god, mocking the Father's ubiquity and spirituality. *The silicon chip is a surface for writing*; it is etched in molecular scales disturbed only by atomic noise, the ultimate interference for nuclear scores. Writing, power, and technology are old partners in Western stories of the origin of civilization, but miniaturization has changed our experience of mechanism.

(Emphasis added)

Film, in a similar way to the silicon chip, can be thought as a 'surface for writing'. It is a 'surface' where human history, from various perspectives and in different voices, is written and rewritten. It is as if a historical event which is not written down and performed on film by scriptwriters, directors, actors, producers and film crew, and which is not watched by an audience, is not completed yet, for it is not yet *textualized*. For example, we remember the state fascism of South America in the 1970s clearly from films such as *Tangos* (1985, dir. Solanas), *Official History* (1986, dir. Puenzo), *Sur* (1988, dir. Solanas) and *Death and the Maiden* (1995, dir. Polanski). They even tend to replace the actual historical events, e.g. Kirk Douglas *is* Spartacus or Elizabeth Taylor *is* Queen Cleopatra. Perhaps the most critical and contradictory aspect of film and textuality is the relation between 'reality' and its simulations (Landsberg 1995).

I will be using an activity-theoretical perspective to read a piece of film text in this chapter, and so I will be analysing the confrontation between the characters, not seen particularly as individuals but as the confrontation between different *modes of activity* existing in society, activity which is embodied in those characters. Activity theory (or the activity school) is a heterogeneous collection of perspectives on human life initially formulated in the former Soviet Union by the psychologists and pedagogues Vygotsky, Leont'ev and Luria from the 1930s to the 1960s, and it has recently gained recognition and been developed in various directions in other parts of the world, especially in continental Europe. According to activity theory, the psychological study of subjectivities has to take individual and collective activity as its primary area of study (Leont'ev 1978); here the concept of activity (societal, mediated) emerges as the relevant necessary subject matter of research and the direct study of the phenomenon of consciousness is being dismissed as an idealist project. In activity theory, activity has to be differentiated from action; where activity has an explicit or implicit motive, while actions are particular and goal-oriented and constitute the activity. For example, when your motive is to gain a degree there are definite actions you have to perform, such as attending the courses, preparing the assignments and taking certain examinations. Each of these is a particular action with particular goals (passing the exams, getting necessary grades etc.). The aggregates of the particular actions are parts of an activity which has a definite motive (of gaining the degree), but gaining your degree itself can be an action rather than an activity, and gaining the degree may have different motives underneath (which are rarely explicit), depending on what you are planning to do with it. Thus, even though two actions may look as if they have exactly the same activity, their overall motive – that is, the activity itself – can be quite different. It is the contradictory nature of human activities which is of interest for activity theory in the study of social life and subjectivity, and here for the study of film.

Text: Wall Street

Films produced by big American studios are characterized by their 'affirmative' character. These 'studio' films are criticized for their normalizing effect on social conflicts, and they are a powerful weapon in the Americanization of global social life, exporting North American values all over the world. Studio films hold the majority shares in the world film market, and are thus a key aspect of contemporary social-cultural imperialism (Putnam 1997). Importance is given to those films here because of their power in also giving us a glimpse into changing conditions of social life, even if it is 'distorted' by them. I will argue that film analysis drawing on activity theory has the potential to decode certain codes in the films and to enable us to read the film, interacting with it in a way not completely determined by the script or the director.

The film of which a section has been chosen to be analysed in this chapter is *Wall Street*. *Wall Street* is an Oliver Stone film produced in 1987 by Twentieth Century Fox Studios featuring Michael Douglas (as Gordon Gekko, a financial investor), Charlie Sheen (as Bud Fox, a young broker), Martin Sheen (Carl Fox, Bud's father, a technician and the union representative of the company Blue Star) and Daryl Hannah (as Darien, an interior designer, Bud's lover and Gekko's mistress) (Kagan 1995).

Bud is a New York University graduate, a young broker working at Wall Street who wants to earn lots of money fast, and is aware of the fact that it is not possible to do this working as an ordinary broker. So, he wants to work with Gekko, a multimillionaire and an expert investor in the market. When he finally manages to get an appointment with Gekko he gives strategic information about the aviation company Blue Star where his father works as a union representative. Bud then starts working covertly as an informer for Gekko. As Gekko starts rewarding Bud for the valuable information he gathers, Bud moves from his small filthy apartment into a big loft in Manhattan's Upper West Side and starts living with Darien. Bud wants Gekko to buy Blue Star, and although Gekko is reluctant at the

The section opens with a foggy and smoggy shot of South Manhattan, the financial district where the real Wall Street is located. Bud's father arrives at the flat, dressed casually with his Blue Star company coat on, and Darien and Bud introduce him to the guests. Carl (Bud's father) objects to the presence of Gekko's lawyer, saying he thought that it would be an informal meeting, and Gekko sends the lawyer out to 'take a walk'. They eat a buffet dinner; Carl sits on a futon a bit remote from the main table, seems not very comfortable with the food, which he is probably not used to, and examines the loft while eating. After the dinner, cigars and informal chat, Gekko opens up the discussion about the future of Blue Star, the major shares of which have been bought by Gekko. Gekko walks around the room as he outlines the situation; he emphasizes the doomed future of the company and its employees, whose contracts and unions were being broken by the management. Gekko's deal is to cut the wages by 20 per cent and add seven more work hours a month. After Gekko has spoken, Bud takes the floor and distributes some handouts describing his plan to return Blue Star to profitability, which he sums up in the words 'reorganize', 'modernize' and 'advertise'. The representatives of the pilots and flight attendants are initially sympathetic to the plan but Carl starts laughing sarcastically and delivers a short monologue regarding the plan proposed by Gekko and Bud: 'The only difference between the pyramids and the Empire State Building is that the Egyptians didn't have unions. This guy [Gekko] is in it just for the bucks and he doesn't take prisoners. The "scum" built this company up from one plane in thirty years.' He then hastily leaves the house, and Bud, who is puzzled by this unexpected response, runs out after his father. They take the elevator, and Bud furiously berates his father for destroying his career: 'Save the workers of the world speech, I heard it too many times growing up.' Carl, looking quite disappointed and hurt by Bud's reaction, replies that he will take the plan to the workers and let them decide. The section ends with another smoggy shot of New York City, but this time focusing on the Brooklyn Bridge.

beginning Bud finally convinces him that the company can be profitable following some restructuring and he becomes the manager of Blue Star.

Gekko, Bud, Darien and Bud's father Carl, along with the pilot and flight attendant representatives of Blue Star, meet to discuss the future of the company. Gekko and Bud offer a deal which includes a wage reduction, extra working hours etc. Everyone except Carl is convinced by the plan. Later it turns out that Gekko changed his mind, and instead of reforming the company he now wants to get rid of it, which means the workers will be laid off. Bud learns this and makes a deal with Gekko's arch rival, in which that person will buy the company and will keep the workers on. After some market deals orchestrated by Bud the market value of Blue Star falls sharply and Gekko loses millions, with the majority of the shares bought by the arch rival. Stock market internal security then arrests Bud for obtaining internal information about the stock market.

A section of the film, approximately six minutes long, has been selected to be analysed in detail. It is the meeting of Blue Star members – two representatives of the pilots and the flight attendants, and Bud's father as the union representative – Gekko and his lawyer, Bud and Darien at Bud's new flat in Manhattan's Upper West Side, to talk about the future of Blue Star.

Reading: activity-theoretical approach

We begin the analysis by differentiating various types of activities, and the various characters who embody those activities. When we talk about the embodiment of activities in individuals or groups, we do not draw an absolute relation between the activity and the individual, as if there is not also a contradictory relation between the two. On the contrary, it is precisely the contradictory character of this embodiment which shapes dynamic social life. And when we talk about activities they are not to be understood as abstract units leading their own life and affecting people arbitrarily; rather, they are concrete social relations located in history and produced by social life and its conflicting priorities.

When we look at the text, in the context of the overall narrative of the film, we are presented with two different opposing modes of activities, embodied in Gekko and Carl. While the dominant activity of Gekko is financial activity – buying and selling shares, 'wrecking' companies 'because they are wreckable', etc. – we see Carl, the father, as a representative of a different activity; he is the union representative of Blue Star, representing the workforce. But why are they two different activities? Perhaps the difference is easily observable, but does this mean that we have to see the interaction as one of opposition? To answer this we have to look at that particular time period in US history (and also that of Europe, and other parts of the world). The film is set in the Reagan years, when the term 'New World Order' has been recently coined, the USA is dealing with its skyrocketing budget deficit, the threat of the Communist bloc has decreased and the final 'victory' of capitalism is close. Globalization and marketization of the world is gaining pace. Similar market transactions – buying and selling companies, laying off workers, breaking unions – represented in the film are, in fact, being played out in the USA at that time.

The opposing character of Gekko's and Carl's activities is more obvious if we bear in mind these background social dynamics. Gekko is part of a rising trend, and Carl's star is falling on the social stage at that time.

The meeting and the interactions between the characters remind us of a chess game. Both Gekko and Carl are very well aware of what that meeting means compared to other characters in the meeting. Gekko has brought his lawyer with him, and the camera shows them talking silently (as if discussing the latest tactics and probable outcomes of the meeting) as Carl enters the room. The presence of the lawyer is challenged by Carl, thus reducing the balance of power on Gekko's side, and the lawyer leaves the flat (and the game, though he stays in the building). Gekko is aware of the fact that Carl is the key person in the room, and will have the key role in the decision-making process. And so Gekko orchestrates his body movements (speech tone, intonation, use of jokes, walking around the room during his speech etc.) to influence Carl. At the same time Carl is on his guard, and he shows his uneasiness at every aspect of the situation; he sits somewhat detached from the group (creating a division within the group), he smells the food before eating (as if checking whether it is poisonous or not) and he is not exactly sure of his son's role in this game. The camera almost always shows Gekko, Bud and Darien in the same frame, as if highlighting the most important parties to the discussion or explicitly highlighting those embodying a mode of activity.

The pilot and flight attendant representatives present an ambivalent response, for while they show a slight reluctance to accept the restructuring plans they seem easily convinced by the promised rosy economic growth scenario. They seem impressed by Gekko, the house, the food and the way they are treated. When Bud gives them the handouts about his plan, instead of reading them they listen to what Bud says. It is Carl who reads the details of the plan and disagrees with it, though he adds that he will take it to his fellow workers for further discussion.

Bud is a living contradiction. While all his education was aimed at being a successful market person, and to get rich as soon as possible, this ambition leads him to being a 'criminal'. Bud has chosen what his main mode of activity will be, one close to Gekko's, and this leads to conflicts with his father's mode of activity and morality, the activity which he was raised on. Though he seeks a reconciliation between these two activities, by convincing Gekko to buy Blue Star and preparing a reform plan which will 'save' both the company and the workers, such a 'reconciliation' fails because of Gekko's secret decision to dissolve the company. Bud is disappointed by his father's reaction, which extinguishes his hopes of any reconciliation. He is also in conflict with his new status in life, easy success and wealth, and from time to time he asks the question 'Who am I?' to himself, echoing the ongoing clashes between opposing modes of activities and moral values.

Disadvantages

How film could be analysed as a text has been a continuous challenge during the discussion and writing processes of this chapter, and one of the aims in designing the chapters in the book was in fact to present the text in the length of one page; this is possible for a photo, a letter or an advertisement, but it is not easy for a film. There were two basic problems: the first was of converting a visual and aural text into a written one, and the second was of choosing a section from the film and keeping it meaningful although it is plucked out from the narrative of the film. A still frame of the film could be used, but that would be unfair to the spirit of the film, and would not carry the flow of the story. Finally, it was decided to take a section of the film and describe it thoroughly in a written form, and in order to prevent decontextualization a summary of the whole film was given. Even though it was intended to be 'objective', the description itself is from a particular vantage point, and more details of the text, missed while describing the scene, are given during the analysis. Thus, there is a technical difficulty, apart from the theoretical aspect, of analysing a film text compared with other visual text. It is technically not possible to put the text on a page, as could be done with a painting or a comic strip, and this prevents an actual experiencing of the text if the film is not viewed elsewhere by the 'reader'.

This film text can be analysed as the confrontation between conflicting activities in the social life of a particular place at a particular time. One of the difficulties for the analysis is the fact that it necessitates sufficient knowledge about the political, economic, historical and cultural conditions of the period when the film is produced. This is crucial in deciphering the dominant stories of that period and in making sense of the activities in which the characters are embodied and the activities which they challenge and reproduce.

Activity-theoretical film analysis is open to critique from psychoanalytic and postmodernist perspectives. A critique from a psychoanalytic perspective would make the point that activity theory underestimates the significance of interpersonal and psychic dynamics which shape the story; for example, the conflicting relations between Bud and Carl, the emergence of Gekko as a new father figure and Bud's Oedipal struggle when faced with these conflicts. More than that, it could also be argued that an activity-theoretical perspective is indifferent to the relation between the film and the audience, the mechanisms in process and who the audience is identifying itself with in the film. That is to say, activity theory is perhaps too much interested with the story as a representation of actual social life and does not take seriously the significance of filming as a voyeuristic activity.

As far as a postmodernist point of view is concerned – and I am aware of the fact that it is hard to generalize postmodernism as a well defined position, and so I limit myself to the critique of modern grand narratives and the problematic character of truth and reality – activity theory is still thinking through grand narratives and tends to be quite structuralist in its analysis of social and personal relations. It does not offer rich possibilities of different ways of reading social interactions, and sticks to a fairly singular explanation of social life at the expense of its fragmented nature. For example, in the analysis of *Wall Street*, class antagonism is still used as *the* important criterion. Activity theory is sensitive mainly to economic conflicts and underestimates other kinds of social conflict.

Advantages

Even though the technical disadvantage of analysing a section of a film, compared to other forms of visual texts which can literally be put in the analysis, is clear, film analysis has been successfully carried out for a very long time in cultural studies. The text can be viewed in cinemas, on video or through other media, for example, and if this chapter had not been in a book but on the Internet as a Web site the chosen section of the film could be added to the text as a moving picture, and thus be viewed without any problem. Although there is a technical disadvantage, I believe it is not essential.

Wall Street is actually eminently suitable for an activity-theoretical analysis. The social oppositions or parties are clear, and the whole narrative highlights the social conflicts in the USA, as Oliver Stone (the director) points out:

> You read about these kids who are making a million bucks, two million bucks a year, it demoralizes the person making $40,000 a year. All of a sudden everybody needs a Porsche or a VCR or a fishing boat. And that is what fuels America, more and more greed. We deal with these issues by staying inside a very small story, one fish in one Wall Street aquarium and what happens to that fish.
>
> (Quoted in Salewicz 1997: 49)

An activity-theoretical approach is particularly useful in analysing texts where social, economic and political oppression is present; that is to say, where oppressive and subversive activities are explicit, as in *Wall Street*, where class positions are relatively clear. But such explicitness is not always the case. Social life is getting so complicated that easy analyses of the quality of various activities is not possible. Activities keep changing their character and motive; class positions are getting blurred, and the qualities of what defines a class are getting harder and harder to observe. There are other social divisions which are now perceived as crucial, such as gender, race and sexual identity. Nevertheless, this does not prevent the effectiveness of activity-theoretical analysis as such, and it is still useful for observing and working out various parties in a contradictory situation. The task is to develop activity theory as an approach which is primarily sensitive to all forms of contradictions and conflictual social activities, whether they are socio-economic, political, racial or sexual. This is important because it is exactly such reified compartmentalization of social life which activity theory opposes as taken for granted realities or positions.

Analysing a film text from an activity-theoretical perspective invites the analyst to locate the story and the characters in actual social life and in history, and rather than looking for set templates, social change and its effect on individual lives is foregrounded. A psychoanalytic analysis, for example, often loses this kind of historical perspective, and the emergence of new conflicts in social life, for the sake of re-establishing an Oedipal framework again and again. There is a tendency of rebuilding the well known psychoanalytical structure in the text, and then it is as if the text loses its importance, its character of telling an original story, and becomes merely a guinea pig where the theory is simply confirmed.

One question that would be pertinent to be posed by an activity-theoretical perspective is why a specific film has been produced at this specific time in history. What is the significance of the production of such a film at this moment? The North American cinema industry is quite consciously keeping the pulse of the social life and each new incident or change in social life brings the production of film with it; for example, the Vietnam war was textualized in *Full Metal Jacket*, *Apocalypse Now* etc., homosexuality appears in *The Wedding Banquet*, *The Kiss of the Spider Woman*, AIDS is represented in *Philadelphia*, capital punishment in *The Last Dance* and even the Million Man March in *Get on the Bus*. Perhaps this is also one of the useful aspects of US studio cinema if we know how to read the films critically.

Art has the potential for capturing and creating new modes of human conduct. Perhaps cinema is one of the most affective and most sensitive forms to detect and thus produce new ways of talking, touching, walking, writing, living. The cinema medium is too important to be left aside by social and cultural studies and understood only as a form of entertainment.

Key readings

Haraway, D. (1991) *Simians, Cyborgs, and Women: The Reinvention of Nature.* London: Free Association Books.
Landsberg, A. (1995) Prosthetic memory: Total Recall and Blade Runner. In M. Featherstone and R. Burrows (eds) *Cyberspace, Cyberbodies, Cyberpunk: Cultures of Technological Embodiment.* London: Sage Publications.

References

Giroux, H. A. (1996) Slacking off: border youth and postmodern education. In H. A. Giroux, C. Lankshear, P. McLaren and M. Peters (eds) *Counternarratives: Cultural Studies and Critical Pedagogies in Postmodern Spaces*. London: Routledge.

Haraway, D. (1991) *Simians, Cyborgs, and Women: The Reinvention of Nature*. London: Free Association Books.

Kagan, N. (1995) *The Cinema of Oliver Stone*. Oxford: Roundhouse.

Kaplan, A. E. (1990) Introduction: from Plato's cave to Freud's screen. In *Psychoanalysis and Cinema*. London: Routledge.

Landsberg, A. (1995) Prosthetic memory: Total Recall and Blade Runner. In M. Featherstone and R. Burrows (eds) *Cyberspace, Cyberbodies, Cyberpunk: Cultures of Technological Embodiment*. London: Sage Publications.

Leont'ev, A. N. (1978) *Activity, Consciousness and Personality*. Englewood Cliffs, NJ: Prentice Hall.

Lotman, J. (1976) *Semiotics of Cinema*, trans. M. E. Suino. Ann Arbor: Michigan Slavic Contributions.

Putnam, D. (1997) *The Undeclared War: The Struggle for Control of the World's Film Industry*. London: HarperCollins Publishers.

Salewicz, C. (1997) *Oliver Stone: The Making of His Movies*. London: Orion Media.

Turner, G. (1993) *Film as Social Practice*. London: Routledge.

PART III

Physical texts

Cities: resident
readers and others

MARTINE C. MIDDLETON

Cities function as a physical celebration of social activity. The changing dynamics of the city sustain the livelihood of those who permanently live and work inside its confines. The man-made conurbation becomes increasingly attractive to those people outside who actively seek to visit a city and experience the place themselves. The city is socially diverse and economically productive in nature. Political governance is often instigated and converted into active policies to facilitate the functional operation of city development. The urban region contains a physical hierarchical framework from city centre to suburbia and its recreational periphery. Social patterns of movement, behaviour and meaning are derived from the physical and social interaction of city and place. Why and how do different people read the city in different ways? The framework for discursive debate focuses on the city as a text, with people as its readers. A distinction is made between residents and tourists assimilating meaning from familiar and unfamiliar surroundings.

The city acts as a repository of people's memories, recalled events and accumulated cultural symbols. Benjamin (1979) identifies criteria of concentration and distraction to understand how people read the urban text. Individuals travel with different states of consciousness towards their surroundings. Benjamin argues that buildings are appreciated in passing, in a state of distraction, as people pass on to elsewhere. Urry (1995) has also investigated the relationship between the social and physical environment, and four approaches to understanding the significance of 'place' are identified by him. They are: restructured as centres for consumption; consumed visually; consumed by significance (e.g. industry, history, buildings); and serving to consume one's identity. He concludes that the economic dimension to tourism emerges from evaluating tourist consumption patterns, but that consumption remains an indelibly social activity.

The city marries the physical and social dimensions of daily life. Foucault (1977) focuses on links between power and knowledge and addresses the manner in which space is physically organized. The object here is the city, and the people within it are the subjects reflecting their knowledge through their ability to orientate, decipher and read the meaning of the place. Residents possess a sense of the known, familiar and mundane experience of everyday life. Tourists, on the other hand, arrive with a sense of urgency to experience the essence of the city. Narratives are fashioned out of a range of experiences. The extent to which the process is logical, sequential and ordered imposes a structure on the experience. Large cities compound the demands made upon finite physical resources that must be organized to accommodate the economic and social needs of others (Law 1993). The institutional bodies of central and local government possess the remit to devise policy and its practice. City planners need to evaluate the physical, economic and social dimensions that combine to provide a holistic approach to environmental management. However, the ideology that underpins policy is not static, nor necessarily the same for each agency. The government assumes the role of safeguarding cultural heritage as a representation of the past, and the ideology of the provider of the experience is a vulnerable one. In addition to this, ideology instigates a sense of identity.

Residents who inhabit an area identify with the place by origin, family connections or knowledge derived through longstanding experience. Tourists, however, seek identity with a place on a temporary basis, without ownership, and are constrained in both knowledge and time. Contradictions emerge from such a juxtaposition between the city provider and individual consumer. Finance is injected into an economy that must cater to an increasing number of people. The temporary and affluent nature of tourists makes tourism an attractive commodity to city management. The relationship between the needs of residents and the wants of tourists is an unstable one that affects the physical environment that they share. The physical form of the city is prone to commodification by different economic and social criteria. Reading the city highlights the details of the physical setting. Discourse analysis identifies patterns of variation within the city between people's experience of familiar and unfamiliar surroundings. To what extent can fact merge with fiction to maintain visitor attraction and remain in keeping with the fabric of the city?

Everyday activity in the city shares one physical location but brings together diverse cultural backgrounds, reflecting different modes of interpretation of the shared environment. The tangible form of the city encompasses a stationary landscape reflecting culture, history and architecture. The intangible form represents the experience derived from travelling around, and seeking visually to consume the city. The diversity of this experience leads to different discourses for different audiences. Soja (1989: 323) suggests that a historical consciousness emerged within social theory such that the historical imagination seemed to be annihilating the geographical. The visual quality of the city has important significance for providing clarity, or legibility, of the cityscape. To understand this we must look beyond the city as an object in itself, to the city as perceived by its inhabitants. Such an approach distinguishes social perception from the physical dimension (Lynch 1960).

The experience derived from the city represents a series of interactions between people participating within the urban form. Participants can possess diverse levels of knowledge and awareness of their surrounding environment. The physical form of the city addresses the elements of familiarity and difference. The urban environment attempts to make that form intelligible to different audiences. City discourse depends upon culturally constructed images depicting a representation of the past. This setting reflects an array of meanings for those who inhabit and visit the city. The physical form of the city consists of buildings, streets and spaces dedicated to fulfilling the economic and social needs of people. However, the city also acts as a magnet to those attracted by the allure of heritage and mystique. The use of architecture, street furnishings and landmarks provides an appropriate backdrop to orientate the tourist around an unfamiliar physical setting. The process of acquiring actual experience of the city also differentiates between social groups. Cultural distinctiveness may be expressed in the organization of the city as a text, and is articulated and transmitted by the use of various discourses. Cultural frames of reference emerge through the participation of diverse social groups within the unified confines of the built environment. In the same way that the city consists of physical zones and boundaries, so flourishing social networks based on common goals are formed.

Text

Tourism has been defined as the set of ideas, theories or ideologies for being a tourist, and the behaviour of people in touristic roles when the ideas are put into practice (Leiper 1990: 17). The nature of the tourist experience is dependent upon individual principles, assumptions and motives. Boorstein (1964) demeans the experience of tourists as being shallow

The city of Manchester has a population of 2.5 million inhabitants and is internationally renowned for its wealth of heritage and cultural resources. This cosmopolitan city attracts visitors from around the world. It is a post-industrial metropolitan city meeting the increasing economic and social demands of today's diverse society. Two photographs of Manchester have been selected to illustrate the physical representation of the city. The first is 'Castlefield Urban Heritage Park', the first of its kind in Britain. The park reflects the diverse heritage of the city, with an emphasis on education. The second picture depicts one of Castlefield's major tourist attractions, Granada Studios Tour. This site offers a fun-filled extravaganza of Hollywood proportions. It celebrates the inauthentic experience by creating staged events to induce pleasure and a sense of escapism. The focus of the experience is one of entertainment as opposed to historical observation.

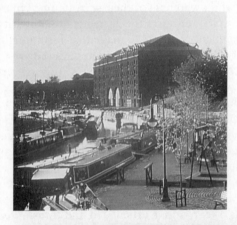

Castlefield: The facts of the city

Granada Studios Tour: The fiction of the city

and superficial. He argues that tourism has compromised authenticity and what is experienced is no more than a number of 'pseudo-events'. This view is contested by MacCannell (1973), who states that the tourist does not seek contrived experiences but desires an accurate and real experience. Both of these opposing views are refuted by Cohen (1979), who questions the existence of 'the tourist' because such a generalization fails to acknowledge the individual's 'world-view' relating to people, place and tourism.

Lowerson (1994) describes tourism as the consumption of place and desired experience. Insight into the tourist as a user of the city embodies the whole process of the interaction of visitor behaviour with the physical environment. The city represents an amalgam of physically defined spaces determined by their use and function. The physical form of the city is often shaped by the economic determinants of the area, which in turn is reflected in the urban landscape. However, the city exceeds the representation of a series of material buildings, streets and landmarks. These physical entities reflect a history rich in diverse cultural and social significance. This composite approach to the city attributes integrity to the form. Here, the city is a representation to which people ascribe meaning. It is in this sense that the city may be perceived as a text, and this warrants a semiotic approach to reading the city, with individuals seeking a quest for urban legibility (Sharpe and Wallock 1987: 17). This legibility can be achieved by reading the narratives, similes and hyperbole available to residents and tourists. Different interpretations emerge from the same physical environment and urban discourse highlights diverse paradigms of meaning and representation.

MacCannell (1976) argues that the cultures of the world have been displaced and altered by the continuous movement of people. From this process two types of displaced thought emerge. The first uses signs and artefacts of cultural difference leading to hybridization of culture in the postmodern world. The second aims to reconstruct tradition, presenting culture as a consumable commodity. Both of these types of thought encompass and utilize the physical surroundings as purveyors of the myth of the city. The tourist attempts to experience the whole vision. A central theme in MacCannell's argument is that the tourist actively seeks cognitively to recreate structures which modernity has destroyed. The breakdown of boundaries between high and popular culture, history and heritage, and scientific and popular narratives leads to a differentiation between resident and tourist.

Reading

The impact of physical and social change is especially evident within older industrial-oriented cities, such as Manchester. The heritage of many northern industrial cities is reflected in the landscape architecture. The image of these cities has been transformed from 'the old dark satanic mills'. The passing of time and the implementation of tourist initiatives serve to increase the economy by promoting the city to tourists. Featherstone (1990) asserts that the everyday life of big cities is becoming aestheticized. In acclaiming the aesthetic potential of mass culture and the aestheticized perceptions of people, visitors are encouraged to participate in the complex sign play of symbolism throughout the built environment and urban fabric of the city. The text example illustrates the open, outdoor nature of the city, with the 'Disneyfication' of the enclosed, artificial environment.

'Flânerie' is associated with the form of looking and observing one's surroundings. Readings of the city are based on the meaning derived from this activity. Observation and reading lead to the production of distinctive forms of texts. Benjamin (1979) examined the role of the 'flâneur' wandering around the city in a distracted and voyeuristic manner. The text example illustrates the polarity of meaning between two 'sights' located adjacent to each other. As the momentum of society continues to advance, physical changes are reflected within the urban landscape. This landscape is visible in space and narratively visible in time. A consistent relationship between the built environment and historical setting provides authenticity to the experience. The modernization of urban space unifies the physical form with social demands. A voyeuristic approach to wandering around the city is nowadays escalated in time and space. The physical environment is continuously changing, often resulting in a lack of coordination or visual continuity. Castlefield celebrates the heritage and culture of Manchester, for example, while Granada Studios Tour advances into the futuristic, high technological age. Physical urban systems of streets, roads and pedestrianized areas enable people to circulate freely around the city with increased ease and speed. It is this notion of the modern city that has altered the physical representation of the city to accommodate social change. Spaces are increasingly areas of social interaction consisting of new public developments: arcades, galleries and cafes. It is a physical environment that becomes more diverse in both form and function. Modern cities encompass varied and numerous periodic settings, often within a limited walking distance. Manchester reflects Victorian architecture, industrial heritage, Roman archaeology and fictional media promotion within one accessible site. To what extent do those seeking to experience it question the physical compression of time and space?

In acknowledging that tourists pursue different modes of experience, Cohen (1979) identifies two problems: what are the chances of *realization* of the different modes of touristic experience; and, from the point of the external observer, what are the possibilities of *falsification* of such experiences by the tourist? The quest for authenticity is not always integral to the tourist experience. The diversionary mode seeks entertainment, while the recreational mode performs a restorative function for the individual

(Cohen 1979). The remaining three modes Cohen identifies (experiential, experimental and existential) all require some degree of authenticity to attain fulfilment. MacCannell (1973: 601) argues that the fate of tourists is to become entrapped in 'tourist space', never able to realize their craving for authenticity.

Form, function and aesthetics affect both resident and tourist. The need to assimilate information and to orientate oneself around an unfamiliar city will underpin the tourist experience. How the visitor interacts with his or her surroundings is dependent upon a number of factors, some more conducive than others. Holloway (1992) identifies three ways in which the tourist is affected by the architecture and cityscape design of the city. There are those who are not only interested in architecture but encouraged by the media to seek and appraise the buildings in question. Another category of tourist is one who is not so design-conscious but keen to improve the overall satisfaction of the tourist experience. The third category is subconsciously sensitive to the surroundings. The implementation of 'wallpaper architecture' enhances a setting without the visitor's conscious awareness of its impact (Holloway 1992). This technique is being widely adopted throughout Britain as numerous city centres adopt the use of black and brass coloured Victorian street furnishings and signage. The Victorian heritage of Manchester is promoted by the same technique. However, such widespread use dilutes visual susceptibility to the significance of the physical surroundings.

Urry (1990) refers to the visual consumption of an unfamiliar place as the 'tourist gaze'. There is no single gaze as such, for it varies by society, by social group and by historical period. However, tourists are a distinct social group with a series of identifiable characteristics. Their approach to the meaning of place differs in anticipation and expectation. The place provides prospects of pleasure derived from its surroundings, surroundings that are removed from everyday experience and involve different forms of social patterning (Urry 1990). The term vacation, by definition, refers to the *vacating* of one's usual space to experience a new and temporary one. Cities may be seen as a series of spaces in which meaning is ascribed. The open space of the city centre facilitates a passive absorption of the built environment. Conversely, the enclosed space of Granada Studios Tour acts as a divertionary force creating excitement and encouraging active participation. The closure of physical space acts as a divisive mechanism between those who enter and are accepted, and those who remain transitory and excluded.

Authenticity is commodified to create the tourist experience. Cities are prone to change and adaptation by professional planners who determine the form and function of the physical environment to accommodate those it serves. This incorporates a system of imitation, reproduction and commodification editing the physical reality and reinforcing the social myth projected by the city. The text example illustrates attempts to preserve heritage for people to enjoy and the powerful commercial presence of lucrative tourist development. The reality and myth of the city are physically presented and visually consumed simultaneously.

Disadvantages

The physical form of the city symbolizes its economic and social history within processes of architectural representation. City development progressively alters the physical embodiment of the past to accommodate the increasing demands of modern life. Different social groups facilitate the use of the city for their own requirements. The onus of evaluating the form and function of city utilization lies with the planners and designers of city management (Urry 1990). The attributes of physical, economic and social demands need to be aligned to optimize the physical provision for social consumption. This is evident in the 24-hour, seven-day week economy that is emerging. Developed service economies are becoming increasingly consumer-led, thereby continually extending the size and scope of social provision. A distinction is made between those familiar (resident) and unfamiliar (tourist) to a place. The reality of the physical environment is utilized in different ways by different groups. The person who lives or works in the city is relatively impassive to the aesthetic values that surround him or her. The resident adopts a functional approach to city interpretation. Alternatively, an incoming visitor has the desire to experience the essence of the city, seeking out the cultural dimension inherent in the physical location. In determining the differences that distinguish social groups from each other, cohesion is the overall goal. Social integration and unity between minority and predominant groups remains a constant objective of effective policy bodies.

The physical environment mirrors diverse meanings to various groups. The urban landscape is commonly determined by an economic output that governs form and function of the city. The composite nature of the city includes a thriving social dimension that encompasses work and leisure demands of society. This is compounded by the growing number of incoming visitors who wish to experience the sites (and sights) of the multifaceted urban landscape. The complexity of socially constructed meanings differs from individual to individual. Cities represent a combination of tangible elements evident by their visual interpretation. The description of places and events is dependent upon the use, adaptation and interpretation of language. This is significant in how the city is marketed to attract people to visit and in what way expectations are met. Therefore, the power of relating experience lies with the choice of words, tone and context in which it is applied. In identifying the tangible form by intangible attributes, words assume a powerful role in describing experience. The experience is between the person and the environment expressed in a second-hand form and thereby prone to inaccuracies and distortion. This is compounded by the complex nature of cities and their significance in visitors' perception and expectation. Cities themselves are associated with a plethora of adjectives, e.g. vibrant, lively, dynamic, uptown/downtown. These words are symbolic of a directional flow indicating motion. However, the oppressive use of language often describes the darker side of city experience (e.g. dirty, dangerous, intimidating). Rhetorical devices conjure up vivid visual interpretations of the experiences of others.

The evaluation of perception, expectation and experience centres on the image of the city (Lynch 1960). This needs to be positive to motivate the person to travel to, and experience, what the city possesses. The city may create or re-create a desired image for itself based on chronological dates and events. Alternatively, a fictional representation may be introduced to complement, or substitute for, previous images. MacCannell (1973) proposes that all tourists seek authenticity but are frustrated because of the creation of inauthentic environments. However, authenticity is not an essential element to a satisfying tourist experience. The description of an experience derived from actual behaviour is dependent upon the power of memory and recall. Lynch (1960) and Pearce (1977) both acknowledge different levels of awareness to the city experience, and highlight this distinction. Each group expresses a different expectation that is often constrained by time. The fulfilment of expectation comes as it turns into direct experience and shifts the description of events from the past into present time. This can provide problems for analysis and a lack of methodological rigour to underpin the study.

What is the 'city as text'? The multifaceted nature of the city embodies buildings, people, policies, planning and much more. The relationship between people and place is compounded by continuous change. People derive meaning from cities yet do not analyse how they are meaningful. Discourse analysis seeks to derive specific meanings, but the nature of the city is dynamic, complex and inspiring. It is difficult to capture this in such a structured mode of reading.

Advantages

The discursive framework provides an analytical insight into experience of the city. It combines the individual elements within the built environment and creates a composite, structured evaluation based on socially derived meaning. It recognizes the power of implicit meanings in the urban environment as understood by its symbolic interpretation. The continued spatial development of cities embodies change and adaptation of the physical attributes that visually represent the tangible city. This process creates and modifies the space we occupy. Discourse is an appropriate approach to identify differences of meaning derived from new places. It addresses the diversity of groups reading the city and questions what people see and do. Cities represent an amalgam of social and cultural attributes that encompass both heritage and modernity. However, Cohen (1979) argues that the correct perception of authenticity is not guaranteed. MacCannell (1973) notes that some tourists, but not others, are upset when they realize the staged nature of tourist provision. It is significant to note that we must not assume that all tourists strive to experience truth.

The understanding of environmental imagery is mediated by the use of signs and symbols. Culler (1981) cites tourism and tourists as an 'exemplary case' which can guide and illuminate the understanding of semiotics; the tourist is not interested in the alibis a society uses to refunctionalize its practices. The tourist is interested in everything as a sign in itself. Culler suggests that in participating in tourist behaviour tourists are the 'accomplices' of semiotics by being engaged in semiotic projects, reading cities, landscapes and cultures as sign systems. Therefore the argument for tourism contradicts physical uniformity, preferring particular place-specific readings.

The physical construction of cities includes recognizable systems of accommodation, transport and services (Ashworth 1992). A discursive approach systematically dissects and examines the political/social dimensions of the categorizations of others. It is by acknowledging significant differences that actions can materialize. In recognizing the level of interaction between the objective physical environment and its subjective social use a greater insight is achieved. Through this process distinct frames of reference are created between those familiar and unfamiliar with their surroundings. This allows perception and experience to be evaluated (Urry 1990). Areas of collective cognition, orientation and behaviour can be explored and patterned. This is especially relevant within the institutional framework of creating policy aimed at the use and capacity of social provision.

City planners need to achieve a sense of order and meaning within urban forms. A holistic, comprehensive approach must be embraced to attain legibility and imageability (Lynch 1960). Cities function through the utilization of political, economic and social systems. The significance of reading the city is dependent upon a series of thought processes. Extrinsic interpretation focuses on the physical surroundings – signs, architecture, urban design – while the individual perception and expectation of the visit determine intrinsic evaluation of the city experience. Experiences expressed through language and within the analysis of texts achieve new depths of significance and acknowledge the diversity of society. We provide a voice to those groups previously absorbed by others and utilize the opportunity to express past experience in modern-day language. The dynamics of discourse harnesses change, significance and progress.

Large cities are important tourist destinations. Geographers continue to seek comprehension relating to patterns in city development and appreciation (Law 1993). The process of urbanization brings together physical development to accommodate economic and social demands. Cities are meeting grounds for diverse social and cultural integration to materialize within a physically determined environment. These places have developed as centres of economic production and social provision. Their significance is magnified as focal points of political power are exercised through the agency of government. It is the remit of local authorities to ascertain appropriate and conducive resources to meet the needs of the city recipients. The study of urban places will continue to occupy those involved with the social sciences. Therefore the city will remain a challenging text within the field of discursive research.

Key reading

Selwyn, T. (1996) *The Tourist Image: Myths and Myth Making in Tourism*. Chichester: Wiley.
Zukin, S. (1992) Postmodern urban landscapes: mapping culture and power. In S. Lash and J. Friedman (eds) *Modernity and Identity*. Oxford: Blackwell.

References

Aase, T. H. (1994) Symbolic space: representation of space in geography and anthropology. *Geografiska Annaler*, 76b(1): 51–8.
Ashworth, G. J. (1992) Tourism policy and planning for a quality urban environment. In H. Briassoulis and J. van der Straaten (eds) *Tourism and the Environment: Regional, Economic and Policy Issues*. Dordrecht: Kluwer.
Barthes, R. (1972) *Mythologies*. London: Jonathan Cape.
Benjamin, W. (1979) *One Way Street and Other Writings*. London: Verso.
Boorstein, D. J. (1964) *The Image: A Guide to Pseudo-events in America*. New York: Harper and Row.
Cohen, E. (1979) A phenomenology of tourist experiences. *Sociology*, 13: 179–201.
Culler, J. (1981) Semiotics of tourism. *American Journal of Semiotics*, 1: 127–40.
Featherstone, M. (1990) Perspectives on consumer culture. *Sociology*, 24: 5–22.
Foucault, M. (1977) *Discipline and Punish: The Birth of the Prison*. London: Allen Lane.
Gunn, C. (1988) *Vacationscape*. New York: Nostrand-Reinhold.
Holloway, J. C. (1992) Cityscape: a comparative evaluation of the new built environment and its influence in generating tourism. Conference Proceedings, Tourism in Europe, University of Durham.

Holloway, J. C. (1995) The tourist as streetwalker: gaze or daze? Conference Proceedings, The Urban Environment, South Bank University.

Ittelson, W. H. (1973) Environment perceptions and contemporary perceptional theory. In W. H. Ittelson (ed.) *Environment and Cognition*. New York: Seminar Press.

Law, C. (1993) *Urban Tourism: Attracting Visitors to Larger Cities*. London: Mansell.

Leiper, N. (1990) *Tourism Systems: An Interdisciplinary Perspective*. Palmerston North, NZ: Department of Management Systems, Massey University.

Lowerson, J. (1994) Celtic tourism: some new magnets. Conference Proceedings, The Romance of Place, Exeter University.

Lynch, K. (1960) *The Image of the City*. Cambridge, MA: MIT Press.

MacCannell, D. (1973) Staged authenticity: the arrangement of social space in tourist settings. *American Journal of Sociology*, 79: 589–603.

MacCannell, D. (1976) *The Tourist: A New Theory of the Leisure Class*. New York: Schocken Books.

Pearce, P. L. (1977) Mental souvenirs: a study of tourist and their city maps. *Australian Journal of Psychology*, 29: 203–10.

Rapoport, A. (1982) *The Meaning of the Built Environment*. Beverley Hills, CA: Sage.

Relph, E. (1976) *Place and Placelessness*. London: Pion.

Sauer, C. O. (1963) The morphology of landscape. In J. Leighley (ed.) *Land and life: A selection from the writings of Carl Ortwin Sauer*. Berkeley: University of California Press.

Sharpe, W. and Wallock, L. (eds) (1987) *Visions of the Modern City*. Baltimore: Johns Hopkins Press.

Soja, E. (1989) *Postmodern Geographies*. London: Verso.

Tuan, Y. (1974) *Topophilia*. Englewood Cliffs, NJ: Prentice Hall.

Urry, J. (1990) *The Tourist Gaze*. London: Sage Publications.

Urry, J. (1995) *Consuming Places*. London: Routledge.

11 Organizations: breaking the body of the text

HEATHER HÖPFL

This chapter is concerned with the interpretation of the organization as text. As such, the methodological issues on which it focuses are to be found in what Burrell and Morgan (1979) have termed *the radical humanist paradigm*, although, of course, many other positions are possible. This paradigm challenges the validity of the assumptions of more functionalist approaches to the study of organizations and seeks to subject to critical scrutiny a range of issues which relate to social order and regulation. Hence, what follows is an attempt to expose meanings which are both subsumed in the texts of organization and present in texts of organization other than those privileged by the organization itself.

There are a number of deconstructionist positions which are relevant to this task. In particular, Derrida's (1978) notion of *différance* provides a valuable way of conceptualizing what is concealed within the privileged text. Here, it is Kristeva's concern for the poetic which is used as a means to give emphasis to the hidden voices of the text. However, in order to bring these concerns closer to the organization *per se*, the poetic is posed in relation to the trajectory of the rhetorical text of the organization. Clearly, this is a more specific focus than Kristeva's (1984) challenge to the symbolic order. Organizations in their strategic assumptions seek to move from one place to another over time, to achieve objectives, to reach a desired future state. The implications of these moves for organizational members are usually secondary to the trajectory of the strategy. In this chapter, the implications of this directedness for organizational members are addressed via the poetic.

So, the concern of this chapter is with the relationship between the persuasive power of organizational rhetoric and the disruptive power of the poetic. Consequently, two contrasting texts of organization are presented: the rhetorical and the experiential. The rhetorical text of the organization is familiar as the organization as encountered in conventional *text*books, normative, functionalist, prescriptive. Organizational rhetoric is used to secure 'appropriate' behaviour and to move organizational members towards corporate goals. The rhetoric of organizations is about the achievement of tasks, about direction and objectives. It is characterized by its purposiveness. On the other hand, there is another organizational text: the experiential or poetic. This may only be present in the rhetorical text to the extent that it is absent from it: for example, the experience of redundancy may be glossed by the matter of fact language of job cuts or the more euphemistic discussion of downsizing and outplacement. The poetic is concerned with what is concealed by the regulation of the rhetorical text. By looking at the way that the management of change is typically described in management literature and contrasting this with the way in which it is experienced, this chapter attempts to give voice to the experiences which are regulated out by the strategic imperative of the management text.

Consequently, the argument presented below has its origins in two distinct but related pieces of work, both of which deal with the notion of heterogeneity. The first, *Heterologies, Discourse on the Other* (de Certeau 1986), provides an insight into the relationship between rhetoric and poetics. The second, *Revolution in Poetic Language* (Kristeva 1984), deals with the threat posed to the ordered world and rationality by heterogeneity and the irrational. Taken together, these two works offer some important perspectives on social regulation, authority and ambivalence, rhetoric and poetics.

Rhetoric is always directed to some end: 'Rhetoric is that faculty by which we understand what will serve our turn, concerning any subject to win belief in the hearer' (Aristotle, quoted in Hobbes Digest 1934: 80). In other words, rhetoric has a trajectory towards its intent and is fulfilled by its outcome. It is directed to an audience (present or absent) and achieves its objective by provoking a response. Rhetoric is *completed* by the other. It is concerned with the skills and strategies of manipulation and here is linked specifically with management strategies.

In management terms, rhetoric involves the construction of the organization as a purposive entity with a trajectory towards a desired future.

Organizational change is about the way in which such a desired state can be reached. In such movement, in the organization, the action takes precedence over the individual and any ambivalence experienced by the individual must be concealed. Of course, there are any number of ways in which this might be found in texts of the organization, from, for example, the explicit use of rhetoric in marketing the products and images of organizations to the construction of statements, strategies and structures. The fundamental characteristic of rhetoric which is employed in this context is its *directedness* and, clearly, there is a relationship between the direction as orientation and direction as command of the organization and the rhetorical trajectory. In a specific sense, the organization as a rhetorical entity *wants something* of the employee, of the customer, the competitor, the supplier, the general public. It requires that its representations – images and texts – are received as convincing by its various audiences. Recent years have seen the elaboration of the rhetoric of change as directed towards employees in the pursuit of greater commitment and in the construction of ornate narratives of organizational performances.

In contrast, the poetic is concerned with the very ambivalence which is concealed and regulated by the text. Here an attempt is made to restore the ambivalent voice, to seed 'an oral transgression through the semantic organization of the discourse, a transgression which displaces or cuts the articulated meanings and which renders the signifier autonomous in relation to the signified' (de Certeau 1983: 53). To the practised ear the poetic is present in every discourse, the 'hidden voices' which cause the 'signifiers to dance within the text' (*ibid.*).

The interplay between rhetoric and poetics can be seen in the relationship between enunciative acts and their place within a system of statements. The 'procedures which articulate these two terms . . . imprinting on them *what the speaking subject wants of the other* . . . is rhetoric, and no longer poetics' (*ibid.*, italics added). Rhetoric, then, is governed by a system of rules, a trajectory through a given text and a designated outcome. This important distinction has implications for the agonistic struggle, which is the site of ambivalence where what one 'wants of the other' is played out. In poetics the meaning is always ambivalent, embodied and resonant with the flux of experience.

Kristeva (1984) confronts many of these distinctions in her work on poetic language, where she deals with the threat posed to the ordered world and rationality by heterogeneity and the irrational. In brief, Kristeva argues that the notion of a unified subject supposes a unified consciousness and that, in turn, this requires an ordered mind. An orderly mind requires an ordering mechanism and this, according to Kristeva, is achieved via syntax. Poetic language can achieve the disruption of this order and ordering at both the literary and the social level.

Text: the contribution of Julia Kristeva

Kristeva's style is predominantly a product of her desire to subvert the phallocentrism of the Cartesian logos. It is this that Kristeva's writing seeks to problematize, since, according to her theorizing, it is in language that oppression originates. Specifically, Kristeva is arguing that it is in the logos of social organization, in the production of meaning, that such oppression is found (Palmer 1994: 376). In *The Revolution in Poetic Language* (1974 in French, 1984 in English), she took the view that what she termed poetic language puts the subject in crisis and disrupts the unity of the symbolic. The poetic thus subverts the dominant social discourse to challenge order, rationality and patriarchal regulation. Kristeva's ambivalence, as theorized, say, in her study of the mother as *the abject* and *the sublime* (Kristeva 1980: 157), seems to have recourse to oppositional structures and the vacillations between them. What this contributes to organizational theory is the capacity to make transparent the effects of the production of meaning and to make the notion of trajectory, strategy and purpose problematic. Coherent and purposive membership of the organization is dissolved by such ambivalence. So in her writing Kristeva oppresses with mastery and subverts via the insinuation of the poetic.

In 'Stabat Mater', she *breaks the body* of the text in order to allow her personal reflections on motherhood to enter and subvert the text. However, the text is constructed to represent these two positions, her own writing on the Virgin Mary and her own reflections on motherhood in dialectical opposition: two columns running down either side of the page, to represent, on one level, the Body on the left and the Law on the right. The Body speaks of rupture, and tearing, and blood. The Law speaks of regulation and representation, of rational argument and rhetoric trajectory. The Body and the Law are both Kristeva in her vacillation between embodied experience and her mastery of language. Her writing splits the Body of the Text, rends the page. Kristeva *breaks the body of the text* and, in doing so, recapitulates the breaking of the physical body of God the Son, the Word made Flesh. In the organization text presented in the text box, the body of the text is likewise broken in order to show what is concealed by the language of organizational change. By this breaking of the text, the implications of the rhetorical trajectory of the text are made transparent. In the illustration of organizational texts given here, this same breaking of the text is used to offer, on the one hand, a conventional view of the management of change and, on the other, a number of short statements about experience. In this illustration, the texts are set against one another. However, as will become apparent, they are implicitly inextricable from each other.

From her position as a revolutionary Marxist in the 1960s, Kristeva has moved through marriage and motherhood to a radically different point of

The first activity involves *motivating change* and includes creating a readiness for change among organizational members and helping them to overcome resistance to change. The second activity is concerned with *creating a vision* for a desired future state of the organization. The vision provides a direction for change and serves as a bench mark for assessing progress. The third activity involves *developing political support* for change. The fourth activity is concerned with *managing the transition* from the current state to the desired future state ... The fifth activity involves *sustaining momentum* for change so that it will be carried out to completion ... (144–5).

Organizational change involves moving from the known to the unknown. Because the future is uncertain and may adversely affect people's competencies, worth, and coping abilities, organizational members generally do not support change unless compelling reasons convince them to do so ... people's readiness for change depends on creating a felt need for change. This involves making people so dissatisfied with the status quo that they are motivated to try new things and ways of behaving. Creating such dissatisfaction can be rather difficult ... Generally, people and organizations need to experience deep levels of hurt before they will seriously undertake meaningful change (146).

At a personal level, change can arouse considerable anxiety about letting go of the known and moving to an uncertain future. Individuals may be unsure whether their existing skills and contributions will be valued in the future. Methods for dealing with resistance to change include at least three major strategies ...' (148).

'I'm sorry this essay is late but it's so close to what I'm experiencing at work at the moment that I couldn't bear to write it.' MA Human Resource Management part-time student and Training Manager, Bolton Institute, regarding a late essay on restructuring and emotional labour.

A senior human resource development manager in a major UK company who was experiencing serious personal difficulties was warned that she should not allow her personal life to intrude into her work as it was *not appropriate to her role* in the company. Likewise, a commercial manager with a UK paper manufacturing company explained how his personal life had atrophied as his career had advanced saying, 'In my job I'm expected *to play the hard man.*'

'My husband was made redundant after working for the same firm for twenty-five years. He was called into his boss's office and asked to leave then and there. When he got home he kept saying that they hadn't even let him go back to his office to collect his coat.' MA student, Bolton Institute.

A regional manager with a large insurance company who was expected to work every weekend over a period of three months asked for one Sunday off to celebrate his daughter's fourth birthday. The request was refused with the reminder 'It's *the price you have to pay for your role* in the company.'

'They gave us a Myers Briggs test and told me I didn't fit the profile. It seems they didn't want a "peaked-cap" image for security so I was out – too old, I guess. I felt completely betrayed.' British Airways security officer made redundant in the late 1980s.

view on political praxis. This has not made her popular with Marxists or with bourgeois or androgynizing feminists. However, she has taken great pains to convey her ideas in both the form and the content of her writing. The issue of praxis is important here since, above all, it seems that this is where she feels the expression of her being human is translated into action. Likewise, in translating her work into an organizational context, it is perhaps best to consider her contribution to the micro activities of day-to-day practice and interaction with others. Her radical contribution to practice is based on the role of love in the psychoanalytical context. The cure for the patient can only be found in transference and, for Kristeva, this means love. This is her ethical position; her *herethics* (Kristeva 1983; Moi 1986: 185). It is a radically different way of being from that conventionally associated with organizational behaviour. What this might contribute to the analysis of organizations is considered below.

Reading: accounts of movement/moving accounts

It is extremely difficult to do justice to the complexity of the issues raised by the theoretical standpoint and its application to the texts in the text box. However, with this caveat, it is possible to indicate a number of emergent themes. The management of change is about moving an organization from one state to another. In the text box, the text down the left-hand side of the page comes from Cummings and Worley's 1993 book, *Organization Development and Change*. It lays the foundations for a motivational approach to the management of change by identifying five activities essential to the process of organizational change. The management text is normative. It explains what should be done to achieve desired objectives. It talks of *motivating change*: moving organizational members towards these objectives. It says that change will bring resistance which has to be overcome, and it talks of creating a vision to guide the direction of the change towards the desired future state. The capacity to move, in various senses of the word, an organization from one state to another is clearly a significant part of the change process and of the rhetoric of change. In the language of everyday experience, people speak of being *moved* by a performance, a visit to a particular place, a story they have heard. Such an expression suggests a change of state, a change of position, a change of experience. Something occurs in the individual's experience which brings about *movement*.

In broad terms, the argument presented here is concerned with the relationship between motivation, and emotion both of which share a common etymological root (Latin *movere*, to move). Movement, therefore, carries the notion of *something moved*, something which has to be *borne or carried*. Of course, in the change literature what is carried is the forward movement of the organization towards its objectives. What is rarely acknowledged in the literature is the inevitable emotional counterpart to such movement, which has to be borne by organizational members. Where the costs of change are referred to, it is, as in the example, as if the consequences of change were unfortunate obstacles to progress and should be overcome. For those affected by organizational change the issue is not so easily addressed. On the right-hand side of the page are texts which relate to individual experience. These all, to some degree, refer to the costs of organizational change as experienced by the individual. 'I can't carry on', 'she has to carry it off', 'he could not bear it', 'his actions were insupportable', 'it was unbearable', 'he bore up', 'she's weary', 'I'm worn out': When people use such phrases to describe how they feel about their lives and work they are describing experiences which must be 'carried', 'borne', 'worn'; experiences which are likened to some burden, pressure, weight or stress. So the MA student says, 'I'm sorry this essay is late but it's so close to what I'm experiencing at work at the moment that *I couldn't bear to write it.*' Likewise, the commercial manager who has to bear the cost in his personal life of the demands his work role places on him, or the regional manager of the insurance company who is expected to place his work role before his family life: these brief examples demonstrate the implications of the rhetoric of change, the left-hand column, for the lives of employees, the right-hand column.

Moreover, the left-hand column, with its concern to overcome resistance to change and its advocacy of the creation of dissatisfaction, implicitly involves an extension of the psychological contract of work. The contract of work now requires not only that people change with the demands of their work roles but that they experience 'a felt need for change'. Inevitably, this has consequences for the individual, but 'people and organizations [*as if these were different from the people who make them up*] need to experience deep levels of hurt before they will seriously undertake meaningful change': this without reflection or critical awareness of the ideological imperative of strategic rationality. The individual is available to the reified (and, in this case, personified) organization, and without question, as an available and consumable collection of attributes: 'the individual learns ... which parts of himself [*sic*] are unwanted and unworthy' (Gouldner 1969: 349). Arguably, the past thirty years have seen an increasingly specific attention to those attributes of the person which are desired and those which are not. Of course, to many this may seem an entirely inconsequential necessity to ensure the predictability of organizational behaviour. However, more is at stake than a simple and necessary classification of behaviours. Only a part of what might be held by the individual to be a coherent identity is required in the construction of the organizational role, so, for example, the categorizations of standardized assessment procedures might appear to be neutral arbiters of selection and allocation. However, as is apparent in the example of the security officer given in the right-hand column, the use of the categorization assisted the organization to make *logical* decisions about its staffing policies during a period of culture change.

One way in which it is possible to look at the two columns is in terms of the relationship between rhetoric and poetics, between order and disorder, between the text of organization and the text of the lived experience, between organization as encountered in the *textbook* and organization as its other. One might see the columns as a series of oppositions. For example:

Rhetoric	Poetic
Direct(ed)ness	Ambivalence
Regulation	Flux
Symbolic	Semiotic
Tyranny	Resistance
Trajectory	Disruption
Male	Female
Penis	Hymen

Organizations have sought to appropriate poetic experience in the service of production. This is irreducibly rhetorical: representational and directed to an outcome. The recognition of the power of poetic language should provide a key to political praxis and resistance to regulation. The agonistic site is the site of ambivalence. It is the locus of poetic power. The texts above demonstrate the trajectory of movement required by rhetoric, accounts of movement, and are set against experiences which as text are also rhetorical but are moving accounts of the implications of the rhetorical trajectory of the organization.

Put simply, women, in Kristeva's analysis, threaten to subvert the symbolic order by liberating the semiotic. The poetic taps the resonances of the semiotic flux. When she argues that women are the silence of the unconscious which precedes discourse, she is saying that women threaten to disrupt the rational ordering of language, that, as the locus of ambivalence, women threaten to disrupt the culturally constituted symbolic order by not 'knowing their place'. When women do not accept this position they are 'put in their place'. In other words, reminded of the 'proper' order (of male discourse). Clearly, there is more to be said about the relationship between the thrust of the phallogocentric text and texts of experience. However, the purpose of this chapter has been simply to open up the discrepancies between the logic of ordering and organization and embodied experience.

Disadvantages

Perhaps the most common criticisms which are made of the theoretical concerns expressed above is that they are not relevant to business problems;

that they are not useful, that they are difficult to apply; that, similarly, they are not prescriptive, they do not offer ways in which organizations *should* act. Moreover, such approaches have often been criticized for being incoherent, lacking in rigour or, indeed, inappropriately rigorous, as instruments of subversion, as valueless self-indulgence and arrogant intellectualism. It is clear that critical approaches to texts are normally regarded with suspicion within traditional functionalist management disciplines. So preponderant is the hegemony of the functionalist paradigm in theories of organizing that it is difficult to see how this could be otherwise. However, for those working within the interpretive and radical humanist, radical structuralist paradigms, the functionalist paradigm offers no comfort in terms of analysis and explanation.

In a period of intense exhortation to vocationalism, the non-functionalist paradigms are viewed with increasing scepticism and criticism for their inability to 'deliver' in performance terms. Such approaches do not support the purposive rationality of organizations by offering techniques which would help organizations to be more efficient or more effectively regulated. Non-functionalist approaches, on the contrary, give attention to the human aspects of organization and, in various ways, pose both challenges and possibilities for alternative modes of organizing. By giving attention to the human aspects of organization, anti-organization theorists privilege the individual over the reified notion of the organization as a purposive entity.

Of course, this leads to a further criticism which has been levelled against the non-functionalist theorists. Functionalists often regard the sort of analysis presented in the examination of the texts above as *romantic* and *unrealistic*, as divorced from the *'real world'* and its problems. Sometimes, and this position has become modish in some university business schools, it is criticized precisely for its inability to enhance profitability or income generation, where Kristeva's ideas on love and practice would be regarded as laughable unless it were possible in some way to incorporate them into a human resource strategy.

Even those who are sympathetic to the analysis of discourse may be irritated by the anti-organization position. There is no promise of purposive coherence and ambiguities may become *unbearable*, meanings unstable, the authorial voice equivocal, the genealogy of the ideas glossed, the stance vertiginous. Ambivalence affords a considerable threat to rational order, yet there may be disagreements within the non-functionalist paradigm about the relationship between the radical position and its implications for practice, about bourgeois concerns and their influence on practice, about gendered positions and their priority, between gendered positions and their practice, about the appropriate level of action. Clearly, there is no easily agreed position and, as the example itself shows, it is difficult to raise the fragmented voices of the non-functionalist paradigms against the loud and exhortatory voice of functionalism.

Advantages

The most important contribution of the ideas above is in their capacity to open up the difference between the language of the organization and the language of experience. In broad terms, the ideas can be located in what Burrell and Morgan (1979) have referred to as anti-organization theory. Anti-organization theory is concerned with the critique of purposive rationality, of rules and control systems, of the language of organizational life, of the ideological mechanisms of work, of technology as surveillance, of the reification of aspects of work which regulate organizational behaviour, often by a process of mystification. Most, if not all, of these concerns are to be found in the texts above. Clearly, as a contribution to anti-organization theory, the work of the post-sructuralists aids the critique of language, purposive rationality and regulation. The critique of the language of organizations provides a useful insight into the relationship between consciousness and the mode of organizing. In this particular example, the radical shift of interpretation required by a deconstructionist approach to the text is *performed* by posing two alternative texts of organization, where the privileged text is that of the *textbook* and what is normally deferred by such text is placed in parallel or restored.

What is presented, however, is not a methodology *per se* but a series of borrowings from theoretical positions which contribute to a critique of language and regulation. Of course, this could be criticized to the extent that it does not offer a coherent theoretical perspective or provide a straightforward methodological tool. What it offers is a way in which the hidden voices within the text can be made audible. As such, it does not present a call to analysis but a call to *praxis*. By first giving attention to the taken-for-granted assumptions of organizational text, this approach exposes the organizational text as ideological, as privileging objectives over individuals, and as regulatory in prescribing behaviours and values which organization members much follow. Second, the approach adopted in this chapter leads to particular assumptions about the implications of what is revealed in the texts for organizational life in general. It is possible, on the one hand, to articulate a position within the radical humanist paradigm (Burrell and Morgan 1979) from which to challenge existing social arrangements and the current modes of organizing and, on the other, to follow Kristeva into defining ethical and feminine practices which might guide the micro-politics of interpersonal behaviour.

Hence there are two important dimensions to the ideas presented here: the process of restoration and the implications for practice. Undoubtedly, the task of restoration is an important one, since it implicitly challenges the rhetorical trajectory of the organizational text. However, there are also problems associated with this. Whenever an area of experience is raised in opposition to the trajectory of the organization, it is rapidly specified as a problem and the disorderliness of the experience is subjected to further regulation via the extension of the psychological contract of work. This has been the case over the past ten years or so with emotional labour: first conceptualized as a problem for the individual but subsequently addressed by the conceptualization of emotional labour as a problem for the organization. Hence, to specify is to endanger, to conceptualize, to capture and to reveal, to subject to regulation. This creates considerable problems for the anti-organizational theorist. The implications for practice present one way around this. In particular, the translation of such insights into interpersonal behaviour suggests a possible symmetry between the restoration of the individual and the translation of that into what Kristeva has termed 'herethics': a praxis based on love (Kristeva 1983; Moi 1986).

Clearly, other approaches to organizations and their texts do little to draw attention to what is concealed or deferred by the logic of organizing. Consequently, conventional textbook approaches are characterized by their normative, prescriptive, functionalist accounts of organizations and are often alarmingly unreflexive. At the same time, conventional approaches to organizations do not tend to question the inevitability of change in the pursuit of organizational objectives or the issue of resistance to be overcome. Such gross assumptions are challenged by approaches which seek to restore what is repressed by the text (Kristeva 1983; Moi 1986). Finally, it is difficult to imagine theorists of work organizations advocating an approach to behaviour based on love, such as Kristeva's, unless such an approach itself was rooted in purposive rationality and the pursuit of organizational objectives. Yet, if work is the primary source of meaning and identity for many if not most people today, it is precisely these issues which need attention.

Key reading

Höpfl, H. (1994) Learning by heart: the rules of rhetoric and the poetics of experience. *Management Learning*, 25(3): 464–74.
Kristeva, J. (1983) Stabat mater. In T. Moi (ed.) (1986) *The Kristeva Reader*. Oxford: Blackwell (for Leon Roudiez's translation).

References

Aristotle (1934) *Poetics of Aristotle, On Style by Demetrius and Selections from Aristotle's Rhetoric with Hobbes' Digest and Ars Poetica by Horace*, edited by T. A. Moxon. London: J. M. Dent.
Billig, M. (1989) *Arguing and Thinking: A Rhetorical Approach to Social Psychology*. Cambridge: Cambridge University Press.

Burrell, G. and Morgan, G. (1979) *Sociological Paradigms and Organisational Analysis.* London: Heinemann.

Cummings, T. and Worley, C. (1993) *Organization Development and Change,* 5th edn. Minneapolis: West Publishing Company.

de Certeau, M. (1986) *Heterologies, Discourse on the Other.* Manchester: Manchester University Press.

Derrida, J. (1978) *Writing and Difference.* Chicago: University of Chicago Press.

Gouldner, A. (1969) The unemployed self. In R. Fraser (ed.) *Work, Volume 2.* Harmondsworth: Penguin.

Hobbes, T. (1651) *Leviathan.* Oxford: Blackwell (1949 edition).

Kristeva, J. (1980) *Powers of Horror,* trans. Leon Roudiez. New York: Columbia University Press.

Kristeva, J. (1983) *Histoires d'amour.* Paris: Denoel (translated as *Tales of Love,* by Leon Roudiez. New York: Columbia University Press, 1987).

Kristeva, J. (1984) *Revolution in Poetic Language.* New York: Columbia University Press.

Lechte, J. (1990) *Julia Kristeva.* London: Routledge.

Moi, T. (ed.) (1986) *The Kristeva Reader.* Oxford: Blackwell.

Oliver, K. (1993) *Reading Kristeva.* Bloomington: Indiana University Press.

Palmer, D. (1994) *Looking at Philosophy: The Unbearable Heaviness of Philosophy Made Lighter.* Mountain View, CA: Mayfield Publishing Company.

Sarbin, T. R. (1986) Emotion and act: roles and rhetoric. In R. Harré (ed.) *The Social Construction of Emotion.* Oxford: Blackwell.

Selden, R. (1989) *A Reader's Guide to Contemporary Literary Theory.* Hemel Hempstead: Harvester Wheatsheaf.

12 Gardens: planning and presentation

SUSAN FORD

The study of the suburb has been doubly hindered by its perceived mundanity on the one hand, and by the privacy, which was the cornerstone of its existence, on the other. A close reading of a garden's plan offers the reader a chance to engage with both the myriad detail and the broader issues concerning the suburban house and garden. Gardens, and especially historic gardens on a domestic scale, are particularly problematic artefacts to analyse. Simon Pugh (1988: ix) has discussed the difficulties encountered when analysing the garden: a garden's fluid and transient nature means that 'it can never be pinned down, fixed, it can never be a definitive text.' Unlike Pugh, whose focus of attention, the gardens at Rousham, Oxfordshire, survive, fieldwork cannot enhance this analysis. Evidential problems of this nature are often intrinsic to the researching of the very private world of the Victorian suburban home. Textual analysis offers a means of overcoming these evidential difficulties. This chapter suggests that the garden plan may be treated as a cultural text and that the materials used in the garden, and the philosophy underpinning its design, may reveal links to the wider concerns of early Victorian urban society.

My reading of the text begins with the premise that garden plans should be treated as artefacts embedded in a series of social, cultural, economic and political structures. Within this frame the garden is understood as a material consequence of a specific negotiation of a relationship between humankind and the natural world. The conscious and unconscious manipulation of such cultural artefacts by society, and the consequent embeddedness of an artefact within the wider matrix of everyday life (Cosgrove and Daniels 1988), makes an excavation of meaning, via a detailed textual reading, an attractive proposition. It is this theoretical manoeuvre that immediately shifts the questions asked about the garden plan. For example, the detail of the bedding-out patterns chosen for a garden might focus on the more traditional horticultural concerns of colour choice and issues of cultivation. However, very different questions might be asked of that same set of flower beds. Did the choice of plants reflect certain social practices and economic constraints? Who cultivated the beds? What was that garden space used for? What issues of self-presentation were facilitated by garden planning?

Theoretical support for close textual reading is provided by Erving Goffman's (1982) *The Presentation of Self in Everyday Life*, which adopts the theatrical metaphor of a performance on the study of social life. Goffman's premise is that human behaviour is often acted out according to cultural and personal preferences. Human interaction is dominated – especially among those who are not well acquainted – by appearances. Thus, Goffman (1982: 13) explains that

> When an individual enters the presence of others, they commonly seek to acquire information about him [*sic*] or to bring into play information about him already possessed. They will be interested in his general socio-economic status, his conception of self, his attitude towards them, his competence, his trust-worthiness, etc.

However, it is not only a person's behaviour that determines the success or failure of any interaction, but also the setting, the props used and the way in which they are 'stage-managed'; an environmental and spatial dimension is thus introduced into Goffman's approach.

For much of the twentieth century, suburbia has been tarnished by pejorative aesthetic and social associations; its links with mass, degraded, culture; and its ordinariness and cloying domesticity (e.g. Silverstone 1977; Thompson 1982). Such a mind set might totally dismiss the idea of seriously researching suburbia. However, I wish to suggest that the suburban garden is a worthwhile object of research for two reasons: first, suburbia was a key site of the renegotiation of gender and class relations within the nineteenth-century city; second, suburban scholarship has been marginalized because of its domestic concerns. The new perspectives afforded by feminist scholars have provided an analytical framework and conceptual justification for refocusing our attentions onto the detail of the suburban scene (e.g. Alpers 1982: Schor 1987).

The suburban villa, physically separated from what was perceived to be the increasingly threatening city, was promoted as the new specialized private space in which the patriarchal nuclear family could dwell, reproduce and relax (Loudon 1836; Ruskin 1901). For those who could afford it, the suburban villa, and its garden, offered the opportunity to design a new way of living, one which would reflect the values of its largely middle-class inhabitants. The domestic landscape of the Victorian bourgeois home may be interpreted as the physical manifestation of an ideology of sexual difference and, as such, was inextricably tied up with the construction of gender identity (Davidoff and Hall 1987). Men and women were assigned gender roles based on what were thought to be the innate biological and spiritual differences between the sexes. Men were deemed most suited to the demands of work and public life, and women's talents could be best exercised within the family home. Thus, it was argued by Ruskin (1901), that the sexes were perfectly complementary in their life skills.

This sexual categorization had profound geographic implications for the way in which the middle classes were supposed to lead their lives. The public world of work was gendered male, whilst the home was a sphere which, although dominated by the servicing and reproduction of the workforce, was sentimentally characterized as the realm of the family. Despite the validity of what has been labelled the 'separate spheres hypothesis', recently challenged by Vickery (1993), the currency of separate spheres is still much in evidence within John Claudius Loudon's (1783–1843) writings on garden planning, the source of the 'text' for this chapter.

Text: Fortis Green

Loudon was a landscapist, garden and agricultural writer, social and cultural critic, and perhaps most notably in the context of this analysis, one of the earliest propagandists of suburban living.

Having established that the suburb was an important part of the changing landscape of the nineteenth-century industrial city, the next problem is to establish the validity of the evidence selected, and the method of analysis. Loudon's didactic literature, with its inherent problems of validity, fulfils a crucial role in the reconstruction of early Victorian suburban space. Personal papers and diaries provide a patchy source of information on domestic design, as personal reminiscences often record details of the social rather than environmental milieu. The literature on household advice and design is split between books concerned with various aspects of household management (see Palmegiano 1976; Attar 1987) and books which are

Plan of Fortis Green. *Source: Gardener's Magazine*, new series VI (1840), pp. 50–1.

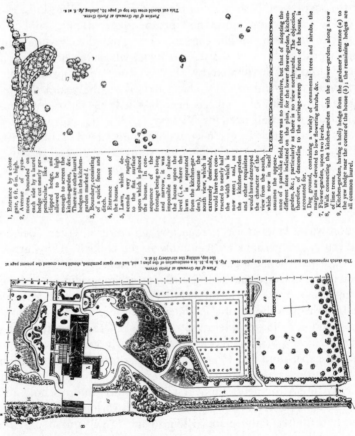

Portion of the Grounds at Fortis Green.

This cut should cross the top of page 52, joining *fig.* 8. at *k*.

Plan of the Grounds at Fortis Green. *Fig.* 8. to *fig.* 51. is a continuation of the plan; and, had our space permitted, should have crossed the present page at the top, utilising the shrubbery 16 &c *x*.

This sketch represents the narrow portion next the public road.

1, Entrance by a close gate, 6 ft. 6 in. high.

2, Avenue of sycamores, bounded on each side by a laurel hedge cut nearly perpendicular, like a clipped hedge, and assumed high enough to screen the kitchen-garden, &c. There are other laurel hedges in the kitchen-garden marked *j*.

3, Dog-kennel, consisting of a quick fence and ditch.

4, Entrance front of the house.

5, Lawn, which descends very rapidly to the surface upon which is placed the house. In consequence of the frontage being so long and narrow, it was impossible to place the house upon the level (i. e. where the lawn is separated from the kitchen-garden), because the south view, which is extremely desirable, would have been contracted to nearly half the width which is now seen; and, as the kitchen-garden and other requisites would have destroyed the character of the view from the south, which now in itself assumed the appearance of a park-like field, there was no alternative, but that of adopting the different sites indicated on the plan, for the lower flower-garden, kitchen-garden, &c.; particularly as there is no view northwards. The objection, therefore, of descending to the carriage-sweep in front of the house, is accounted for,

6, Dug ground, containing a variety of ornamental trees and shrubs, the margin devoted to low flowering shrubs, &c.

7, Flower-garden, upon two levels.

8, Walk connecting the kitchen-garden with the flower-garden, along a row of lime trees.

9, Kitchen-garden, having a holly hedge from the gardener's entrance (*a*) to the yew hedge near the corner of the house (*b*); the remaining hedges are all common laurel.

10, Melon ground and pond.

11, Orchard, and potato and mangold wurzel ground, &c.

12, Belt of spruce and Scotch firs.

13, Gardener's communication with the public road, when manure and other materials for the gardens are wanted to be brought in.

14, Approach to the stable-yard.

15, Grass drying-ground, on a lower level than the approach, and screened by a dense mass of evergreens, &c.
   k, House-yard.

16, to figs. 8, 9, and 10, Boundary plantation, fenced towards the field with furze (kept clipped), concealing from the flower-garden a sheep-hut and little stack-yard (*e*).

17, in *fig.* 9, Groups of thorns and other trees.

The frontage of the villa adjoining Mr. Nesfield's at *c* in *fig.* 10. is the same size as his own; and, as both places were built by the same architect (A. Salvin, Esq., Mr. Nesfield's brother-in-law), and laid out at the same time, care was taken that where the ground was planted thinly in the one villa, it was planted thickly in the other; an *vice versâ*; so that each villa might aid the other in producing its general effect, and in sacrificing as little ground as possible in planting.

The field belonging to Mr. Nesfield embraces the frontage of both houses; and the land attached to both, being 8¼ acres, is subdivided as shown in *fig.* 10. In this figure, *a b* show the land occupied by Mr. Nesfield, and containing in all 4¼ acres, *a* being that part which comprises the house, kitchen-garden, &c., and *b* being the grass field; *c* is the house and garden of the adjoining, occupier; and *d* his grass field, to which he has access by the road *e*; *f* is the public road, and *g g* are the entrance-gates to the two houses. This arrangement (on purchasing the land) was made in order that each house might enjoy the effect of space as much as possible, and, by dividing the ground with the wire fence (*h*), which is scarcely visible from either house, the breadth of effect is not cut up, as it would have been, had the division been made longitudinally. The boundary hedge (*i*) winds considerably, and there are several very fine trees in it, which, in consequence of the winding, group most admirably, as shown in the view, *fig.* 11. The wood at *k*, in *fig.* 10., belongs to the Earl of Mansfield's grounds, at Kenwood, and, together with the spire of Highgate church, adds greatly to the beauty of the landscape, as shown in the view above referred to (*fig.* 12.).

concerned with the architectural issues (see Archer 1985). One is left to extrapolate the detailed environmental context in which such contrived social relations took place. Loudon's texts are particularly useful, in that they combine environmental detail with pertinent social information.

The plan of Fortis Green's garden comes from an article published in Loudon's *The Gardener's Magazine*. The ten-page article contains plans, engravings and a description of Fortis Green, a suburban dwelling in Muswell Hill, North London, owned and landscaped by the landscape designer and watercolourist, William Nesfield, whose work was admired by Loudon (1840). The details of the Fortis Green's plan were intended to be carefully scrutinized by the readership of *The Gardener's Magazine*. A detailed reading of the design and use of domestic space will demonstrate the way in which garden design reinforced privacy, propriety and gender distinction, values which were the domestic sphere's organizing principles. The following analysis of the plan is a small part of a larger project which attempts to create a feminist account of the suburb. Detailed textual analysis is central to this project in two ways: first, the intimate level of engagement with the text dovetails with feminist epistemology; second, the paucity of evidence demands an intense engagement with available sources (Ford 1991).

Reading: a tour of the garden

My reading of Fortis Green takes the form of a tour around the garden guided by the plan. For although Fortis Green was a modest establishment, lacking the size and variety of the great country house garden, a careful reading reveals that its materiality is replete with statements about its owners and their wider social interests.

I will begin my analysis by considering the villa's entrance. Careful attention had been devoted to the entrance front of Fortis Green (marked 1 on the plan) to ensure that it gave the right impression. Access to the villa from the public road was guarded by a 'close gate, 6 ft. 6 in. high'; thus, it was not possible for passers-by to see into the property, either through the gate or through the dense hedging which shielded it from the road (Loudon 1840: 50). The boundary hedges were slightly set back from the road. This reflected well on the landowner and 'convey[ed] the idea of there being no want of room within ... and of his possessing that liberal spirit and abundance of wealth, which render two or three poles of land ... of no consequence of him' (Loudon 1835: 56). The boundary of the property was further screened by the trees of the orchard shown on the plan. The careful concealment of the villa from the outside world heightens the notion that the villa was a distinct and private space, and a place of retirement from the outside world.

Once through the gate, a long avenue of trees, which were back-planted with shrubs, led the visitor towards the house, which was hidden by the gentle sweep of the drive (2 on the plan). The dense interplanting of the avenue masked the fact that the villa's land stretched only to the west, the shrubs to the east concealing the adjacent property. Judicious planning with the adjacent villa meant that space was saved by removing the need for both residences to be thickly planted on all their borders. The curve of the drive masked the dimensions of the grounds and maintained visitors' sense of expectation and suspense, waiting for the precise moment that the view of the house was to be revealed. The drive's curve also protected the owners from the 'derogatory' experience of being looked down upon (Loudon 1835b: 56).

The drive of Fortis Green branched off towards the stable yard before the house was reached. In front of the house, it broadened to form a turning space for carriages. The villa's facade was framed in a picturesque manner by a collection of evergreen trees and shrubs. These were testament to the healthy position of the house, for such shrubs only flourish in well drained, dry places. Complex arrangements of flower beds were considered inappropriate for the front of a villa, for their detail would draw the eye away from what should be the focus of this view, the house itself. As another author remarked 'what gives perfect grace and luxuriance to the private grounds has an air of ostentation when exposed to the daily gaze of an "admiring public"' (Hibberd 1987: 363). The tower of the house draws that gaze towards the area occupied by the family, while the servants' offices are partially hidden by vegetation.

The productive activities of the garden, the melon ground and pond 10, orchard 11 and kitchen garden 9, are enclosed to the west of the drive. These activities were hidden – and thus separated from leisured lifestyle of the owners – behind the approach road's hedging. The narrowness and sloping nature of the site prevented this area being located closer to the servants' domain. The design of the areas devoted to the production of foodstuffs, in contrast to rest of the garden, was dominated by geometric forms, having never thrown off the 'sixteenth century yoke of formality' (Larkham 1979: 139). The trees of the orchard were geometrically arranged, while the straight-sided boundaries of the kitchen garden hint at the formality which was probably contained within the neatly planted hedging. Loudon noted that the 'kitchen garden, as well as [being] a garden professedly ornamental, ought to be an agreeable place to walk in, as well as [being] profitably cultivated' (Loudon 1835a: 746). Aesthetic appreciation of this space was framed in the utilitarian discourse of fitness-for-purpose. The owner's enjoyment would come from surveying the neatness and order that he or she had facilitated by the employment of a competent gardener. The management of a kitchen garden was compromised when the gardener's judgement was questioned by the 'constant and irksome

interference of masters and mistresses' (*ibid.*). Where the proprietor of a
residence wished to be the gardener in charge, he or she should employ
only garden labourers, rather than a gardener whose professional integrity
would be stifled. However, Loudon thought that this arrangement generally produced ill-managed and poorly cultivated gardens (*ibid.*).

A successful kitchen garden aimed to produce a wide variety of fruit and
vegetables. The simulation of climatic regimes of other lands was facilitated by the vast improvements which had been made to the stove, hot-
house or greenhouse. Loudon was a keen advocate of gardening under
glass, having published a number of works on the subject (Loudon 1817,
1822). The use of the greenhouse enabled the cultivation of exotic varieties
imported from the Empire and fruit and vegetables out of season, thereby
testing the skill of the scientific gardener. Although such gardening feats
were a further way of displaying wealth, the display was tempered by the
notion that such activities could be justified as a scientific exercise. The
amount of space devoted to food production had to be carefully balanced,
for an over-concentration on an activity of economic worth would be out-
of-step with the genteel suburban existence being pursued at Fortis Green.

The shrubbery of Fortis Green masks the paddock, stable yard and
servants' offices from the flower garden. The plan shows a dense plantation of trees, shrubs and herbaceous plants, planted for their beauty and
fragrance. The path down the eastern side of the shrubbery (16) adds to
the range of scenes that the ideal garden was expected to contain. The
more architectural and formal elements of the garden – the terrace, the
conservatory and the flower garden – were to be connected to the house.
Fortis Green's flower garden is carefully enclosed by hedges separating it
from the more public front of the house. It was overlooked by the most
important rooms of the house, the dining room and the drawing room.
Steps, grassed terraces and the conservatory bridge the transition from
culture to nature; that is, from house to garden. The views from the back
of the house are threefold: one window looks out into the conservatory,
while through the french windows the detail of the flower garden as well
as the more distant prospect of rolling countryside may be surveyed. Visible fencing, rather than a ha ha, separates the cultivated garden from the
area in which livestock roam.

The precise curving geometry of the flower beds would have contained a
carefully attended display of blossom and foliage throughout the year.
These beds were edged with box and were set out upon gravel. A reserve
garden would be required to keep the flower garden in perfect order. One
acre would be necessary to furnish the 36 varieties of flowers deemed
necessary to produce a reasonable border display (Loudon 1835a). The
absence of a reserve garden at Fortis Green suggests that a nursery sup-
plied the bedding, further evidence of the owner's wealth. The flower garden
was adjacent to the drawing room, the place where the lady of the house

would receive visitors and spend the greatest part of her day. Loudon (1826: 614) had long eulogized the benefits of gardening for men and women, hoping that 'every lady have her flower garden and conservatory . . . [and] every gentleman have his arboretum'. Sexual categorization needed to be observed even in the garden.

The grassed area below the flower garden contains only a few beds of more hardy shrubs. The garden at Fortis Green thus maintains the essential ideal that, as one moves away from the house, the garden should become more natural. The park describes the area used for the growth of timber and for pasturage, also adding 'grandeur and dignity' to the residence. Fortis Green's park was at the rear of the property (areas 16 and 17 adjacent the main plan). The field to the back of the plot completes the transition from the garden, the landscape of home, to the 'natural' countryside of the outside world.

Disadvantages

It is hoped that the previous reading of Fortis Green's plan has drawn attention to the benefits yielded by close textual reading. The shortcomings of my reading can be divided into two categories: the first concerned with the theoretical and empirical choices made; and the second bound-up in the materiality of the text itself.

There are many other avenues and themes which could have been explored in this reading. The relationship between housing and class; the linkages between the suburban garden, the plant trade and Empire (Brockway 1979; Fisher 1982); or a detailed study of gardenesque aesthetics are three such avenues which the brevity of this chapter has made it impossible to explore. However, the method of analysis used does not preclude other choices being made. Different contextual material pertinent to the topic being researched could provide the reader with different questions to ask of the plan.

The act of interpreting the plan reinscribes it into the present, and this process brings with it a series of cultural associations and value judgements. My reading is very specific and detailed, which is simultaneously its strength and weakness. I have attempted to reconstruct a very small domestic fragment of London, choosing not to focus on the experiences of the vast majority of Londoners or the landscape of the city as whole. This decision was born out of personal choice. It was a reaction to the broad brush stroke of much social history, coupled with an urge to interrogate a particular environment with a feminist agenda. Indeed, it should be noted that the choice of feminist analytical framework is rooted in the predilection of the Western academy of the late twentieth century. Similarly, the rejection of psychoanalytic approaches to the text, and in particular the relationship between nature and society, is a product of the author's background in cultural geography and the methodologies of anthropology and art history.

The plan's reproduction in the article is not high quality, and there is an inordinate amount of detail in such a small illustration, both of which make it difficult to read. Printing this plan was a cheap and relatively effective means of communicating Loudon's ideas. Plentiful illustrations, whose cost was mitigated by using cheaper woodcuts, had been a distinguishing feature of Loudon's work for some time. As early as 1811 he remarked that a small plate would 'communicate more accurate ideas ... than the most copious details of a letter press' (Loudon 1811: 14). There are obvious problems associated with trying to reassemble a sense of a living and dynamic piece of landscape from a two-dimensional, black and white plan. To founder here, however, would be to miss the point of the article's publication.

Advantages

The Fortis Green plan forms part of a larger corpus of Loudon's work which provided what might be termed an etiquette of landscape. The plan and associated description were intended to promote good practice.

Richard Sennet (1986: 167) takes a similar tack to Goffman's (1982) work, mentioned earlier, and draws attention to his particular relevance to the kind of reading presented here. He notes that the Victorian bourgeoisie's increasing concern with the minutiae of appearance was an obsession rooted in the 'notion that all appearances speak, that human meanings are immanent in all phenomena'. Appearances mattered, especially to those whose position in society was not guaranteed by birth, but who were anxious to secure socially a way of life funded by trade and business activities. These people, the aspiring middle classes, were the audience at which Loudon's work was explicitly aimed. They were most in need of guidance on how they could achieve the appearance which would reflect their upwardly mobile aspirations. There were fine distinctions between what was considered good and bad taste. In personal dress, for example, although in fashion terms the 1840s were seen as a particularly unremarkable decade, the marker between good taste and bad could be still read by those versed in the intricacies of etiquette. Subtle indicators such as the way in which a cravat was tied, the quality of a garment's cloth or the cleanliness of a neck band could be decoded by those initiated in what constituted desirable appearances.

The details of Loudon's texts, when read in this theoretical context, make more sense, for they were guides to planning and decoding visual statements made in the suburb. Loudon's plan can be seen as providing information about the idealized setting and the 'props' which aided middle-class behaviour. From here we might begin to extrapolate the symbiotic relationship between the suburban environment and society.

In answer to gender-sensitive questions, the plan yields material on the complex relationship between gender, space and social practice. A close reading of the plan and other contextual material offers a way into the brief, but persistent, references to women and gardens in the literature. For, as Waters (1988: 241) notes, 'surprisingly little attention has been given specifically to the part played by the association of women and gardens in the construction of female stereotypes, and in the legitimizing of women's domestic and decorative functions.' A survey of the garden literature of this period has revealed the extensive promotion of gardening for 'ladies'. Women's interest in the flower garden was fostered through botanical and horticultural texts written specifically for women, such as Lindley (1834) and Loudon's own wife Jane (1840). Gardening and botany were ideally suited to genteel women, for they were home-based activities.

The development of a garden terminology familiar to women further encouraged women gardeners. Terms were poached directly from needlecraft, for example circular flower beds were called 'pincushion beds'; whilst for regular borders 'ribbon gardening' was recommended and border edging plants were called 'fringing' (Hibberd 1987: 353–4). Gardening was even recommended as a suitable form of gentle exercise for ladies, and garden tools were designed to take into account their specific needs. The hand flower gatherer enabled a 'lady' to hold her parasol in one hand and tend to her flowers with the other, without pricking her fingers or soiling her gloves (Loudon 1830). However, alongside this more practical literature was a close metaphorical association of women and flowers. Flowers and women represented beauty, frailty, fertility, both needing careful nurturing within a confined and controlled environment if they were to be brought to full bloom. Flower gardening was promoted for women because, as one writer in *The Amulet* put it, 'Flowers are the teacher of gentle thoughts, promoters of kindly emotion . . . The very utility of flowers is their excellence and great beauty; for by having a delightfulness in their very form and colour, they lead us to thoughts of generosity and moral beauty detached from, and superior to, all selfishness' (cited in Loudon 1832: 25).

This chapter has argued that a garden plan can reveal much about a society's obsessions and cultural choices. A close textual reading allows the researcher to become immersed in the text and more familiar with its nuances and subtleties. It might be concluded that debate surrounding the construction of gender identies was therefore actually self-consciously inscribed upon suburban soil. As Ann Bermingham (1987: 166) has suggested, the 'suburban house and garden became the repository of the owner's personal iconography'.

Key reading

Cosgrove, D. and Daniels, S. (eds) (1988) *The Iconography of Landscape.* Cambridge: Cambridge University Press.
Davidoff, L., L'Esperance, J. and Newby, N. (1977) Landscape with figures. In J. Mitchell and A. Oakley (eds) *The Rights and Wrongs of Women.* Harmondsworth: Penguin.

References

Alpers, S. (1982) Art history and its exclusions: the example of Dutch art. In N. Broude and M. D. Garrard (eds) *Feminism and Art History.* London: Harper and Row.
Archer, J. (1985) *The Literature of British Domestic Architecture 1715–1842.* Cambridge, MA: MIT Press.
Attar, D. (1987) *A Bibliography of Household Books Published in Britain 1800–1914.* London: Prospect Books.
Bermingham, A. (1987) *Landscape and Ideology: The English Rustic Tradition 1740–1860.* London: Thames and Hudson.
Brockway, L. H. (1979) *Science and Colonial Expansion: The Role of the British Royal Botanic Garden.* London: Academic Press.
Cosgrove, D. and Daniels, S. (1988) Introduction: iconography and landscape. In D. Cosgrove and S. Daniels (eds) *The Iconography of Landscape.* Cambridge: Cambridge University Press.
Davidoff, L. and Hall, C. (1987) *Family Fortunes.* London: Hutchinson.
Fisher, J. (1982) *The Origins of Garden Plants.* London: Constable.
Ford, S. (1991) Landscape revisited: a feminist reappraisal. In *New Words, New Worlds: Reconceptualising Social and Cultural Geography.* Conference proceedings of Social and Cultural Geography Study Group of the IBG.
Goffman, E. (1982) *The Presentation of Self in Everyday Life.* Harmondsworth: Penguin.
Hibberd, S. (1987) *Rustic Adornments for Homes of Taste.* London: National Trust (first published 1856).
Larkham, J. (1979) Kitchen and vegetable gardens. In J. Harris (ed.) *The Garden: A Celebration of One Thousand Years of British Gardening.* London: Mitchell Beazley.
Lindley, J. (1834) *Ladies' Botany.* London: James Ridgeway and Sons.
Loudon, J. C. (1811) *Design for Laying out Farms and Farm Buildings.* London: J. Harding and Longman, Rees, Hurst, Orme and Brown.
Loudon, J. C. (1817) *Remarks on the Construction of Hot-houses.* London: J. Taylor.
Loudon, J. C. (1822) *The Different Modes of Cultivating the Pineapple, from Its First Introduction to Europe to the Improvements of T. A. Knight, Esq.* London: Longman.
Loudon, J. C. (1826) View of the progress of gardening. *Gardener's Magazine*, I: 609–38.

Loudon, J. C. (1830) Gardening operations for ladies. *Gardener's Magazine*, V: 587–9.

Loudon, J. C. (1832) Thoughts on flowers. *Gardener's Magazine*, VII: 25.

Loudon, J. C. (1835a) *Encyclopaedia of Gardening*. London: Longman.

Loudon, J. C. (1835b) Remarks on improving the approach road to a small villa which is now undergoing alteration. *Gardener's Magazine*, new series, II: 53–6.

Loudon, J. C. (1836) *The Suburban Gardener and Villa Companion*. London: H. Bohn.

Loudon, J. C. (1840) A description of the suburban residence of Fortis Green. *Gardener's Magazine*, new series, VI: 50–6.

Loudon, J. W. (1840) *Instructions on Gardening for Ladies*. London: John Murray.

Palmegiano, E. M. (1976) *Women and British Periodicals 1832–1867: A Bibliography*. New York: Garland Publishing.

Pugh, S. (1988) *Garden, Nature, Language*. Manchester: Manchester University Press.

McLeish, G. (1829) Observations on the improvement of flower gardens. *Gardener's Magazine*, IV: 48–9.

Ruskin, J. (1901) Of Queen's Gardens. In *Sesame and Lilies*. London: George Allen (first published 1865).

Schor, N. (1987) *Reading in Detail*. London: Methuen.

Sennett, R. (1986) *The Fall of Public Man*. London: Faber.

Silverstone, R. (ed.) (1997) *Visions of Suburbia*. London: Routledge.

Thompson, F. L. M. (ed.) (1982) *The Rise of Suburbia*. Leicester: Leicester University Press.

Vickery, A. (1993) Golden age to separate spheres? A review of the categories and chronology of English women's history. *The Historical Journal*, 36(2): 383–414.

Waters, M. (1988) *The Garden in Victorian Literature*. Aldershot: Scholar Press.

13 | Sign language: space, community and identity

JOHN ALLBUTT, SARAH GRAY AND BEVERLEA SCHOFIELD

This chapter discusses the representation of sign language in discourse analysis and promotes the need for culturally sensitive research into deafness. Throughout this chapter we follow the convention proposed by Woodward (1972), where the term 'deaf' refers to deaf people who hold an audiological understanding of deafness and 'Deaf' refers to deaf people who hold a cultural understanding of deafness. The term 'deaf' will also be used when it is necessary to refer to all people with a hearing loss.

Two important developments in the area of deafness research have been the recognition of British Sign Language (BSL) as a real language and the political campaigning by Deaf people to be seen as a cultural/linguistic minority rather than a disabled group. Thus skill in BSL and knowledge of Deaf culture are essential to a discourse analyst working in this area. The ideal profile for such a researcher is that of a Deaf discourse analyst who has native sign language skill.

Sign language can be defined as 'A visual means of communication used within the deaf community and learned naturally by interaction, which is not dependent on spoken language' (Miles 1988: 111). Communication in sign language involves the use of the hands, arms, shoulders, chest, abdomen, face and head and is almost always made in the signing space around the top half of the body. The unit of sign language most closely corresponding to a word is the sign. Signs can be of three types: (a) manual signs, which are made using the hands; (b) non-manual signs, which are made with other parts of the body, e.g. the face; and (c) multi-channel signs, which are made using the hands and other parts of the body. On occasions individual letters or words may be spelled out using signs from a sign alphabet. This aspect of sign language is called finger spelling, and makes up a small part of signing. Sign language is of equal communication capacity to spoken language, being capable of expressing both concrete and abstract concepts. The sign language of the British Deaf community is BSL. This is a distinct language with its own lexicon of signs and grammar. Other sign languages exist in other countries, with a particular sign language typically being named after its country of origin, e.g. American Sign Language (ASL).

Communication in the visual modality offers greater potential than in the auditory modality for relationships between the physical form of a sign and its referent than a word and its referent. Brennan (1987) describes four types of relationship in sign language: (a) iconic-pictorial, where a sign is a pictorial representation of its referent, e.g. the sign PHONE in Figure 13.1; (b) conventional, where the link to the form of the sign is through a meaning commonly associated with the handshape, e.g. the sign GOOD in Figure 13.2; (c) metaphorical, where a sign is a visual metaphor for its referent, e.g. the sign CONFUSED in Figure 13.3, where the circular motion of the hands acts as a metaphor for the disordered thought processes of the mind; and (d) arbitrary, where there is no disernible link between the form of the sign and its referent, e.g. the sign WHAT in Figure 13.4.

The greater potential for links between form and meaning in sign language has caused some researchers to question the linguistic status of sign languages. However, in the immediate production and comprehension of sign language non-arbitrary relationships are of little importance to native sign language users. Of more importance to the signer and receiver are the relations between signs and the language's grammar (Gregory and Miles 1991).

The capacity for the simultaneous transmission of linguistic information in a visual language is great. This can range from the combination of manual and non-manual features in multi-channel signs to the signing of two separate signs at the same time by different hands. This feature of sign language is called simultaneity. The primary linguistic structure in BSL is topic–comment. Thus the English sentence 'What is your name' would be signed NAME WHAT YOU, with the topic of the sentence preceding the comment. In BSL locations in space can be used to refer to objects such as people, and to communicate ideas relating to time. Thus objects can be

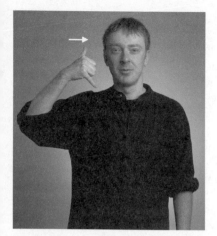

Figure 13.1 PHONE.

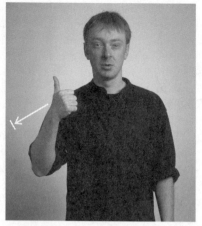

Figure 13.2 GOOD.

Figure 13.3 CONFUSED.

Figure 13.4 WHAT.

Directional symbols

▶   Movement to the left or right or up and down
>   Movement towards or away from the signer
▶▶   Repeated movement to the left or right or up and down
◀◀ ▶▶   Repeated movement from side to side or up and down

Path symbols

————   Hand or part of a hand moving in a line
————| Firm movement
═══════   Fast movement
◯   Circular movement. Each circle shows the movement of one hand, unless two hands move along the same path, in this case one circle shows the movement of both hands.

Interacting movement symbols

◯   The hands maintain contact throughout the movement. If direction and path symbols are attached to the circle, then the hands are held together and move together accordingly.

placed at a location in the signing space by signing and pointing to the location or just signing at the location. Subsequent reference to this point by pointing or nodding is sufficient to indicate the involvement of the object in a specified grammatical relationship.

Signing systems exist that draw on the signs of BSL but not its grammar, and so are not distinct languages. These systems involve the use of signs together with spoken or mouthed English. The most commonly used system is Sign Supported English (SSE).

There is no everyday written form of BSL. BSL is not alone in this, as approximately two-thirds of the world's spoken languages have no written form (Kyle and Woll 1985). Systems of picture-like symbols for writing sign language called Sign Writing (Sutton 1981) and a computerized system called SignFont (Newkirk 1987) have been developed in America, but they have not been widely used. However, there are a number of other possibilities open to a researcher to represent BSL as a transcript.

The meaning of BSL signing can be translated into written English. Ideally, this should involve two phases: forward- and back-translation. Forward-translation involves a signer translating BSL into written English. Back-translation involves a different signer translating the English back into BSL. The two sign language transcripts can then be compared for equivalency and discrepancies corrected.

Signs can also be represented by glosses which are words or phrases. By convention, glosses are written in capitals and if they are made up of more than one word then the words are separated by hyphens. Glosses may not relate to words in a simple one-to-one way. If a sign has more than one meaning then the gloss will represent only one of these meanings. Equally, the word or phrase used to gloss a sign may itself have more than one meaning. Thus a gloss is not directly equivalent to a word. Glosses have been used in books about sign language to indicate single signs or short BSL phrases. Finger spelling may be glossed by using uppercase with hyphens between individual letters (Lucas 1989), and aspects of an utterance which are not communicated by the hands glossed by lowercase words (Miles 1988).

Pictures or photographs of BSL signs have often been used along with glosses to illustrate the meaning of a sign or demonstrate an aspect of BSL use. Symbols such as arrows are used to indicate the direction and type of movement.

Finally, phonetic notation systems have been developed by researchers of sign language. These systems are designed to represent signs in a systematic way. All notation systems code signs in terms of location (Tab), handshape (Dez) and movement (Sig). Some systems also code for additional information such as the orientation of the hands. Notation systems are typically used to represent single signs and are not easily accessible to people unfamiliar with them.

Text

The researchers included a hearing psychology lecturer who has knowledge of the academic literature relating to social constructionism, deafness and sign language, a Deaf final year psychology student who has expertise in sign language use and a Deaf tutor for the deaf and sign language teacher who has expertise in sign language use. Thus across the team is a complementary combination of skills and experience. All three authors occupied equal status roles and made equally valuable contributions.

The text shown here is made up of a very short extract from an interview between the hearing author and a Deaf participant. The participant was a friend of the hearing researcher. She was born partially deaf and became profoundly deaf at age 15. She had hearing parents, learned BSL from her Deaf grandmother and now teaches sign language. She has good oral skills. The interview was conducted in SSE at the request of the interviewer, but during the course of the interview the participant used a number of BSL features such as the placement of signs in the signing space and non-manual features. We asked the participant to repeat one of the extracts from the interview which had contained placement in full BSL for presentation here.

The interview was a pilot study for an ongoing research project into the positive aspects of Deafness. We were primarily interested in Deaf people's accounts of what is good about Deafness, when it is better to be Deaf than hearing as well as more implicit positive imagery in Deaf people's talk about their culture, community and identity. The rationale behind this approach is that discussion of what is good about Deafness and when it might be better to be Deaf than hearing can operate as a challenge to the negative images of the dominant medical discourse and hence as a stimulus for change. Ultimately, the responses of Deaf participants might provide useful material for deaf awareness courses.

The extract from the interview was chosen to illustrate the possibilities for the construction of identity through the use of *space* in sign language. The participant drew on two resources in the extract with which to construct her identity. The first was the positioning in the signing space of the Deaf and hearing worlds. The second was two discourses of social relationships. Through the use of these resources, the participant was able to account for her differing loyalty to the Deaf and hearing worlds.

The text is represented through the use of photographs, glosses and an English translation. The photographs involve the first Deaf researcher producing a visual transcript of the participant's signing. We adopt this approach to maintain the anonymity of our participants. With the exception of signs involving pointing, all photographs were taken from the starting point of the sign.

Prior to this extract the participant located the Deaf community on the right side of her signing space and the hearing community on the left side of her signing space. After this, pointing to one of these places is enough to indicate that the signer is talking about what has been located at that point.

Deaf world
The deaf world is my family

Family

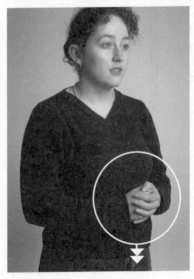

Hearing world
The hearing world my friends

Friends

Reading

The analysis offered here is necessarily brief and only aims to highlight possible interpretive avenues an analyst might explore.

Sign language makes use of all four dimensions: the three dimensions of space and also time. Space in BSL can serve to communicate a number of types of information. Spatial relationships such as proximity can be shown by how close the hands are to each other and lend themselves to depiction in a visual language. More abstract relations like status can also be coded through the relative height of placement in the signing space. Thus in some circumstances details of the physical separation and relative height of signs will be of importance.

Early in the interview the participant placed the Deaf community on the right side of the signing space and the hearing community on the left side of her signing space. In BSL this allows the signer to link these spatial positions with the referents. Subsequent reference to these positions by looking at them or pointing to their location indicates that the signer is talking about them. This process initially takes time in the laying out of the signing space but subsequently allows rapid and economical communication. By default a signer following the conventions of placement will place entities as far apart as possible to make the signing clear and will place the entities on the same level. Here this creates an image of two separate communities with no overlap or links being depicted. Two features of the placement stand out as interesting: the separation of the two communities at opposite ends of the signing space and their placement on the same level. In this instance the most plausible reading is that the signer is simply following the conventions of placement and that these are not significant aspects of the signing, but it is possible that in other instances these features could be important. The distance between the two communities could symbolize the degree of separation between the two communities, for example in terms of language or culture. The relative heights of the communities could also be of importance in communicating the relative standing to the individual of the communities.

After placing the Deaf and hearing communities in the signing space, the participant drew on discourses of the family and friendships to construct the nature of her relationship to the two communities and to explain the relative strength of her ties to each community. In the text which follows the interview extract presented here the participant used these discourses to account for her greater loyalty to the Deaf community by virtue of the greater strength of family ties compared to the ties between friends.

The representation of the Deaf community as a family promotes an image of the community as a nurturing, supportive environment that a Deaf person would want to belong to. Similarly, the depiction of the hearing community as friends implies good relations with hearing people.

These images contrast sharply with alternative possible constructions of the Deaf community as an escape or retreat from the hearing world by people who have given up trying to integrate. Thus the family and friendship discourses act to construct a positive identity for the participant.

The separation of the two communities in the signing space acted as a resource for the participant's talk following the extract shown here. Later in the interview the positioning of the two communities was used to depict the participant's active construction of her identity by selecting parts from the right side of the signing space (Deaf community) and parts from the left side of the signing space (hearing community). This depicts an image of an agent able actively to construct her own identity from elements of the communities she inhabits.

The family discourse was also used later in the interview as an accounting device. The participant used this as a metaphor to explain a norm in deaf culture, where Deaf people support each other when they need help in the same way that members of a family might help each other because of kinship ties. The metaphor was also used to account for disagreements between members of the Deaf community, depicting them as the 'normal' tensions that would take place within a family and not sufficient to threaten the ties between them.

The analysis of the text has outlined some features of the use of space which might be important to the reading made by a discourse analyst working with a BSL text. Positive imagery, here in the form of family and friendship discourses, can be drawn on by Deaf people to account for aspects of their lives, and identity is depicted as actively constructed. Such positive imagery does not fit well with a medical discourse which sees deafness as something negative.

Disadvantages

Taken in isolation, each of the forms of representation we used to depict the sign language extract have drawbacks. The English translation will at best only preserve the meaning of the sign language text. Meaning may be lost in the translation as some signs, such as multi-channel signs, may be difficult to translate.

The English glosses preserve information about the sequential order of signs from the signing. The use of glosses involves the use of one language to describe another. On their own, combinations of glosses used to represent a signed utterance would generally not be understandable to English speakers, as they may not communicate the full meaning of the signing. Thus it may not be apparent to an English speaker that the BSL utterance NAME WHAT YOU means 'What is your name?' Knowledge of BSL grammar is needed in order to translate such a signed message. Further, the glosses used will give no indication of the exact form of the signs used. Factors such as regional variation in sign use and the way that signs may differ from citation forms in actual use mean that even a BSL user may not be able to say exactly what form a sign took by just looking at a gloss.

The photographs preserve some visual information about the signs used. However, fundamental limitations are placed on what a photographic or pictorial representation can show by their being two-dimensional static representation of a three-dimensional moving process. A photograph or picture will represent only one angle from which the sign can be viewed at one instant in time. If a sign changes greatly in shape in the course of its production then more than one picture may need to be used to depict it. Movement involved in the sign may be represented by the addition of artwork to the photograph, but this may not be easy for a reader to interpret. It may also be difficult to represent errors and variation in people's signing using existing artwork.

In order to maintain the anonymity of our participant, we attempted to copy her signing in the photographs. This placed additional limitations on what could be depicted, since the re-creation of the participant's signing would be dependent on the quality of the original video recording and the researcher's signing skills. Also the artificial nature of posing for still photographs makes it difficult to re-create accurately a person's signing.

The text we have used is very short and does not address representational issues which would become apparent with longer texts, such as where and how English punctuation such as the use of question marks might be used. Some Deaf people may object to the forms of representation we have chosen here, as they all, with the exception of the photographs, use some form of English. They may prefer representational forms that are only associated with sign language, and so emphasize the status of BSL as a language separate to English.

The approach taken in this article is to see deafness as a social construct. Some readers may question this. If deafness has a physical basis how can it not be a disability, and so why are we championing the cultural cause?

Advantages

The problems associated with the individual representational formats discussed above are true, but we feel that either they are offset by the combination of the three forms or this combination offers the best option we have available. The photograph's strengths lie in its being the best medium for depicting how a sign was produced by the signer, glosses can convey sequential aspects of the BSL grammar and the English translation opens up the text to people not familiar with BSL. Photographs were preferred over drawings here to represent the signs visually. This was because of their greater capacity to represent non-manual features of signing clearly.

It may not always be essential to use all three of the formats we used. The form of representation adopted will depend on whether the researcher wants to represent the signing as it was signed or not, the use to which the transcript is to be put and the intended audience.

Analysis of the kind we offer helps to identify discourses of deafness and to give 'voice' to the Deaf community. There are currently two main discourses of deafness (Woodward 1972). These are the medical or pathological discourse and the cultural or linguistic discourse. The medical discourse constructs deafness in audiological terms, and is the understanding that most hearing people have of deafness. Deafness is seen as a deficiency and therefore something negative. Within this framework, hearing values and behaviour are seen as the norm and the problem of deafness is located within the individual. The cultural discourse constructs deafness in cultural terms. Aspects of the Deaf community such as the use of BSL and the existence of distinct Deaf social norms, customs, traditions, games, humour and art forms are used to argue that Deaf people form a distinct cultural group separate from hearing people. In this construction deafness is seen in a more positive light: Deaf people are different rather than deficient. The two discourses impact on Deaf people's lives through their link to social practices. Thus, if deafness is considered to be a disability then appropriate support would be to try to correct the deficit using such devices as hearing aids or cochlear implants. If deafness is seen as a cultural phenomenon then appropriate support would take a different form, such as the provision of interpreters and sub-titles on television.

In response to people who would question whether deafness can be seen as a cultural phenomenon, we would argue that it is a social construct and as such its meaning is not fixed. Researchers such as Groce (1985) and Padden and Humphries (1988) have documented situations where deafness was not experienced as a notable characteristic of a person or associated with ideas of deficit or pathology. These studies argue for the socially constructed nature of the word 'deaf'.

Accepting the validity of a cultural identity for Deaf people is often difficult for hearing people. This is because of a number of factors, such as the fact that the major institutions in hearing society (medicine, education and law) tend to promote a medical discourse. Also Deaf people are less likely than hearing people to achieve good levels of English language literacy and occupy positions of power in society, resulting in the accounts of Deaf people being less likely to be written down. Thus hearing people are only used to thinking of deafness in medical terms, and tend to know little about Deaf culture or BSL.

We would justify championing the cultural discourse of deafness for two reasons: (a) The majority of deaf people see themselves as Deaf rather than deaf (Lane 1992); and (b) an identity based on a cultural discourse offers a more positive identity than an identity based on a medical discourse. The focus on positive aspects of Deafness in our research and our support for a cultural discourse of Deafness does not mean we are saying that Deaf people do not face real difficulties, but rather that a significant part of these difficulties stems from disabling attitudes and the barriers put up by hearing society.

An important feature of our work that we want to promote was the attempt to carry out research in an informed and culturally sensitive way. This was reflected in the composition of the research team and the attempt to research deafness from a cultural perspective. This is an approach that we would wish to encourage.

Note

We would like to thank Adrian Greenhalgh for taking the photographs, Kevin Bradley for his help with the artwork and both Guy Barnard and Chris Mellor for their helpful comments on an earlier draft of the chapter. We would also like to thank David Brien for giving permission to sample the artwork from the BSL dictionary.

Key reading

Brien, D. (ed.) (1992) *Dictionary of British Sign Language/English*. London: Faber and Faber, pp. 1–114.

Dant, T. and Gregory, S. (1991) *The Social Construction of Deafness*. Milton Keynes: Block 3, Unit 8, of the Open University Course D251, Issues in Deafness.

References

Brennan, M. (1987) British Sign Language: the language of the Deaf community. In T. Booth and W. Swann (eds) *Including Pupils with Disabilities*. Milton Keynes: Open University Press.

Gregory, S. and Miles, D. (1991) *British Sign Language, Communication and Deafness*. Milton Keynes: Open University Press.

Groce, N. (1985) *Everyone Here Spoke Sign Language: Hereditary Deafness on Martha's Vineyard*. London: Harvard University Press.

Kyle, J. G. and Woll, B. (1985) *Sign Language: The Study of Deaf People and Their Language*. Cambridge: Cambridge University Press.

Miles, D. (1988) *British Sign Language: A Beginner's Guide*. London: BBC Books.

Newkirk, D. (1987) *SignFont Handbook*. San Diego: Emerson and Stern Associates.

Lane, H. (1992) Constructions of deafness. *Disability and Society*, 10(2): 171–89.

Lucas, C. (ed.) (1989) *The Sociolinguistics of the Deaf Community*. San Diego: Harcourt Brace Jovanovich.

Padden, C. and Humphries, T. (1988) *Deaf in America: Voices from a Culture.* London: Harvard University Press.

Sutton, V. (1981) *Sign Writing for Everyday Use.* Newport Beach, CA: The Sutton Movement Writing Press.

Woodward, J. (1972) Implications for sociolinguistic research among the deaf. *Sign Language Studies*, 1: 1–7.

PART IV

Subjectivity in research

14 **Bodies:** reading the body

DAVID J. NIGHTINGALE

This chapter focuses on three key themes or questions. (a) What does it mean to suggest that we can discourse analyse bodies in the same (or similar) ways to written or spoken texts? (b) Are bodies amenable to forms of analysis developed for written or spoken texts, or do they present us with unique methodological and/or theoretical difficulties not present or evident in other forms of discourse analysis? And, finally, (c) in what ways can an investigation of bodies further our understanding of the methodological practices and theoretical foundations of discourse analysis? The chapter considers biological, social constructionist and phenomenological explanations of the body, through reference to Williams syndrome (a 'genetic learning disability'), and concludes that phenomenological analyses of the body provide a potentially fuller and more useful account of the body than other perspectives. However, it is also argued that this approach needs further theoretical and methodological development if it is ultimately to provide a coherent and politically useful model of the body.

Biological approaches to the body are commonplace within many arenas of contemporary Western thought and will not be described in any great detail within this chapter. Suffice it to say that the idea that the body is originary with respect to such widely disparate notions as emotion, sexuality, self-image and intellectual performance is reflected within all medical and medically derived disciplines and many of the human sciences as well, in particular the various branches and perspectives of traditional psychology. What these approaches share is the belief that the body, as a concrete, observable phenomenon, (a) can be described acontextually *in and of itself*; and (b) will readily give up its nature to a rigorous and objective scientific analysis. An extreme example of the biological perspective is the Human Genome Project, an international project to map the sequence of nucleotide bases that are strung along the DNA molecule of the human genome. New 'discoveries' arising from this project include the identification of specific sequences that predispose individuals to illness or disease (Friedman *et al.* 1992).

The human sciences have shifted focus from processes of representation to processes of signification; from the ways in which knowledge is seen as a veridical and unmediated 'mirror' of reality (Rorty 1979), a representation of some externally existing world that can be captured, reflected in talk, theories and words (and ultimately explained), to the ways in which knowledge can be seen as structuring and constitutive of that which it purports to describe: 'The argument is that the reality represented does not determine the representation or the means of representation. Instead, the process of signification itself gives shape to the reality it implicates' (Henriques *et al.* 1984: 99). In this sense, discourses are not talk *about* some external pre-existing reality (just waiting to be discovered through the judicious application of the right procedures) but *are* 'practices that systematically form the objects of which they speak' (Foucault 1972: 49), in this instance, bodies.

Social constructionist approaches to the body can be seen as both an elaboration of key theoretical concepts within a particular perspective (anti-essentialism, anti-realism etc. (see Burr 1995) and a form of political activity, the undermining of dominant and hegemonic discourses that position the human subject through matrices of institutional power and knowledge. Constructionist analyses seek to undermine the originary power of the body as object and source of meaning, and seek, instead, to demonstrate the ways in which the body is constructed within particular disciplinary practices and webs of institutional power. Knowledge of the body, within this framework, is knowledge of the workings of power, who has constructed the body and in what ways.

For example, feminist research has demonstrated that notions of female embodiment and practice have been traditionally defined in biological and pathological terms: the notion of menstruation as 'curse' (Ussher 1989), the ideological aspects of PMT (Laws 1983), deconstructions of biomedical explanations of osteoporosis (Klinge 1997), issues of female sexuality (Kitzinger 1987) – all these share a fundamental understanding as to the essentially social origin of meaning with respect to the body and its practices. Likewise, within contemporary disability theory, the notion that disability arises as a necessary consequence of a physical or mental impairment has been shown to be incorrect. Disability theorists have argued that impairment is 'individual limitation', whereas disability is a 'socially imposed restriction' (Oliver 1983). In this instance, the lived experiences of disability are recast as a social rather than biological or physical phenomenon, arising through the limitations imposed by others (professionals, medical personnel) or by factors within the environment (Swain *et al.* 1993).

Central to the majority of discourse analytic or social constructionist approaches to the body is a belief that the 'nature' of the body can be better explained as a consequence of the social, moral and political realm within which it resides than as a consequence of any inherent or pre-existing essences within it. This decoupling of the 'nature of the body' from the 'body as object' has enabled critical theorists and practitioners to mount successful challenges to institutional and traditional knowledges that have served to disempower, pathologize and oppress the marginalized groups they purport to describe and explain. Through demonstrations of the fundamentally relativistic nature of such knowledge, many groups have been given the theoretical, practical and political means whereby they might challenge both their oppressors and the discourses that legitimate their oppressive practices.

However, while social constructionism has (at least within critical academic circles) achieved a fundamental deconstruction of all things bodily, it has done so at a cost. Perhaps the major, and potentially most damaging, critique of current constructionist accounts regarding the fundamentally social nature of the body is the 'uniform plasticity' of the body that *must* hold true if constructionist accounts are to appear coherent. By this I mean that all bodies (young/old, male/female, able-bodied/impaired) must be comparably write-able, so similar as to drop out of the equation, sufficiently malleable and homogeneous that bodily discourses may write over or through them as though they were not there. This unidimensional (or non-dimensional) body is, I would suggest, an analytic device that bears no relation to lived experience – a theoretical fiction without which constructionist theories become untenable. The cost, then, is the exclusion of the physical body (in and of itself) from contemporary theories of the body within psychology. However, while the body may have been expunged from (or marginalized within) theory, it remains a stubborn reality. For example, within disability theory, bodily impairment (as mentioned above) is reconceptualized as 'individual limitation', but as Hughes and Paterson (1997: 326) have noted, 'the social model . . . actually concedes the body to medicine and understands impairment in terms of medical discourse.' Descartes would have been proud: not only have experience and the body been separated, but they have now also been relegated to entirely separate disciplines. In other words, responsibility for the messy physicality of the body (in and of itself) has been either brushed aside as inconsequential, epiphenomenal or unreal, or abrogated to other disciplines; rendering its theoretical significance, as an active and inherent component of lived experience, null and void.

In response to these difficulties, a phenomenological approach (of which no more than a preliminary sketch can be presented here) would seek to reintegrate the *subjectivism* of many constructionist accounts (i.e. that reality is no more than a negotiated consensus of talk or deed) with the *objectivism* of mainstream scientific accounts (that reality exists independently of our talk, perceptions and social activity) – not in the sense of maintaining or promoting such a dualism, but through the recognition that while our subjectivities and discourse do indeed shape reality, they are, in turn, dependent upon and formed by such a reality. The basic argument is that our perception of the world, and our activities within it, are based upon an interaction between our mental faculties and the nature of the world but cannot be reduced to either. The implication, as I hope to demonstrate, is that the nature of the body cannot be dismissed (as many constructionists would have it), or given over to other disciplines (as in the medicalization of impairment), but must be reintegrated into a basic theoretical account that will allow for an analysis of the body as other than epiphenomenal or peripheral to discourse. These issues will be elaborated throughout the remainder of this chapter by reference to the chapter's specific text – Williams syndrome. (For a more detailed explanation of phenomenology, and its relevance to psychology, see Spinelli 1989.)

Text: Williams syndrome

The specific text that forms the basis of this chapter is an extract from a newspaper article that discusses the nature and defining characteristics of Williams syndrome, a 'genetic learning disability' (Bower 1997: 48). While a piece of text is clearly not a body, and this chapter is purportedly about the discourse analysis of actual bodies, it may seem as though (yet another) piece of text is somehow secondary to our major concern and not really what the chapter should be about. However, the body, as should now be becoming clearer, cannot be reduced to the 'body as object', it is neither a simple collection of anatomical bits that can be (re)presented on a page and analysed as a biological or pictorial fact, nor, as I have argued, a purely textual consequence of cultural knowledges and practices. As a dissected frog refuses to jump and a butterfly collection no longer flits around a warm summer garden, so the body as object, image or text (in and of itself) is no more capable of explaining the lived experience of the human body than a corpse in the library with a lead pipe beside its head.

As Terry Eagleton (1996: 70) notes, the body 'is the hinge between Nature and Culture', by which he means that it inhabits and exists within,

The following extract appears towards the end of the article (entitled 'The gift of the gab', *Independent on Sunday*, 11 May 1997), and is highlighted within a box that spans two columns of text. The box is entitled 'Picking up the clues'.

The classic clinical and behavioural signs of Williams syndrome were fully described in 1987 but, says Dr Orlee Udwin, consultant clinical psychologist at Lambeth Healthcare and part of the team that spelled out the full exotic profile, many doctors remain unaware of the condition and families often endure months, even years, of anxiety before diagnosis.

GP Dr Mike Wolfman and his wife Fran, whose seven-year-old son Freddie has Williams Syndrome, spent nine months trying to persuade paediatricians that they were not 'over-anxious professional parents', while Carol Mathurin, who has a filing cabinet of background information on her daughter Nikki's condition, spent nine years trying [to] persuade consultants and authorities that she was not a neurotic mother.

For a knowledgeable clinician, there are multiple clues:

- Facial features – wide mouth, retroussé nose, slightly bulgy eyes – often referred to as 'elfin' features.
- Very high calcium levels at birth. Babies often vomit frequently, don't feed well sometimes because of difficulties in sucking, are restless sleepers and grow very slowly.
- Supravalvular aortic stenosis.

Almost all Williams syndrome people have a narrowing of the arteries going to the heart.

- Hypersensitivity to sound. Can be extremely distressed by sounds such as washing machines, vacuum cleaners and planes, and by certain individual tones.
- All development is retarded. Language starts late but advances quickly to the characteristic fluency and adult-like phrasing and excessive chatter.
- Extremely emotional, swinging from exaggerated displays of fear, excitement, sadness, happiness.
- Short attention span, highly distractable [*sic*] but also subject to all engrossing obsessions.
- Over-friendly and tactile and lacking recognition of social boundaries.

For all this catalogue of difficulties, the one word consistently used by family, carers and clinicians to describe Williams syndrome people is 'charming'. As Nikki Mathurin says: 'People who know me like me for who I am not what I am, they like me for my personality. I think people think of me as a hard worker who does well on my courses, and as a very bouncy person who's very friendly and easy going to be with.'

between and across the spaces between the two. It cannot be captured and described as purely a biological object or as a reductive consequence of cultural knowledges and practices. It is with this in mind that the extract was chosen, not because it somehow ideally captures the 'nature' of the body, but because it allows us to explore the tensions that differing accounts of the body make evident – the ways in which bodies transcend their physical boundaries but are none the less physical, corporeal beings; the ways in which bodies are more than their descriptions but are none the less suffused by such descriptions; the ways in which bodies are simultaneously both artefact and reality.

Reading: making sense of Williams syndrome

What follows represents an analysis of the text example from the perspectives introduced earlier. The biological analysis is supplemented with further material from the article. The constructionist argument brings to bear issues of pathologization and seeks to deconstruct the ways in which this syndrome is manufactured within social and disciplinary knowledges and practices. The section on phenomenological approaches to the body sketches out the necessity to redraw the boundaries between body and culture, and reiterates the need to transcend purely biological or purely textual analyses of the body.

The article from which the extract is taken is constructed as an explicit challenge to certain assumptions within contemporary cognitive science, but, as will be evident, it also represents an implicit endorsement of the biological model underpinning such accounts. The first sections of the article discuss the ways in which Williams syndrome presents a radical challenge to everyday conceptions of intelligence, by stressing the highly fluid and advanced grasp of language demonstrated by Williams syndrome children (normally taken as a good index of intelligence), in comparison to their 'obvious' deficits in other areas (counting, visuo-spatial ability etc.) and typical IQs of between 40 and 70; 'By school age many of these children talk like angels, in flowing, descriptive language, using long words and adult language' (Bower 1997: 48).

In a general sense, the presentation of the text example represents a classic medical model of the 'disabled' person: a set of symptoms, ranging from the genetic (lack of a 'chunk' of the DNA on chromosome 7), physiological (congenital heart problems), through psychological ('all development is retarded'), to the social ('over-friendly and tactile and lacking recognition of social boundaries'). The arguments mobilized to explain the 'differences' in higher order psychological and social functioning include both neurobiological and genetic explanations, both of which share a common conception of such differences as, in some way, directly attributable to the physiological or genetic 'abnormalities' that Williams syndrome children share. This is the kind of rhetoric that the disability movement has fought hard to challenge, the systematic categorization of people and their (dis)abilities as a function or consequence of impairment.

At the heart of critical deconstructions of biological accounts of the body is a break from the notion of the 'body as object' that can be explained *in and of itself*, an object that can be decontextualized from history and culture and observed (and subsequently explained) through the mechanisms of scientific practice, to a recognition that the body is immersed within cultures and practices that shape or determine our experiences of our own and others' physical realities. In terms of this framework, the discourses employed within this article to describe Williams syndrome children can be deconstructed in a number of readily apparent ways. The implicit assumptions regarding the aetiology of psychological and/or social difference and the rhetoric of such terms as 'over-friendly' and 'extremely emotional' indicate typical ways in which we could begin to demonstrate the fundamentally social origins of Williams syndrome. The term 'syndrome' is surely enough to raise the, almost certainly, socially constructed hackles of the best of us. While there are clear gains for Williams syndrome children and their carers in such deconstructions, particularly in terms of the depathologization of difference that these accounts offer, is this a sufficient explanation, or indeed an always useful one?

The ever-present danger of attempting a reintegration of the biological, particularly in terms of groups that have fought hard to challenge the domination that biologistic models of the person present, is that *any talk at all* concerning the biological or physical nature of the body can be seen as a form of capitulation or used by those who would seek to maintain or support such oppression. However, in this particular instance, it can be seen that the social model of disability does not offer a sufficiently coherent framework to explain adequately this 'condition'. As mentioned above, the social model of disability (Oliver 1983) conceptualizes disability as 'socially imposed restriction' – a person who requires a wheelchair for mobility is not disabled by the impairment but by an inadequately accessible environment; a visually impaired person can have access to the written word through adequate provision of large print books and computer facilities.

What these examples share is a recognition of the disabling consequences of an inadequate environment. However, as Sally French (1993: 18) has argued, modifications to the environment may not always be entirely effective or even possible for every impairment (e.g. modifications that would enable certain groups may further disable others). While she notes that some of these difficulties can be overcome she also suggests that some 'are difficult (perhaps impossible) to replace' (*ibid.*). An example she utilizes that allows us to explore the phenomenological or lived experience of visual impairment relates to the difficulties she experiences in perceiving non-verbal communication. What this implies is that her lived experience would be different if she were not visually impaired and that this difference is tied in with her visual impairment in complex ways, not merely as a socially imposed restriction, but as a fundamental phenomenological component of such an impairment.

Can we adequately explain Williams syndrome in terms of 'socially imposed restriction' (and consign any impairment to the medical personnel), or do we need to move beyond such dualistic interpretations of the physical and mental towards a more phenomenological analysis? The descriptions of Williams syndrome children in the text example present us with a charming, friendly, affectionate, linguistically fluent but 'cognitively limited' child. In the remainder of this chapter the strengths and weaknesses of both (purely) discursive and phenomenological approaches will be discussed with the aim of providing some preliminary suggestions for how we might conceptualize the phenomenological aspects of this 'syndrome' and the nature of embodied experience(s) more generally.

Disadvantages

As should now be evident, a phenomenological account offers the potential for a more coherent theoretical stance with respect to the body. However, it has been suggested that current political concerns outweigh the need for possible (future) theoretical coherence (see, for example, Sampson 1993). When the subject matter is the embodied nature of groups that have been consistently oppressed within dominant discourses of genetics, biology and medicine, a call for a return to such topics may be seen as counterproductive and politically naive. However, while radical theorists have gained ground within academia and, to a lesser extent, within the world at large, these achievements, in failing to address materiality of embodiment, are likely to remain peripheral to mainstream concerns. While they may be rallied around and serve as an organizing principle for political and social activity, they are unlikely to offer much in the way of reconstructive critique.

A further difficulty relates to how this approach might be developed to provide a coherent research strategy, particularly in terms of the development of a suitable methodology. A major strength of the constructionist approach to the analysis of social reality is its unequivocal stance with respect to the status of the knowledge its seeks to describe. Through conceptualizing psychological and social phenomena as *always* social in origin and *always* embedded in discursive practices, it presents an internally coherent theory and a clearly specified methodology. In contrast, a phenomenological approach adds a significant layer of complexity, in terms of both theory and method. While a phenomenological account of the body would recognize that all psychological phenomena are semantically mediated and embedded in culture, it also stresses that they are simultaneously embedded in the physicality of the material body. In what ways can the relative importance of the two be assessed and their interrelationships unravelled? How might we operationalize such a study and what methodologies might we use to explore such complexities? As yet, there are no clear answers to these questions. Perhaps the best we can hope to achieve is a sensitization to the body, a recognition that not all bodies are the same and that discourses, and the ways in which they shape and form social reality, are constrained and shaped in their turn by the physical realities they describe.

Advantages

While these difficulties represent very real concerns, the deficits of the alternatives are fraught with equally unpleasant consequences. As Eagleton (1996: 37) points out: 'it is impossible to say what kind of world our discourse or beliefs are *about*, any more than those who regard the Grand Canyon or the human body as wholly "constructed" are able to say what is being constructed. For them, the question is bound to remain as much a mystery as crop circles are for those who lack a sense of humour.' There is a clear sense in which current constructionist accounts of the body are as univocal as the biological accounts they purport to supersede. The 'body' of these accounts has all the character and vitality of a high-street mannequin – a lifeless, self-identical thing upon which the 'social' may hang its terms. Even this may be going too far, for the 'body', as any sort of 'thing' at all, seems almost inexplicable within this framework. No blood, breath, bone or sinew, just a 'position' or 'epistemological construction', a nexus of social practices and discourses.

I suppose that the sophisticated constructionist rejoinder to the above would be that it isn't the case that nothing is constructed but that no *thing* is constructed – at least no thing with a clearly discernible essential nature. Rather, the various discourses of the body construct our perceptions and practices concerning the body, such that women's experiences become regulated by, for example, gynaecological discourses (generated by predominantly male gynaecologists) that pathologize their experiences in terms of medical dysfunction. Or that people with impairments are excluded from certain practices and opportunities as a consequence of a disability that is supposedly coterminous with such an impairment. Within this framework there is a necessary move away from a static, object-based view of human reality, towards an analysis of process and practice, to the ways in which we, as people, are embedded within the flow of ongoing, constructive social activity. Is this sufficient to explain all aspects of embodied being?

In the text example we can see that parents of two Williams children spent considerable time and energy to find some objective explanation of their children's behaviour. As mentioned earlier, a characteristic 'feature' of Williams syndrome children is their adult-like proficiency with language. Elsewhere in the article, it is suggested that such fluency can often lead to a misrepresentation of the children's learning difficulties as 'just pretending, or that they're lazy or naughty' (Bower 1997: 49). It would seem as though an account of Williams syndrome as a purely biological or genetic disorder cannot adequately explain the lived experiences of Williams syndrome children and their carers; nor would a purely discursive account adequately address the years of 'anxiety' that many parents express prior to 'diagnosis'; nor does it seem to offer a coherent account of the different ways in which Williams syndrome children appear to confront their worlds. It would seem as though the inclusion of the biological, in this instance, offers us an enriched understanding of the body that transcends a purely social analysis.

Biological approaches to this text, in and of themselves, offer little more than a mechanistic and reductive analysis of this phenomenon. Purely discursive or constructionist analyses present us with: (a) a politically powerful means whereby we might destabilize the oppressive ways in which contemporary culture constructs the body; and (b) no body (or at best a pale reflection of one). If, as I have suggested, we attempt to develop a phenomenological theory of the body, we: (a) run the risk of aiding and abetting our political adversaries and those who would seek to maintain their oppressive practices that have 'disabled' or persecuted countless thousands of people; but (b) retain some notion of the lived body as a 'real' and integral component of our analyses. In terms of 'illuminating the text', it would seem as though an account that offers the potential to reconcile the physical *and* the social – the body *and* culture – offers greater scope to explore the nature of embodiment as something other than a thing in itself or a mere epiphenomenon or reductive consequence of discourse, and consequently offers a means whereby we might reassess our notions of how bodies are constructed and actively (or passively) take part in these constructions.

Key reading

Hughes, B. and Paterson, K. (1997) The social model of disability and the disappearing body: towards a sociology of impairment. *Disability and Society*, 12(3): 325–40.

Spinelli, E. (1989) *The Interpreted World: An Introduction to Phenomenological Psychology*. London: Sage.

References

Bower, H. (1997) The gift of the gab. *Independent on Sunday*, 11 May.
Burr, V. (1995) *An Introduction to Social Constructionism*. London: Routledge.
Eagleton, T. (1996) *The Illusions of Postmodernism*. Oxford: Blackwell.
Edwards, D., Ashmore, M. and Potter, J. (1995) Death and furniture: the rhetoric, politics and theology of bottom line arguments against relativism. *History of the Human Sciences*, 8(2): 25–49.
Foucault, M. (1972) *The Archaeology of Knowledge*. London: Tavistock.
Freidman, G., Reichlet, R. and Shera, K. (1992) *Los Alamos Science No. 20: The Human Genome Project*. Los Alamos: Los Alamos National Laboratory.
French, S. (1993) Disability, impairment or something in between? In J. Swain, V. Finkelstein, S. French and M. Oliver (eds) *Disabling Barriers – Enabling Environments*. London: Sage.
Henriques, J., Hollway, W., Urwin, C., Venn, C. and Walkerdine, V. (1984) *Changing the Subject: Psychology, Social Regulation and Subjectivity*. London and New York: Methuen.
Hughes, B. and Paterson, K. (1997) The social model of disability and the disappearing body: towards a sociology of impairment. *Disability and Society*, 12(3): 325–40.
Kitzinger, C. (1987) *The Social Construction of Lesbianism*. London: Sage.
Klinge, I. (1997) Female bodies and brittle bones: medical interventions in osteoporosis. In K. Davis (ed.) *Embodied Practices: Feminist Perspectives on the Body*. London: Sage.
Laws, S. (1983) The sexual politics of pre-menstrual tension. *Women's Studies International Forum*, 6(1): 19–31.
Oliver, M. (1983) *Social Work with Disabled People*. London: Macmillan.
Popper, K. R. (1979) *Objective Knowledge: An Evolutionary Approach*, rev. edn. Oxford: Clarendon Press.
Rorty, R. (1979) *Philosophy and the Mirror of Nature*. Princeton, NJ: Princeton University Press.
Sampson, E. E. (1993) *Celebrating the Other: A Dialogic Account of Human Nature*. London: Harvester Wheatsheaf.
Spinelli, E. (1989) *The Interpreted World: An Introduction to Phenomenological Psychology*. London: Sage.
Swain, J., Finkelstein, V., French, S. and Oliver, M. (eds) (1993) *Disabling Barriers – Enabling Environments*. London: Sage.
Ussher, J. M. (1989) *The Psychology of the Female Body*. London: Routledge.

Ethnography: reading across culture

MIKE HUMPHREYS

Geertz (1973: 10) argues that 'Doing ethnography is like trying to read (in the sense of "construct a reading of") a manuscript – foreign, faded, full of ellipses, incoherencies, suspicious emendations, and tendentious commentaries, but, written not in conventionalized graphs of sound but in transient examples of shaped behavior.' This chapter takes up these themes and applies them to an ethnographic study of organizational culture across wider, national, cultural differences.

Finding a consensual definition of organisational culture presents a problem. Brown (1994: 5) speaks of an 'embarrassment of definitional riches' before presenting 15 alternatives as a 'selection of some of the best known and widely promulgated definitions [which] reflect very different understandings of what culture is' (Brown 1994: 6–7). However, one of the most widely used definitions is Schein's (1992: 12): 'The pattern of basic assumptions that a given group has invented, discovered or developed in learning to cope with its problems of external adaptation and internal integration, and that have worked well enough to be considered valid and therefore to be taught to new members as the correct way to perceive, think, and feel in relation to these problems.'

Although qualitative research is a relative newcomer to international management research (Wright 1996), recent opinion (Brannen 1996) suggests that ethnography can be a particularly powerful research methodology for the investigation of organizational cultures when the *problem* entails 'taking a holistic viewpoint – where context and behaviour are interdependent' (Cassell and Symon 1994: 6). Watson (1994: 8) sees such organizational ethnographic research as a natural extension of 'what we do all the time as human beings', in that it involves activities such as reading signals and ambiguous messages in confusing circumstances, while maintaining a network of relationships. The one thing that *is* clear from the burgeoning methodological literature on writing ethnography is that there are no stylistic rules: as Fetterman (1989: 104) says, 'ethnographic writing comes in a variety of styles, from clear and simple to Byzantine.' Hammersley and Atkinson (1995: 258) are even less prescriptive in their advice that 'there are no right and wrong ways of writing ethnography', and Van Maanen (1988: 35) produces a 'phenomenological war whoop' when he declares that 'there is no way of seeing, hearing, or representing the world of others that is absolutely, universally valid or correct. Ethnographies of any sort are always subject to multiple interpretations. They are never beyond controversy or debate.'

This chapter locates an ethnographic reading of the organizational culture of a Turkish university faculty in the context of broader cultural issues, specifically that of Turkish culture, still suffused by the symbols of Atatürk's charismatic leadership. This is evident throughout urban Turkey, particularly in public establishments. His mausoleum, a huge Parthenon-like building containing his tomb, dominates the capital Ankara. It is protected 24 hours a day by a rigidly disciplined ceremonial guard and there is a constant stream of Turkish visitors to view the display of his possessions, including, for example, his cars, clothes, library, cigarettes, rowing machine and photographs. Throughout the country his statues and busts feature in front of buildings and in town squares, and his portrait hangs in every office, classroom and lecture hall. His image appears on currency, postcards, carpets, wall-hangings, calendars, sets of photographs, slide packs, brooches, cufflinks, key-rings, lapel badges, television screens and university prospectuses. Hence, although he died nearly sixty years ago, his symbolic presence is maintained by a national industry supplying his likenesses and also by the fund of stories surrounding him. For example:

I was in primary school and one of my sisters was a history teacher and she always used to invite the whole school to see Atatürk's farm on May 1st. They had a picnic and my sister took me along too. I was very small and Atatürk was amongst us and he said 'who are you'? I was quite nervous. (How old were you?) Maybe 7 or 8. He put me on his lap and talked to me and I always wish I had a picture of this moment. When I look at his eyes I feel a kind of fear – he had very deep blue eyes and I remember this more than anything else.

(Retired teacher)

As in all the educational establishments in Turkey, each classroom in the faculty I studied has a portrait of Atatürk and a Turkish flag, and most have a framed calligraphic Turkish version of Atatürk's address to Turkish youth. A professor from another faculty, looking up at the portrait of Atatürk above her desk, which had been painted by her father, said with emotion 'He was the *true* prophet – but we are not allowed to talk like that any more' (Istanbul University).

Three days after Atatürk died in Istanbul on 10 November 1938, his body was transferred by battleship and train to Ankara with a Turkish flag (this is the flag referred to in the text box), covering the ebony coffin. On arrival in Ankara the body was laid out before the Grand National Assembly Building and then transferred to a temporary grave site in the Ethnographic Museum (about 200 metres from the site of the original women's teacher training school which evolved into the faculty). It remained there until 1953 when it was placed in the sepulchre of the special memorial complex, known as Atatürk's Mausoleum, on a hill overlooking Ankara. To Kemalists (followers of Mustafa Kemal Atatürk), he continues to symbolize a glorious past of battles won, a move towards modern technological society, strength, nationalism, military power, stability, leadership and emancipation for women (Pope and Pope 1997).

Text

The text here is a vignette extracted from an ethnographic study of the professional culture of a Turkish university faculty. At its simplest level, the study attempts to represent the professional culture of this faculty in such a way that 'if the reader goes for the first time into the social setting that they have read about, either as a manager or as an academic observer, they will feel better placed to cope than if they had not read it' (Watson 1997: 8). This study is ethnographic, not only in Van Maanen's (1988: 14) terms as a 'written representation of culture' in that it is 'concerned with cultural interpretation', but also, like Watson's (1994: 2) text *In Search of Management*, it attempts to 'tell a story' and fulfil Sackmann's (1997: 5) advice that such research should 'contribute to a better understanding of cultural complexity, as well as some of its implications for management'. Thus the 'ethnographic focus' (Spradley 1980) of this case is the professional life of a group of academics in a university faculty.

The role adopted by the researcher was one of 'active membership' (Adler and Adler 1998) as an educational consultant to the faculty and as an organizational ethnographer. Data collection strategies included participant observation, semi-structured interview, documentary evidence collection, writing field notes and compiling an interpretive diary. The researcher disclosed this dual role to all staff.

We are shown into the Head of Department's office. The Head of the Handicrafts Department is a woman in her early fifties and the two other teachers are of a similar age; the research assistant is in her twenties. All are dressed in Western suits, looking very much like women staff in a British further education college business studies department. Everyone shakes hands and exchanges formal greetings, the Head seats herself behind her large desk under the ubiquitous Atatürk portrait, D, my interpreter, and I sit facing each other at the other side of the desk, with a low coffee table between us. The two teachers position chairs at our sides and the research assistant sits at a large table behind me. I explain the nature of my research and D translates with the facility that she has developed over our months of working together. The Head explains in English (with some lapses into Turkish when she glances at D and receives instant translation) that she has asked the others to be present to enhance the data. I ask if they would allow me to tape record the interview. They say yes without hesitation, I place the recorder on the Head's desk and the interview begins. My initial fears of group inhibition disappear quickly as the 'inverview' becomes a three, four and five way conversation, in Turkish and English with D at full stretch in deep concentration. The women seem to reinforce each other's honesty and candour. I am wondering how to raise the issue of the headscarves when one of the teachers brings it up as a major problem for them. At this point I notice that the tape recording indicator has gone out – the new batteries straight from the packet must be dud. The Head of Department notices my distress and immediately stops the interview and telephones a secretary, who, in turn, summons a student to the office. The student, a young woman in jeans and sweater, comes in, head bowed deferentially, the HOD explains the problem, I give her a 250,000 TL note (about £3), show her the failed batteries and she runs off. The 'conversation' resumes and the staff become very excited about the headscarf issue. I try to make notes but feel that I am losing crucial data and I am extremely relieved to see the student arrive back after only five minutes with some new batteries. I am so pleased to be back recording that I try to get her to keep the change (80,000 TL, £1) but she refuses with a shy smile. We continue to discuss the issue of headscarves. The staff explain that in their view the increase in headscarf wearing students is a socio-economic problem, being exacerbated in Hero University by the targeting of students by the Islamic Refah Party who, they said, were providing funding and halls of residence places for students who wear Islamic dress. A male servant in a blue jacket brings in tea on a silver tray. After tea I raise Atatürk as a theme. One of the teachers suggests that their school had been in the vanguard of Atatürk's push for the education of women, and that she felt that the school had been linked to him from the beginning. I mention that yesterday I had visited the Ethnographic Museum in Ankara where Atatürk's body had lain after his death until the building of his mausoleum. I tell them that I felt that the proximity of the museum to the original building where the women's education institution was based suggested that the school was symbolically connected to Atatürk. They agree passionately and tell the story of the flag and the 24-hour vigil of staff and students awaiting the arrival of his body in Ankara.

> When he died the flag made in our school was sent to cover his coffin, it was a very valuable hand made flag, even the crescent which had a 1.5 metre diameter was made by hand. One of my teachers had it made by the students and it was a very special time. Of course people loved him and we never thought that things would change after his death.
>
> (From interview transcript)

The emotion generated by this story is quite overwhelming and my translator D is overcome with tears, telling us that her mother had been involved in the vigil when she was a student at the school. The Head orders more tea for us all. After everyone recovers we spend some time discussing the role of language and then at the end of about two hours the research assistant interviews me about technical teacher training in the UK. I finish off by thanking them all and saying from my heart how much I have appreciated their honesty and openness. I am surprised by the tears and joy that this seems to provoke from these professors and assistant professors, and very moved as they thank me for allowing them to speak about their problems and for reawakening their faith in Atatürk's principles, which 'will never die'. I leave with D, trembling with emotion and excitement myself, the passion of these women had been astounding. They saw Atatürk as having given them rights and freedom greater than women in Europe at the time and they were beginning to see that freedom eroded; our interview, it seems, had reawakened some of their feelings. D and I go to the hotel bar for a glass of wine to calm down and discuss the experience.

The ethnography itself is designed to move the interpretive focus from a macro to a micro view at several levels. It begins with an account of the history of the Turkish Republic, then of higher education within the country, and focuses eventually on the university and the specific faculty. Core themes are then used to explore the nature of academic life within the faculty. A concluding section aims to integrate the exploration of the core themes, responding to Delamont's (1996: 148–9) 'challenges to familiarity' in using an ethnographic approach to the study of higher education in other cultures and, in the process, answering the question 'what is it like to work as an academic in this faculty?' In order to enhance the understanding of the *'story'*, vignettes, described by Van Maanen (1988: 136) as 'personalized accounts of fleeting moments of fieldwork case in dramatic form', are used to provide narrative voice and give access to Richardson's (1995: 208) 'uniquely human experience of time' in terms of everyday, autobiographical, biographical, cultural and collective experiences. The example text is one of the vignettes.

Reading

We will look at four possible readings of this text. The first reading will be that of a generalized other: that is, how the piece is likely to be read by a naive reader. The second will use some of the 'backstage' information possessed by the ethnographer and the third will consider, in passing, the implications of a transcendent reading. The fourth, final reading will put the text in the wider context, and reveal how the vignette can be set in a deeper field of research and interpretation.

Reading 1: the naive reader

This is an account of a visit to a college, involving a meeting of academic colleagues from different countries. This is reflected in the relative informality of the exchanges. There is clearly a reciprocity at work where the experience of the visitor is familiar to the hosts, who may have been in similar position in colleges they may have visited abroad. In particular, notice the way the hosts display their openness, their doing things with due deliberation such as the introductions, the tea and, of course, dealing with a dud battery. There is a clear will to have the data-gathering proceed, and it almost seems that the hosts are enjoying just seeing a researcher at work. An air of relaxation grows, as does the depth of interaction. The last section is unique in that the communication now includes emotion and the account is aware of this. There is also sentimentality here, in that the writer mentions tears, most unusual for anyone from a British culture in an academic encounter.

Reading 2: the ethnographer speaks

The ethnographer is actually in possession of a great deal more of what was happening 'off camera' and this can add meaning to the vignette and generate further questions. First, the researcher had a dual role during this visit, as World Bank consultant for his own organization and as an ethnographer for his personal research. How much of the response of the interviewees is influenced by such factors as perceived access to aid funds, represented symbolically by the British Council *uniform* of navy blue blazer, grey trousers and Samsonite briefcase? Second, in having a professional interpreter present, the meeting had a device to ensure immediate translation, which meant that social interactions were not slowed and the pace of events is, it is hoped, similar to how it would be if all spoke the same language.

Another feature missing from this reading is the feeling of power that can be read into the flag immediately behind where the interviewee sat, the close-up portrait of Atatürk on the wall immediately behind her and the desk with its pens and name plate, underlining that this is where the buck stops. She is very much a public official. Perhaps the biggest symbolic issue here is dress. The discussion of this is most animated, and was regarded by the interviewer as being of the greatest relevance. In talking about dress he is writing about the most momentous issue of the day, and this is perhaps the most important subtext. The interviewer focuses on the 'headscarf' issue, but what are the subtler issues of dress and its relationship with Islam, Kemalism, power and status? The women being interviewed are conforming with government rules for wearing Western suits, but how do they dress in their home environment? How is the interviewer dressed? How is the interpreter dressed?

The emotional response of the women was a great surprise to the researcher and attributed to the particular situation. However, how much of the response was cultural, and how much visible emotion is acceptable in Turkish academic circles? Is the interviewer ethical in generating and using such emotions as data? He was also surprised by his own emotions, which may reflect how overwhelming the situation was and also suggests that the interviewer had succeeded in getting at some very significant issues.

Reading 3: a transcendent reading

We could continue to add readings in the interests of reflexivity, so how do we stop and at the same time achieve an adequate data capture? It is suggested that some means is found to judge how well this can now be incorporated in the wider ethnography. Hammersley (1992), in arguing the merits of realist, postmodern and reflexive perspectives, implies a need to have a reading which takes due account of not only the intended meaning in the text, but also the presence of the ethnographer and what he or she brings. Hence, there is a need for a reading which embraces obvious content (our first reading) and the presence of the researcher (in the second reading). As a way of dealing with this, we could now present a reading of the previous reading, our transcendent reading, and so an infinite regress starts which if you are not careful can result in you disappearing up your own orifice. So instead we turn to the fourth reading.

Reading 4: reading in context

Clearly there is a need to have a final reading that completes this ethnography for the researcher. This reading is one in which the detailed context of the research is present. In other words, the author gives the reader access to his wider research material. In this reading the wider scene is presented by considering aspects of one of the major themes within the ethnography, the issue of dress.

Dress is a constantly occurring theme in Turkish life. Certainly, the fez and veil are regarded as symbols of Islam and were banned in the 1925 Turkish Hat Law. Atatürk, in the early days of the Turkish Republic, attempted to create a unified nation and culture by the imposition of draconian measures, including the hat laws, dress codes and changes in the written script. However, as Robins (1996: 70) points out, 'Kemalism was an ideology imposed on the people from above.' A paternalistic and authoritarian regime was established which attempted to stifle the diversity and pluralism inherent in the popular culture of Turkey. However, popular culture re-emerged in the form of political Islam and left-wing socialism, and was subdued by military coup (1960, 1971 and 1980) followed by legal statute (e.g. Higher Education Law 2457 in 1981).

For Turkish women wishing to show their allegiance to Islam publicly, the banned 'veil' has become replaced by the Islamic 'turban' or headscarf. This has become an issue for the faculty academic staff. Whatever their political or religious persuasion, they are prohibited, as are all female government employees, from wearing the headscarf, but within the faculty there is a continuing increase in the number of students wearing the headscarf. Many of the staff, taking the Kemalist line, see this as a regressive phenomenon. The recent political success of the Refah Party would seem to support Gülalp's (1996: 178) view that 'Islamism is ascending' and that its real source of strength in contemporary Turkey is its 'critique of modernism in an age when modernism is in global decline'. Islamic dress, therefore, is a visible symbol of the conflict and cultural dissonance within the faculty, which is itself a metaphor for the national struggle between secularist Kemalism and political Islam. In organizational terms, the headscarf, as a symbol of the rise in political Islamism, can also be seen as a critique of the original values of the teacher training school and therefore of the values of the academic staff of the faculty.

Disadvantages

General criticisms of ethnographic research centre on issues of subjectivity and representation. At one end of the critical spectrum it is suggested that ethnography 'only captures surface appearances and not the underlying reality' (Hammersley 1990: 13). Conversely, ethnographies have been criticized as being merely rhetorical constructs or 'fictions crafted by their authors and shaped by "literary" conventions and devices' (Atkinson and Hammersley 1998: 123). Furthermore, cross-cultural ethnography, particularly in studies of Eastern or Islamic cultures, has attracted criticism drawn from the notion of cultural imperialism. Said (1978: 325), for example, poses the question, 'is the notion of a distinct culture (or race, or religion, or civilisation) a useful one, or does it always get involved, either in self-congratulation (when one discusses one's own), or hostility and aggression (when one discusses the "other")'? This worry about the position of the Western observer as Author, using the 'privileged gaze that reproduces authorial omniscience – where the voice of the ethnographer is privileged and that of Other is muted' (Atkinson and Hammersley 1998: 123), is paralleled by feminist critiques which 'challenge narrative realism and traditional naturalistic ethnography' (Denzin 1998: 334). In support of this, Denzin and Lincoln (1998: 28) advocate a more 'reflexive multi-voiced text grounded in the experiences of oppressed peoples'.

As well as the above general criticisms, which could be levelled at any piece of cross-cultural ethnographic research, there are specific criticisms which pertain to this particular organizational case study. Language is crucial in this instance because the researcher had access to the voices of the researched only via an interpreter. This raises questions about whether culture can be transmitted effectively in another language, and how much depends on the class, background and attitudes of the interpreter herself (in this case, a middle-class Turkish woman from a military family). There is also a methodological imperative here, compelling the researcher to examine his or her own subjectivity, cultural background and research strategy. Thus a white British male with a background in science, technical education and organizational behaviour has an obligation to explore, in his methodology, the answers to important questions. How much of the research was an appropriation of culture by the researcher for his own ends (getting 'good' data for a research project)? How much was he instrumental in setting up 'scenes' for his own research, in what Sayer (1992: 245) acknowledges has, in some aspects of ethnographic research, given rise to such epithets as 'empty-headed fishing expeditions'? How was the issue of reflexivity managed? Were the subjects of the research given an opportunity to read the ethnography in progress and add their views and comments? What are the implications of a male researcher working in a women's faculty? There is also the issue of the use of what Stake (1995:

130) refers to as the 'atypical and often extreme representation of persuasive vignettes which over-focus on rare and vivid moments'. Although these questions have been noted here under the heading of 'disadvantages', the self-awareness and reflective cycle of interpretation that they generate for the researcher may actually be seen as a strength.

In the end, the reader of a piece of ethnographic research must concern himself or herself with what Hammersley (1990: 70) refers to as 'the two criteria for the assessment of any social research – validity and relevance'. As Butler (1997: 928) puts it, 'the essence of empirical inquiry, is to draw an audience into a collective experience – in which a version of the true is demonstrated for that collective to judge.' Thus organizational ethnographers and the readers of their work must attempt to answer the question posed by Tsoukas (1989: 551): 'to what extent can organisational knowledge acquired through explanatory idiographic studies, be regarded as valid?'

Advantages

As Stacey (1996: 261) puts it, a 'residual notion that a researcher is some kind of independent, objective observer has to be abandoned. Intervening in an organisation always affects it.' Easterby-Smith *et al.* (1991: 38) suggest that, in research into organizational culture, ethnographic fieldwork can 'create understanding of meaning systems, extend conventional wisdom and generate new insights into human behaviour'. The advantages of such an approach are reinforced by Bryman (1988: 29), who says that the results 'tend to be sensitive to the nuances of what people say and to the contexts in which their actions take place. The emphasis tends to be on understanding what is going on in organisations in participants' own terms rather than those of the researcher.'

In this particular piece of research the approach is consciously polyphonic, multivoiced and interpretive in an attempt to 'elicit interviewees' views of their worlds, their work, and the events they have experienced or observed' (Rubin and Rubin 1995: 35). The ethnography and, more specifically, the example vignette are intended to act as the link joining culture and fieldwork, and this link, as Van Maanen (1988: 4–6) puts it, 'entails far more than merely writing up the results – a culture or cultural practice is as much created by the writing as it determines the writing itself'. Rosen (1991: 280) describes the process as an interpretation of what the ethnographer observes, experiences or is told, 'recording this cultural data in field notes and consciously or unconsciously letting it settle against a tableau of meaning structures within his or her own imaginings.' The research account and the vignette may usefully be examined using Butler's (1997: 930) theatrical metaphor, which suggests that there are three types of participant in any social inquiry, *the inquirer* or *narrator* (the researcher and writer of the study), the *actors* (the subjects of the inquiry) and the *audience* (the various users or readers of the inquiry's findings). Vignettes which illustrate the research process by discussing, describing and explaining the feelings and experiences of the inquirer are therefore placing the inquirer firmly in the *play* itself, as one of the actors. The audience is therefore being asked to judge the validity of an autobiographical account of the inquirer's research experience. As Butler (1997: 933) puts it: 'to accept this position is to accept that the inquirer is "of the data".' Van Maanen's confessional and impressionist tales, for example, are certainly conscious examples of ethnographers creating what Hammersley (1992: 2) refers to as a 'product of their participation in the field rather than a mere reflection of the phenomena studied'. Let us briefly examine each of the readings in this light.

Reading 1 is certainly a plausible reading and serves to clarify a good deal of this encounter as an intercultural exchange, telling a small story, creating an atmosphere and setting up questions in the reader's mind. This glimpse of a private world could be a piece of journalistic reportage, an example of oral history, an extract from the fieldworker's diary or a piece of narrative fiction. It is seductive, with an air of spontaneity and drama often missing from academic discourse. It is also dynamic, in that it reaches a dramatic climax and could therefore be 'performed' as a monologue or a scene in a play. In reading 2 the ethnographer acknowledges his own presence and provides the reader with some answers as well as some new questions which perhaps increase the depth of the discourse between reader, researcher and text. Finally, in reading 4 the contextual reading not only highlights the richness of the data in the vignette but also shows how the vignette itself places the research process and researcher presence on the wider stage of theory, literature, historical and political context. The reader is encouraged to ask further questions, but also, perhaps, to investigate areas of particular interest and create new research and discourse.

Hence arises the final question, is the vignette a legitimate representational device in ethnographic research into organizational culture? Schein (1992: 187) argues that the main concern of the researcher into organizational culture should be the 'discovery and accurate description of the phenomenological reality as experienced by both the outsider and the insider' and, although there is no formula for this, the description should be 'objective in describing artefacts and espoused values and empathic in describing basic shared assumptions as they are experienced by insiders' (*ibid.*). Hammersley (1992: 2) suggests that the validity of 'realist' ethnography lies in its superior 'ability to capture the nature of social phenomena'. The vignette clearly 'thickens' (Geertz 1973) the description, and gives the reader access to the natural and spontaneous reactions of researcher and researched, thereby creating an atmospheric story. Such moments are essential in the representation process, providing the reader with the experience of excitement and spine-tingling feeling of recognition which make ethnographic fieldwork worth doing. The vignette is the thread connecting researcher, researched and reader in a discourse of shared human experience.

Key reading

Butler, R. (1997) Stories and experiments in social inquiry. *Organisation Studies*, 18(6): 927–48.
Watson, T. J. (1997) Theorising managerial work: a pragmatic pluralist approach to interdisciplinary research. *British Journal of Management*, 8: 3–8.

References

Adler, P. and Adler, P. (1998) Observational techniques. In N. Denzin and Y. Lincoln (eds) *Collecting and Interpreting Qualitative Materials*. Newbury Park, CA: Sage.
Atkinson, P. and Hammersley, M. (1998) Ethnography and participant observation. In N. K. Denzin and Y. S. Lincoln (eds) *Strategies of Qualitative Inquiry*. London: Sage.
Brannen, M. Y. (1996) Ethnographic international management research. In B. J. Punnet and O. Shenkar (eds) *Handbook for International Management Research*. Oxford: Blackwell.
Brown, A. D. (1994) *Organisational Culture*. London: Pitman.
Bryman, A. (1988) *Research Methods and Organisation Studies*. London: Routledge.
Butler, R. (1997) Stories and experiments in social inquiry. *Organisation Studies*, 18(6): 927–48.
Cassell, C. and Symon, G. (eds) (1994) *Qualitative Methods in Organisational Research: A Practical Guide*. London: Sage.
Delamont, S. (1996) Just like the novels: researching the occupational culture(s) of higher education. In R. Cuthbert (ed.) *Working in Higher Education*. Buckingham: SRHE and Open University Press.
Denzin, N. K. (1998) The art and politics of interpretation. In N. K. Denzin and Y. S. Lincoln (eds) *Collecting and Interpreting Qualitative Materials*. London: Sage.
Denzin, N. K. and Lincoln, Y. S. (eds) (1998) *Strategies of Qualitative Inquiry*. London: Sage.
Easterby-Smith, M., Thorpe, R. and Lowe, A. (1991) *Management Research: An Introduction*. London: Sage.
Fetterman, D. M. (1989) *Ethnography Step by Step*. London: Sage.
Geertz, C. (1973) *The Interpretation of Cultures*. New York: Basic Books.
Gülalp, H. (1995) The crisis of Westernisation in Turkey: Islamism versus nationalism. *Innovation*, 8(2): 175–82.

Hammersley, M. (1990) *Reading Ethnographic Research: A Critical Guide*. London: Longman.

Hammersley, M. (1992) *What's Wrong with Ethnography? Methodological Explorations*. London: Routledge.

Hammersley, M. and Atkinson, P. (1995) *Ethnography: Principles in Practice*, 2nd edn. London: Routledge.

Pope, N. and Pope, H. (1997) *Turkey Unveiled: Ataturk and After*. London: John Murray.

Richardson, L. (1995) Narrative and sociology. In J. Van Maanen (ed.) *Representation in Ethnography*. Newbury Park, CA: Sage.

Robins, K. (1996) Interrupting identities: Turkey/Europe. In S. Hall and P. Du Gay (eds) *Questions of Cultural Identity*. London: Sage.

Rosen, M. (1991) Scholars, travellers, thieves: on concept, method and cunning in organizational ethnography. In P. J. Frost (ed.) *Reframing Organizational Culture*. London: Sage.

Rubin, H. J. and Rubin, I. S. (1995) *Qualitative Interviewing: The Art of Hearing Data*. London: Sage.

Sackmann, S. A. (ed.) (1997) *Cultural Complexity in Organizations: Inherent Contrasts and Contradictions*. London: Sage.

Said, E. (1978) *Orientalism*. London: Routledge, Kegan and Paul.

Sayer, A. (1992) *Method in Social Science: A Realist Approach*, 2nd edn. London: Routledge.

Schein, E. H. (1992) *Organisational Culture and Leadership*, 2nd edn. San Francisco: Jossey Bass.

Spradley, J. P. (1980) *Participant Observation*. London: Holt, Rinehart and Wilson.

Stacey, R. D. (1996) *Complexity and Creativity in Organizations*. San Francisco: Berret Koehler Publishers.

Stake, R. E. (1995) *The Art of Case Study Research*. London: Sage.

Tsoukas, H. (1989) The validity of idiographic research explanations. *The Academy of Management Review*, 14(4): 551–61.

Van Maanen, J. (1988) *Tales of the Field: On Writing Ethnography*. Chicago: The University of Chicago Press.

Watson, T. J. (1994) *In Search of Management: Culture Chaos and Control in Managerial Work*. London: Routledge.

Watson, T. J. (1997) Theorising managerial work: a pragmatic pluralist approach to interdisciplinary research. *British Journal of Management*, 8: 3–8.

Wright, L. L. (1996) Qualitative international management research. In B. J. Punnet and O. Shenkar (eds) *Handbook for International Management Research*. Oxford: Blackwell.

16 **Silence:** absence and context

CHRISTINE NOBLE

Researchers have yet to focus on the language of silence, yet in many situations silence is already automatically interpreted by the reader. Reading the meaning of silence in a text intimately involves the reader's subjectivity and the context in which he or she is positioned. The following brief examples illustrate the practical reading of silence and its forms, situated in socio-historical and cultural contexts. Silence can actively be used to demonstrate or defend a plethora of relationships. On BBC Radio Four's *Survivors* (May 1997), for example, an autobiographical account was given of one youth's struggle to stay free, and to stay alive, in Uganda under Idi Amin's regime: 'Dogs were barking, cows mooing, buses running, people getting ready for work. The sounds of pots and pans . . . woken by silence. Dogs stop barking because either a leopard is about or soldiers trampling and trucks and engines. Soldiers shot dogs, pigs, hens, chickens and women.' Silence signified the arrival of the soldiers and the narrator was captured and held for five years. Here, the meaning of silence is embedded in a cultural and historical context and is dependent on this. It lies between the sound of normal life and the action of danger. It transforms the noisy calm into violence. Here the discourse of silence can function as a precursor to two potential sources of human destruction: animal and human threats, leopards and soldiers. Silence is an intermediary between peace and war and is integral to the text's meaning.

Here is another example of culturally bound silence where a Malawian native exclaims: 'I woke to a glorious sound this morning: the sound of no rain' (BBC Radio Four, *Today*, April 1997). Here, the meanings of silence can be made explicit by the following connections. An unseasonably late monsoon rain increases the mosquito population and leads to maize rotting, culminating in the threat of famine and disease. Without food there is widespread socio-cultural disruption when there is a secondary danger of the people being unable to perform their cultural rituals and social practices. Life experiences are diverse and influence the context of silence. Silence is constructed to construe the effects of no rain on the population. Its presence functions effectively to transform rain as a danger to the silence of no rain as a source for celebration following relief.

Language is reflexive and unites cognitive perceptions and experiential repertoires. Like being human, speech is unstable and unpredictable; it is active and possesses its own evolving form. The experience of being human cannot be categorized into hierarchies of knowledge; each person's experience should be taken as equal and subjectively valid. The concept of objectivity should have no place in the study of humanity. Emphasis is placed here on the narrative accounts given by an individual, which represent a given experience that alters circumstances, relationships and possible outcomes in people's lives. The emerging discursive repertoires provide the data for discourse analysis, which explicitly relies on the role of intuition and interpersonal interaction (Gilbert and Mulkay 1984).

The silence of oppression disempowers people. Many assume that people are equal, but disparities of wealth, power, values, attitudes and beliefs render societies unequal. Oppression occurs worldwide and is sometimes enforced by gang activity. Politically, government bans and censorship conceal existing injustices and power inequalities, where completely 'open talk' is punishable and there is an incitement to silence.

For example, Carl Rogers and Ruth Sanford in South Africa advocated talking as a successful ingredient for the psychotherapeutic process (Swartz 1986). Psychotherapy relies on a hermeneutic circle where language facilitates a process of interpretation-action, the action leading to a return to dialogue (Fruggeri 1992). This process involves reflexivity as language is exchanged between the two participants and brings about change. 'Completely open talk' is endorsed by Rogers and Sanford. However, talking itself can be used as a defence strategy, caused by an asymmetry in the relationships in which clients are encouraged to talk about their private selves. If the therapist offered an account of his or her life narrative, for example, it would contravene the philosophy of the therapeutic process. Swartz (1986) argues that 'Talk in the context of silence can become little more than a smokescreen for that silence.' Arbitrary issues are avoided by silence, which can thereby provide an authentic and arguably a more powerful antidote to discourse. Silence can have a dual function. Silence can act as a defence or it can be a precursor to resistance when primary issues fail to be raised. Silence may therefore render language impotent during the course of a therapeutic encounter. In hospital settings, the 'therapeutic effect' of the relationship is also outweighed by institutional power.

When I worked on hospital wards for many years, dangerous situations did not produce fear and I was able to respond in an emotionally detached way. Here lies the paradox of care in community care homes. On the wards there is at least the opportunity for support from staff and patients to combat isolation, while in the often privately run community home environment violence is neither accepted nor anticipated. Should it occur, the nurse is expected to act her role and an objective response is anticipated by the residents. There is a danger of the nurse being lulled into a false sense of security, and the residents are also unable to predict the consequences of a specific behaviour. Conflict can arise even though the nurse should not use violence, even in the case of self-defence, while residents sometimes do have the right to do so. Equal status and power cannot totally be shared for legal reasons. The nurse possesses power with status. This involves holding keys to the office and drugs cabinet. To give residents this responsibility is in breach of the law. Staff members have their own 'staff' toilet, implying that their wastage differs from the residents'. Many staff members use staff cups; again suggesting discrimination and fear of contamination.

These are some reasons why the merging of theory and practice is illusory in institutional settings, why the two cannot be totally reconciled. In the hospital setting equality in relationships is not endorsed by staff who derive reward from the power obtained from the unbalanced distribution of status. Staff also become institutionalized and must accept a hierarchical structure whose members range from the domestics to the hospital Managing Directors. Domestic jobs are described using a small 'd', in contrast to large 'M' and 'D' for Managing Directors, highlighting the differences in the roles they play. Nurses at ward management level are discouraged from talking to patients by being kept busy with administrative bureaucracy, having to rely instead on nursing assistant or student nurse feedback.

Text

The text here is my own account of an event in a nursing home for those diagnosed as 'chronic schizophrenics', where the verbal sharing of experience is encouraged. The philosophy of care endorsed by the nurses directly opposes that of a therapeutic regime where the therapist's life narrative is absent.

After lunch Malcolm refused to wash his plate. 'You're an arse,' the obsessional Barry churlishly repeated. 'I know,' Malcolm mumbled and strode into the dining area where he rapidly paced the floor. Up and down. Tony entered the lounge quietly and sat in an armchair. His feet were shaking involuntarily. After kicking the lamp down, Malcolm lay on the couch opposite Tony. His eyeballs were flickering, seeking escape. Many self-derogatory voices swept through his mind. Both men were silent and the air was attacked by a thick, lingering smog. The younger Malcolm tossed ash on to the carpet. Barry was tinkering around in the kitchen, religiously preparing his meal. Tony's feet tapped rhythmically. Four minutes felt like thirty. Malcolm sprang up. His eyes glared; his pupils piercing like pissholes in the green snow. 'Stand back Tony.' Tony rose and precisely shielded his face using his arms. His dancing stopped. He clenched his teeth. The pair froze in time like sculptures exuding adrenalin waves. Silence again . . . Malcolm resumed his horizontal stance and unexpectedly chuckled to himself for hours. He apologized to Tony. Barry had silently vacated the vicinity.

The site is a communal home for the rehabilitation of chronic schizophrenics. There are six male members and one female member of staff. Only three residents feature in the text. The relationships formed between the three residents are as follows. Barry is a member of the Hindu-based Hari Krishna movement and through time his beliefs have gained acceptance and respect. He was initially labelled a schizophrenic following an attempted self-castration during his first year studying mathematics at a Midlands university. Malcolm is considered by all to be the most 'disturbed' because of his violent acts and his self-neglect. Tony is new to the group. He has experienced many years in a hospital and is coping well with communal life.

In this vignette, Barry upsets Malcolm by shouting obscenities at him. This may appear surprising since he is a religious devotee, but Malcolm knows that Barry frequently behaves in this way. Barry's outburst is seen as an exhibition of his misdirected and misplaced internal anger. Malcolm cannot control his embarrassment legitimately and projects his frustration onto Tony to defend his credibility. Tony realizes the warnings and responds actively. Malcolm can remember the tensions he created a few weeks previously. The victim was absent in this extract, where Malcolm wants to see Tony's response. Perhaps he knows that he cannot be penalized because of his long-term mental history. Pressing criminal charges was discouraged by the police following Malcolm's assault after the previous incident. The victim then sat passively in a chair while he was punched in his face, nose and mouth.

Silence cannot be accessed directly, so I have *created* this text. It is a fiction, a representation designed to evoke silence. It is based on events in a real community home, but the names have been changed to honour residents' confidentiality. In this description, silence, like language, is changing and dynamic; it progresses and develops. It occurs in the presence of others and becomes a form of discourse. Like discourse, silence requires interpretation and incorporates action. The analysis of silence and action here is discourse analysis.

Reading

Silence can be more powerful than speech. The opening paragraph shows how a speech act can provoke or instigate violence but silence defuses and dissolves the danger or threat. 'Tony enters the lounge quietly . . .' The fact that Tony's behaviour is quiet suggests that he is not a threat to others and may be vulnerable to danger should it emerge. Later he becomes a potential victim. The action of his feet is ambiguous and could have two separate meanings. Either he is acutely anxious or it is an effect of prescribed drugs. This suggests that Tony may not be reacting to fear as the reader might initially interpret.

Next comes a real threat of danger manifested when Malcolm actively kicks a lamp down. Again silence appears and because of the action of Malcolm's eyes he appears disturbed. If his eyeballs are seeking escape, then so too is his aggression. Then, accompanying silence we have further signs of mental distress: 'Many self-derogatory voices swept through his mind.' Intrusive phenomena are thought to affect Malcolm's thoughts and his subsequent action. Non-smokers will appreciate the next sentence and the activity of cigarette smoke. The scene is silently set for combat just as in an old Western film where two cowboys silently prepare themselves.

Malcolm again manifests 'inappropriate' behaviour by not using an ashtray. After initiating the incident with his rudeness, Barry is safely in the kitchen playing with his pots and pans. Tony continues to incur side-effects from his medication. Time stands still. And then 'silence snaps', just like when the 'straw breaks the camel's back'. Time and silence are personified. Again, Malcolm's eyes show his immediate propensity to violence.

Until now the three characters have been physically isolated from each other. Instead of sharing their potentially intersubjective space they create separate, individual spaces. Usually, Malcolm would sit near Tony and initiate conversation. Their detachment symbolically suggests that something is wrong. Tony and Malcolm are in close proximity and facing each other only when there is potential physical danger. Before this Tony was sitting down, but he neutralizes the physical imbalance by standing.

Tony defends himself by raising his arms to shield his face. This symbolic action suggests that he is not unduly anxious and he is focused on fighting; Tony 'throws down the gauntlet'. There is silence while the two are embroiled in their confrontation. Barry, realizing silent danger, leaves the situation. The interrelations represented by silence and shared by the characters are integral to the outcome. There is an anticlimax when danger disappears. As Malcolm chuckles, silence dies. It is difficult to interpret Malcolm's behaviour. Malcolm always displays uncharacteristic behaviour prior to acts of violence. He paces the floor rapidly and swears to himself and at others. His speech becomes incoherent and hostile and he punches his fist forcefully against a wall.

Staff were not present during the initial act of violence but one member was present during the course of the present event. Malcolm glimpsed the nurse, who was positioned sitting in a nearby chair. And then Malcolm chuckled and the danger disappeared. All residents have experienced hospital life. Once an inpatient, the individual is stripped of responsibility for himself or herself and is expected to play the provided role. Residents become actors who are forced to play accepted parts. They are stripped of their individuality and their sense of self is concealed by their masks. As people, they cease to exist. The individual then shares a united identity, belonging to the group of patients (Goffman 1959).

Major tranquillizers have two forms of coercive power (or, using the psychiatric terminology, 'action'). Power in this context is psychological and physical. Their main effect is sedation, yet foot tapping actions may occur. Tony also makes a noise like a braying horse. Medication and the hospital experience effectively complement each other to encourage 'irresponsible behaviour'.

The variability of discursive silence is evident in this extract, where silence substitutes for speech. Initially, silence is passive as Tony enters the lounge, but it develops and constructs patterns and shapes with differing tensions. Barry's vulgarity at the beginning causes tension. Malcolm feels tense and embarrassed and does not seem to possess the vocabulary to express himself. Tony observes Malcolm's behaviour while Malcolm paces the floor, knocks down the lamp and flicks ash on the carpet. When Tony is verbally threatened everyone feels tense; the nurse was aware of potential danger from the beginning. When Malcolm chuckled there was an abrupt cessation of tension. Because of the characters' interrelationship they knew by the sound of Malcolm laughing that he was no longer hostile. And Barry, the instigator, was absent.

Silence with its various layers develops through the use of metaphor. During silence, the air is 'attacked by a thick, lingering smog'. The atmosphere is dense with smoke as if it could be cut with a knife. Then Malcolm's eyes are personified as they glare; they represent Malcolm as a whole being with accompanying tension and anger. They are silently active and function as a sign of danger. 'The pair froze in time like sculptures exuding adrenalin waves.' It might seem that both are in a state of catatonic stupor but the mention of adrenalin is another indication of stress and the potential for action (in this case aggression) in the presence of silence. During this time, silence renders sound impotent. Barry was harmlessly 'tinkering around in the kitchen'. Silence by now elicits more power; silence is an explicit threat, sound is harmless.

Disadvantages: power, subjectivity and silence

Because of institutionalization and medication regimes in community care homes, residents' behaviour and motor skills appear bizarre. They walk with a gait and sometimes salivate. Their speech can be incoherent and its content unintelligible. These can be modified with time but it may be years before a resident ceases to be defined as coming from 'that funny house'. People they meet adopt a superior status because of their claims to normality. However, their attitude is just as demeaning as those of senior hospital staff. Consequently, residents realize that as individuals they are neither welcome nor accepted by others.

They perceive their environment as hostile, especially if their presence is totally ignored, as if they did not exist. Their invisibility fails to create any form of social comparison and their rights as members in the community are confiscated by others. This results in mutual dissatisfaction and distrust and they feel alienated in their new world. It is easy for one diagnosed as a 'paranoid schizophrenic' to possess 'suspicious ideation' correctly.

During my analysis I have omitted my own silence. I thought this was because I had problems with uniting myself and the residents and was creating a 'them/me' syndrome. On reflection, I was actually embarrassed by the motives for my silence. I was trying to attain objectivity when I was subjectively involved as a potential victim of violence. Even though I didn't withdraw from the situation, I have found my own fear too personal to explain. Another omission was my failure to expand on the metaphor, 'His pupils were like pissholes in green snow.' Here again I felt awkward because of my lack of written refinement. However, I am not apologizing and trust that the metaphor speaks for itself (by the way, Malcolm has green eyes).

So far I have given a reading of a real life event which is dependent on several contextual factors. I have provided a critical analysis to help the reader to understand the dynamics and progression of the text. I have been positioned as privileged, where my role is that of the 'expert'. I have access to the residents' notes even though they have all individually retold their life narratives to me. To be truly critical I should point out my own doubts about the process of writing this chapter. As mainstream psychologists endlessly criticize research dominated by the 'turn to language' and the lack of rigour in investigation, I myself am aware of possible problem areas in this field. One problem with analysing my own prose is the difficulty in working with subjectivity, since it is *my* account and my version of reality is the one that is 'empowered' by the text. If the extract is subjective, my reflections and interpretation are therefore hearsay.

One predominant disadvantage with discourse analysis concerns interpretation. I was unable to provide multiple readings from those who shared the same experience; they do not possess the potential to retell the event in a 'normally' coherent form. As a self-elected representative, my gloss is solely available for the reader's inference. No matter how easy I find it to be subjective in an ethnographic setting (owing to my honorary membership), my interpretation is based on one life narrative. I have therefore alternated between comparative subjectivity, where I am able to be authentic, and objectivity, whereby I deny any emotion and feeling and wear a mask to conceal my individuality.

Although I have explained the changing facets of silence *per se*, I have not described how both speech and silence in this extract have altered social relationships. Since the event, changes have been intangible. There have not been any salient changes to the group as a whole but instead there exists an addition to each member's life narrative.

Advantages, and other reflections

My life narrative differs from the others. I qualified as a psychiatric nurse 16 years ago and am granted respect and prestige from other residents. I am the 'knower'; one whose role is to act should a crisis occur. I am inaccurately judged by others as having knowledge of the truth as a whole, instead of possessing just one form of collective knowledge. During various discussions with residents I am frequently asked for advice and reassurance.

Despite sharing the same social world as the residents for five and a half years, subjectivity is difficult to value, especially because of my training, when I was constantly taught to be objective at all times. Subjectivity and objectivity are bipolar terms, whereas in the social world such extremes are equally unattainable. Therefore a carer's approach in any working context is a combination of the two. By being aware of and questing for subjectivity I have a baseline for my endeavours. Consciously developed subjectivity produces a template for my philosophy of care. Because I felt tense and apprehensive during this potentially explosive incident, subjectivity became obvious and pressing.

It is also now possible to work reflexivity with the construction and analysis of the text. Silence as discourse externally creates objects which can aid or limit the subjective experience. I have been able to offer my reflections on the text while I described the experience of other characters and make it clear that I am the one who has storied them into being. The use of both simile and metaphor helps to construct interpretive resources and then open up the possibility of evoking and displaying part of the life world of the home.

Pragmatically, this writing facilitated the resumption of my existing relationship with Malcolm, as I was no longer hindered by apprehension and fear. Our relationship is mutually authentic, in which positive regard is encouraged for the first time in Malcolm's life experience.

Initially I had the notion of writing a follow-up about a different event and of comparing changes in the functions of silence. But I wouldn't consider this exercise valuable unless I anticipate that silence will itself change. I would merely be creating a set of different and independent silences and I am aware of the probability of multiple outcomes.

Like knowledge, two silences are never the same. Repeated reading of the text creates superimmersion leading to overinterpretation, when the researcher may become incarcerated by her own imagination. I have curtailed the analysis abruptly so as not to contaminate it excessively with my expression of personal frustration, caused by my endeavour to seek pure subjectivity (and objectivity), which people are incapable of. My analysis stopped when my dilemmas seemed to take precedence over anything else.

The advantages of interpretation are multifaceted. It is a tool of analysis (Nikander 1995). It explains identifiable problems and diverging perspectives of a marginalized population and helps the group to find a collective voice. It makes explicit the ordinary experiences of participants to the reader (Denzin 1989) and facilitates an understanding and clarification of their collective life world.

Through interpretation, the language of silence provides an illuminating insight into group interaction and relationships. Without the provision of a version of meaning the reader would gain only a superficial understanding of the text. Although this action-based form of inquiry has been ignored by mainstream psychologists, its technique remains rigorous since it involves observation and the defining of existing issues. It also formulates rules of behaviour and social life while retaining its critical potential.

The analysis of silence reveals the function of non-linguistic communication, while the analysis of aspects of institutional silence reveals structures of power and oppression. This can improve the services available to the characters in the text by formulating ways of including individual choice and thereby improving quality of life.

Interpretation also highlights one main disadvantage with all theoretical frameworks: they cannot be applied directly to people because of the unfixed nature of the social world. I have treated my own text as an ongoing vehicle for change and correspondingly addressed the notion of reflexivity. I have aimed to create the potential for personal and social change. Readers' beliefs and attitudes may be modified but I have not enhanced the residents' lives on a micro level, and none of the readers are likely to meet them.

However, I hope that the reader will gain insight into the enigma of 'schizophrenia' in order to benefit those collectively described as 'schizophrenic'. This requires an understanding of the pervasive effects of power and control following imposed institutionalization and the administration of neuroleptics, culminating in exclusion from mainstream society. We have no equation or computer program to map the dynamics of our species; only the resources of our own interest and involvement. Without these, change is impossible.

Key reading

Nikander, P. (1995) The turn to the text: the critical potential of discursive social psychology. *Nordiske Udkast*, 2: 3–15.
Swartz, L. (1986) Carl Rogers in South Africa: the issue of silence. *Psychology in Society*, 5: 139–43.

References

Denzin, N. K. (1989) *Interpretative Interactionism*. London: Sage.
Fruggeri, L. (1992) Therapeutic process as the social construction of change. In S. McNamee and K. J. Gergen (eds) *Therapy as Social Construction*. London: Sage.
Gilbert, N. and Mulkay, M. (1984) *Opening Pandora's Box: A Sociological Analysis of Scientists' Discourse*. Cambridge: Cambridge University Press.
Goffman, E. (1959) *The Presentation of Self in Everyday Life*. Reading, MA: Cox and Wyman.
Goffman, E. (1961) *Encounters*. New York: Bobbs Merrill Company.
Nikander, P. (1995) The turn to the text: the critical potential of discursive social psychology. *Nordiske Udkast*, 2: 3–15.
Stringer, E. T. (1996) *Action Research: A Handbook for Practitioners*. London: Sage.
Swartz, L. (1986) Carl Rogers in South Africa: the issue of silence. *Psychology in Society*, 5: 139–43.

17 Action: self-advocacy and change

DAN GOODLEY

This chapter reflects upon part of a wider research project that examined self-advocacy groups in the lives of people with learning difficulties (Goodley 1997, 1998a, b). The term 'learning difficulties' is used to describe people who have been labelled at some point in their lives as requiring specialist 'mental handicap services' (Walmsley 1993: 46). Typically, self-advocacy groups are made up of members with learning difficulties ('self-advocates') who attend meetings voluntarily, supported by non-disabled supporters ('advisors'). Experiences, good and bad, are divulged, opinions are shared and action is taken by the group, for and with members. Part of my research aimed to find out how self-advocacy groups work, how they were organized, what processes occurred, what support was offered and what self-advocates got out of involvement. My study drew upon various reference points, some of which are outlined below.

First, a methodology was needed that dealt with the qualitative richness of group dynamics. Ethnography appealed. Ethnographic study has been used to examine the processes and actions in various social contexts where members are people with learning difficulties (e.g. Edgerton 1967, 1984a, b; Braginsky and Braginsky 1971; Bogdan and Taylor 1982). Ethnography is a useful technique for discovering beliefs, meanings and *practices* within a culture (Glaser and Strauss 1967). Social settings can be seen as having cultures: a set of traditional ways of feeling, thinking and *acting* (Edgerton 1984b: 501). To get at these cultural artefacts, ethnography employs a whole host of qualitative methods, including participant observation (Edgerton 1967), in-depth involvement (Atkinson and Williams 1990), interviews (Potts and Fido 1991) and story collection (Angrosino 1994). For my study, the ethnographic project relied mainly on participant observation and qualitative description in field notes, though the form of observational method adopted in ethnography involves more than simply observing a social context. It requires interaction with a social group, becoming part of the group's processes, to understand the symbolic nature of meaning within social action (Sidell 1993: 109).

Second, my ethnographic study aimed to ground understandings of self-advocacy groups in the actions of group members. Ethnographers attempt to grasp the native's point of view, relation to life and vision of the world (Malinowski 1922). This involves getting to know people by being there, alongside them, during ordinary days, to try to capture their experiences at first hand (Atkinson 1993: 59). Ethnography is an immersion within the deep culture of a social group that attempts to find hidden treasures and submerged dangers. In theory, ethnography is committed to representing the *actions* of insiders, in this case self-advocates and their supporters in self-advocacy groups. Moreover, ethnographers ground their analyses in everyday realities of social groups, thus making for 'bottom-up' explorations (see Lincoln and Guba 1985). A dialectical process is formed as the ethnographic enterprise goes beyond behaviour to inquire about attached and associated meanings. The artefacts and natural objects of a culture are described and considered in terms of the meanings that people assign to these objects. These 'grounded theory' analyses start with data and remain close to data (Glaser and Strauss 1967; Charmaz 1995), but the ethnographer goes beyond the data to discover the meanings of subjectivity and action to cultural members. In theory, then, ethnography's links with grounded theory and bottom-up analyses fit the aims of examining self-advocacy in action from the inside.

Third, my study was guided by an adherence to a social model of disability. This model redresses ideology which creates the illusion that disability resides within the impaired individual (Oliver 1990, 1996). Instead, disablement that inhabits every walk of life in late capitalism is opposed through the self-organization of the disabled people's movement (see BCODP 1992). Self-advocacy groups are part of this wider new social movement and their actions thus feed into the development of a social model that deconstructs and reconstructs disabling ideas and actions (Goodley 1997). Consequently, I aimed to consider the actions inside groups in terms of how they reflected and perhaps built upon a social model of disability in practice.

Fourth, the theorizing and actions of proponents of the social model, and disabled activists like self-advocates, parallel Karl Marx's notion of revolutionizing practice:

> The materialist doctrine that men [*sic*] are products of circumstances and upbringing, and that, therefore, changed men are products of other circumstances and changed upbringing, forgets that it is men who change circumstances and the educator must himself be educated. Hence this doctrine is bound to divide society into two parts, one of which is superior to society. The coincidence of the changing of circumstances and of human activity can be conceived and rationally understood only as revolutionising practice.
>
> (Marx 1968: 28)

Self-advocacy groups can be seen as vehicles for social change driven by people with the label of learning difficulties themselves. Indeed, as my ethnography progressed, it became increasingly apparent that the actions of self-advocates, and their supporters, were revolutionizing in the sense that bit-by-bit the subject positions of people with learning difficulties (and indeed supporters) were undergoing change. My analysis of action aimed to pick up on these nuances and subtle changing relations of power.

Previous literature on self-advocacy groups has tended to focus on constitutional and structural facets like *group type* (service-based versus independent; see Crawley 1988) and various *positions of advisors* (professionals versus volunteers; see Worrel 1988). Advisors who are professionals (care assistants, social workers, psychologists etc.) have been attacked on the grounds that their professional accreditation, or the professionalized structures that they work within, inevitably stifle the development of self-advocacy within groups (Hanna 1978). Hence, though there has been an increase in the number of groups, this does not necessarily relate to an increase in tangible and meaningful opportunities for self-advocacy and self-determination (Crawley 1988: 47). My study, orchestrated by an ethnographic attention to action, picked up on the subtle and free-floating dynamics of self-advocacy groups in action. Specifically, one major theme emerged – the 'support' offered by non-disabled supporters (advisors) in the group – which became the focus on my discursive analysis.

Text: 'action texts'

The texts that are analysed in this chapter are taken from a broader discursive analysis of the actions of supporters in self-advocacy groups (see Goodley 1997, 1998a, b). According to Fairclough (1989), discourses are social phenomena in the sense that whenever people speak, listen, write, read or *act*, they do so in ways which are determined socially and have social impacts. Moreover, a relationship exists between social events and more durable social structures that shape and are shaped by these events. In this sense, then, *discourses* and *practices* are inseparable: both refer to either what people are doing on a particular occasion, or what people habitually do given a certain sort of occasion. That is, both can refer to either (linguistic) action or convention:

> The social nature of discourse and practice always implies social conventions – any discourse or practice implies social conventional types of discourse or practice . . . people are enabled through being constrained: they are able to act on condition that they act within the constraints of types of practice – or of discourse. However, this makes social practice sound more rigid than it is . . . being socially constrained does not preclude being creative.
>
> (Fairclough 1989: 28)

Fairclough makes an important point here about discourse and practice: that where there is power there is also *resistance* (Foucault 1975). This notion of resistance to oppressive discourses recognizes a key issue associated with power. We are not simply empty vessels receiving powerfulness or powerlessness. More than that, we *reproduce* power in various ways, with good or bad effects upon others and ourselves. As Oliver (1996: 144) points out: 'Understanding societal responses to long-term disability is no simple task and requires us to analyse ourselves and the discourses we use in order to talk about out world.'

Taking advisors' actions – or interventions of support – within groups, I examined how they reflected and reproduced discourses of disability (see Goodley 1998b). It appeared that advisors were open to reversing, changing, moving, building upon and rejecting altogether ways of acting. Throughout my ethnography it was as if 'good' and 'bad' interventions were available to advisors, just as different discourses float above and between us, meanings slipping and sliding (Howe 1994: 522). For me, there were no 'good' or 'bad' advisors. If anything, there were some who appeared to be more prone to act upon discourses that assumed individual pathology on the part of self-advocates, while others seemed more able to link practice clearly with assumptions of competence.

Such an ethnographic exploration of action requires outsiders to formulate understandings that are in tune with the interests of insiders as well as those of the researcher (Peberdy 1993: 54). Consequently, Halfpenny (1984: 3–8) suggests that researchers should show how their interpretations are bound up with the study of a culture by detailing descriptions of activities, verbatim accounts of talk, key illustrations of their interpretations and a chronology of research experience. In doing so, a reflexive account can consider to some extent the interplay between the researcher's subjectivity, cited incidents of the culture and the analyses that are made. However, reflexivity only captures select examples of interplay. When notes are taken, life is

These two vignettes are taken from my observational field notes of one of the four self-advocacy groups that I was involved with. These supporters, Julia and Dennis, were paid by the group to support the members at meetings and at training days offered by the group. Their actions are interesting because as paid workers they had had much time to conceptualize their roles, their support and consequently their actions:

> Robert, Jonny and Andy went to the bank to pay in some money. We stood at the counter, along with Dennis the supporter. The clerk looked up to catch the eye of Dennis. However, Dennis must have anticipated this and was looking over at Robert. The clerk noticed this and asked Robert what she could do for him.

> The British Telecom engineer walked into the office. Looking around the room his gaze finally fell upon Julia [the supporter]. 'I've come to sort the phones out, is that right?' he asked. Julia shrugged her shoulders and looked over to one of the members Robert. Robert responded, 'Yes that's right, we need the phones fitted upstairs and downstairs.' The engineer and Robert went upstairs and were still chatting away half an hour later.

In terms of presentation, two points emerge from this text. First, I have used written text (the frozen word) to make sense of action (animated movement). Immediately the timing, movement and 'moment' of the actions are stripped away. Second, notice how the spoken word enters the description, giving necessary context and detail. While this might not always be the case, combining action and spoken word obviously invites clarity but also raises questions about analysing action alone. With respect to my analysis, the reference points outlined above are called upon and into question by these two 'action text' examples.

summarized, distorted, discarded, ignored and storied (Plummer 1983). Further, as much as I made conscious efforts not to, my observations were in part directed by the aforementioned reference points in mind. Schatzman and Strauss (1973: 99–103) acknowledge that ethnographers will inevitably combine 'observational notes' (the who, what, when, where and how of human activity) with 'theoretical notes' (interpretations, inferences, hypotheses and conjectures) and 'methodological notes' (the timing, sequencing, stationing, stage setting and manoeuvring of research). The interplay of various 'research questions' raises issues about the description and analysis of actions.

Reading: making sense of support as action

Now to read the texts in relation to the reference points outlined above.

Ethnography

The texts highlight some cultural artefacts of self-advocacy groups. Both advisors appeared to use subtle actions that invited self-advocates into frames of activity. However, as I was a participant of the frames I noticed how the advisors would also, at times, interact with me in ways that avoided contact and overinvolvement. I was necessarily pushed away from the action, put back into my place, an outsider looking from afar. While the symbolic nature of the meaning of the social action that I observed appeared pretty transparent – to get self-advocates at the fore of group activity (Hanna 1978) – to make sense of the action required going beyond the activity. I was to move away from the tacit and perhaps pre-discursive moment of the action, to a moment of discursive analysis. This had implications in terms of the next reference point.

Grounded theory

Ethnographers attempt to grasp the 'native's' point of view, relation to life and vision of the world. However, as ethnographic study goes beyond behaviour to inquire about the meaning, my analysis of the texts problematizes the notion of 'grounded theory'. My analysis was applied as soon as I turned from animated movement to spoken word – when I looked and saw 'significant action' and later, as I will show below, when I referred to the texts as examples of particular types of action. Then, as the social context became a research context, it changed. Consequently, I was applying my abstractions to actions that could have been the product of, or at least affected by, my involvement at the scene.

The social model of disability

Both the vignettes were understood as actions that reflect what I termed the *experience* position – a key component of the social model according to Oliver (1996) – where the experiences of disabled people are worked from, instead of the experiences of non-disabled 'experts'. Other labels could have been applied: like 'knowing why you are there in the first place', or 'passing the buck to self-advocates', where supporters give primacy to the actions of self-advocates. Julia's skilful prodding of Robert ensured that he took on the role of negotiator. The BT engineer changed in his interaction from a chap seemingly unsure of himself and the situation, to someone who felt comfortable to chat away. Dennis changed the social relations of power and intervention, by passing responsibility on to Robert, Jonny, Andy and the bank clerk. Giving space and time for people to speak out is a necessary part of self-advocacy's beginnings and links into the collective responsibility and identity components of the social model (Oliver 1996: 34), where bonds and commonalties are forged with one another and disabling actions are challenged. The texts display facilitating tactics where 'the other' is encouraged to act. In (post-)structuralist terms, the social model of disability highlights the 'other' side of disability – the experiences and resistance of disabled people in spite of a disabling society. Action texts can re-present active elements of the binary opposite (the social model) to the dominant representation of disabled people (the individual model).

Marxism

The texts exhibit the revolutionizing actions of Julia and Dennis changing circumstances, challenging conventions, roles, rules and subject positions within the social interactions. Their support was specific, fluid and open to change. An attention to action allowed me to take forward an analysis that was less concerned with individualized, static notions of 'bad' or 'good' advisors and more involved with specific incidents of bad (dominant oppressive understandings of disability) and good (social model) interventions (Goodley 1998b). This analytical turn reflected the views of a self-advocate that I spoke to: 'Some professionals are ... *professionals*, others are ace – they know where the users are coming from ... it depends on the person' (Jackie Downer, italics in original, Goodley 1998a: 157). Attention was paid to supporters educating themselves and others.

Disadvantages

My analysis of the actions of advisors creates a number of dilemmas and raises a number of questions.

First, a contradiction emerges in my analysis of action between learning from the culture (grounded theory analysis) and applying models to the material in the search for meaning (social model analysis). Schatzman and Strauss (1973: 110) illustrate this tension when they assert that the model grounded theory researcher starts analysing very early on in the research process. There is a danger that researchers immediately pin down incidents of action to various typologies or discursive themes. While this may seem unavoidable – after all description itself is an act of theorizing and analysis (Fairclough 1992: 229) – it appears that no sooner has an action ended before it is shoe-horned into a waiting discrete analytical category. Perhaps a theory-driven approach reflects the analyst trying to capture 'the moment' of the action. Nevertheless, such an analytical move seems at odds with 'grounded theory' and, moreover, to strip bare the essential qualities of a pre-discursive action.

Second, it could be suggested that the written form of a dynamic action renders an 'action text' a fictional, storied and fragmented re-presentation. Perhaps this is not a bad thing. Some proponents of narrative inquiry would assert that stories are *the* central component of experience and reality (Didion 1979; Sarbin 1986; Bruner 1987; Hoffman 1993). Narrative is seen as producing experience, and vice versa. People impose structure and give meaning to their lives through the use of stories (Hoffman 1993). People tell stories in order to live (Didion 1979: 11), in both the telling and doing of self. Others would suggest that because human beings are story-tellers (*Homo narrans*) and life is story put into practice (Gillman *et al.* 1997: 680), so people are texts. However, questions remain about action texts: what are we analysing, 'action as story', 'story as action', fact, fiction or 'faction'?

Third, the 'knowing' position of the researcher in relation to the actions of research participants is called into question. Certain strands of feminism argue that only women researchers can truly grasp their female participants' worlds because they, like their participants, experience and 'know' what it is like to be a woman in patriarchal society. Stanley and Wise (1993: 227–8) describe this experience of 'knowing' as an 'epistemological privilege', with women researchers having access to an *a priori* knowledge of their female informants' subjective realities by virtue of their shared experiences of patriarchy. Another way of viewing 'knowing', according to Stanley and Wise, is that women researchers may feel that they are 'knowers' of women interviewees' realities because their experiences fit with their own life experiences. This type of a 'knowing subjectivity' is formed on a *post hoc* basis with one 'ontological preference' of researchers being an identification with their informants' lives (Stanley and Wise 1993: 228). However, the objects of my analysis – self-advocacy groups – are positioned in the register of 'other' by disabling society. Consequently, is the only ontological preference available to me, a non-disabled person, that of 'not knowing'? Was I therefore capable of picking up on the significance, meaning and symbolic nature of action?

Fourth, concerns about missing actions that are significant to participants are raised. The texts presented here were taken out of a section of my work that was concerned with advisor interventions (see Goodley 1997, 1998b). Later I was to focus on the revolutionizing actions of self-advocates. However, for some time during my involvement with the groups, I was undoubtedly fixated with what advisors did, so that self-advocates' actions were ignored. Two questions emerge from this confession. First, are those actions that the researcher picks out that significant to the workings of a culture? Again, this draws us back to the problems of theory-driven analysis and a 'not knowing' position. Second, what about those actions that are unconventional actions. For example, what about the person who sits still and apparently contributes nothing in terms of activity to the group? What do action-focused researchers have to say about people that may be superficially defined as 'not acting'? There are problems with any piece of research that is preoccupied with the actions of the dominant and ignores the actions of the dominated (see Freire 1970).

Advantages

The above section raises questions about the doing of action-focused research. I will now take up these criticisms to make a case for a focus on action in critical and political research.

First, discursively analysing actions, particularly actions of individuals that have been previously excluded, pathologized or dismissed, permits an analytical turn towards wider conceptualizations of activity, co-activity, co-dependence and collective action. Take, for example, the following observational vignette from one of the self-advocacy groups that I was involved with: 'Rachel does not speak often. She spends her time quietly and apparently contentedly smelling her fingers and looking around the room. At break-time Bill asked her if she would like a cup of coffee or tea. Erica, who lives with Rachel, replied, "She likes coffee don't you Rachel?" Bill looked at Rachel, "Coffee then?"' Rachel's solitary actions provided a catalyst for other self-advocates to act. Indeed, without Rachel's apparent 'inactivity', a chance for interdependence would have been lost. In this sense, then, a turn to action invites a reconsideration of our assumptions about 'the inactive'. People with learning difficulties are the object of assessment strategies that belittle, patronize, pathologize and objectify. Their (in)actions are understood as the behavioural consequence of some embodied 'impairment'. 'They' are split off from culture ('us'), viewed as individual tragedies, while paradoxically being considered to constitute a homogeneous, infected, naturalized deficient group. Nevertheless, a turn to action, when accompanied by recognition of the social relations of disablement, invites us to view the resilience of people with learning difficulties that emerges against the odds.

Second, a turn to action challenges what I would see as a tendency of discourse-oriented analysts to talk a good talk but offer very little in the way of praxis-based conclusions. Action is essentially pragmatic, thus potentially practice-oriented. Moreover, other fields and arenas for and of action are brought in where good and bad practice may be identified (see Boal 1994). For example, the self-advocacy of people with learning difficulties may take many forms, including drama, mime and dance, as people present themselves through media other than the spoken and written word.

Discourse theory can be made workable and useful to people involved in practical settings, drawing together 'the academy' and everyday activity. Discourse analytic work that takes as its starting point the (political) actions of disabled people can put forward what may be termed a 'correct' way of viewing disability – rather than simply alerting us to the intimation connections between meaning and power and knowledge (Foucault 1983). It is all very well recognizing power inequalities, but what are we going to do about them?

Third, following on from pragmatism is the question of starting points. Personally, I have found much overlap between the orientation of some discourse analysts (for example, Fairclough 1989; Burman and Parker 1993) and the approach to the analysis of disabling society offered by disabled activists (see Oliver 1990; BCODP 1992). However, I would argue that an academic project will ultimately fail if it does not take as its starting point the actions of those social members that it purports to understand and embrace. The actions of marginalized groups, like disabled people, exist prior to abstracted theorizing and must surely be taken as a starting point in a de/reconstruction of disabling society. Radical theory can be built up from the actions of the oppressed (Freire 1970). This approach opens the door to Marxist understandings of those material actions that exist beneath and resist the oppressive structures of capitalism, thus offering opportunities to work with the power of action as a revolutionary, reconstructing and deconstructing force. Perhaps the point is to start with action, to turn to text, then to discourse, and to retrace the steps back to action. As unfashionable as it may sound, our aim must be not only to understand the world but also to change it. We should remember, however, that people are already changing aspects of their lives without us. We need to recognize such resistance and avoid getting caught up in a (postmodern) politics of identity and materially ungrounded discursive formulations.

Finally, the subtleties of action are often perplexing and confusing. To become more sensitive to action may mean that researchers are encouraged to get more and more involved with the context under investigation. My research prompted me to make links with a self-advocacy group as a supporter. A hands-on approach alerted me to the contradictions and complexities of power relations within self-advocacy groups generally, and the notion of support specifically. While my findings may be merely fictional re-representations of action, their authenticity was continuously reassessed from my stance as a supporter – a 'getting to know' position if you like. Theorists need to be wary of throwing misunderstood actions into a melting pot of cleverly framed discursive repertoires, thus ignoring the authenticity of the combativity by oppressed groups.

In this chapter I have considered an analysis of action texts. Critical discourse work rips apart assumptions, problematizes aims and raises questions about truth, fact, findings and analysis. Simultaneously, as problems inflict the researcher, the boundaries between researcher and participants can be challenged. Moreover, focusing on action further deals with the subtleties of social relations and recognizes the revolutionizing actions that exist beneath many oppressive discursive and social practices. We should remember that people empower themselves. The question is: how do we as researchers stand in relation to such incidents of self-emancipation?

Key reading

Erlandson, D. A., Harris, E. L., Skipper, B. L. and Allen, S. D. (1993) *Doing Naturalistic Inquiry*. Newbury Park, CA: Sage.
Marx, K. (1968) Theses on Feuerbach. In K. Marx and F. Engels, *Selected Works*. London: Lawrence and Wishart.

References

Angrosino, M. V. (1994) On the bus with Vonnie Lee: explorations in life history and metaphor. *Journal of Contemporary Ethnography*, 23: 14–28.
Atkinson, D. (1993) Relating. In P. Shakespeare, D. Atkinson and S. French (eds) *Reflecting on Research Practice: Issues in Health and Social Welfare*. Buckingham: Open University Press.
Atkinson, D. and Williams, F. (eds) (1990) *'Know Me as I Am': An Anthology of Prose, Poetry and Art by People with Learning Difficulties*. Kent: Hodder and Stoughton in association with the Open University and MENCAP.
BCODP (1992) *Introduction to the British Council of Organisations of Disabled People*. Belper: BCODP.
Boal, A. (1994) *The Theatre of the Oppressed*. London: Pluto Press.
Bogdan, R. and Taylor, S. (1982) *Inside Out: The Social Meaning of Mental Retardation*. Toronto: University of Toronto Press.
Braginsky, D. and Braginsky, B. (1971) *Hansels and Gretels: Studies of Children in Institutions for the Mentally Retarded*. New York: Holt, Reinhart and Winston.
Bruner, J. (1987) Life as narrative. *Social Research*, 54: 11–32.
Burman, E. and Parker, I. (eds) (1993) *Discourse Analytic Research: Repertoires and Readings of Texts in Action*. London: Routledge.
Charmaz, K. (1995) Grounded theory. In J. A. Smith, R. Harre and L. V. Langenhove (eds) *Rethinking Methods in Psychology*. London: Sage.
Crawley, B. (1988) *The Growing Voice – a Survey of Self-advocacy Groups in Adult Training Centres and Hospitals in Great Britain*. London: Values into Action.
Didion, J. (1979) *The White Album*. New York: Simon and Schuster.
Edgerton, R. B. (1967) *The Cloak of Competence: Stigma in the Lives of the Mentally Retarded*. Berkeley: University of California Press.
Edgerton, R. B. (1984a) Introduction. In R. B. Edgerton (ed.) *Lives in Process: Mentally Retarded Adults in a Large City*. Washington, DC: American Association on Mental Deficiency.

Edgerton, R. B. (1984b) The participant-observer approach to research in mental retardation. *American Journal of Mental Deficiency*, 88(5): 498–505.

Fairclough, N. (1989) *Language and Power*. London: Longman.

Fairclough, N. (1992) *Discourse and Social Change*. Cambridge: Polity Press.

Foucault, M. (1970) *The Order of Things*. London: Tavistock Publications.

Foucault, M. (1975) *Discipline and Punish*. London: Allen Lane.

Foucault, M. (1983) The subject and power. In H. L. Dreyfus and P. Rabinow (eds) *Michel Foucault: Beyond Structuralism and Hermeneutics*. Chicago: University of Chicago Press.

Freire, P. (1970) *Pedagogy of the Oppressed*. Harmondsworth: Penguin.

Gillman, M., Swain, J. and Heyman, B. (1997) Life history or 'care history': the objectification of people with learning difficulties through the tyranny of professional discourses. *Disability and Society*, 12(5): 675–94.

Glaser, B. G. and Strauss, A. L. (1967) *The Discovery of Grounded Theory*. Hawthorne: Aldine.

Goodley, D. (1997) Locating self-advocacy in models of disability: understanding disability in the support of self-advocates with learning difficulties. *Disability and Society*, 12(3): 367–80.

Goodley, D. (1998a) Appraising self-advocacy in the lives of people with learning difficulties, PhD thesis, University of Sheffield.

Goodley, D. (1998b) Supporting people with learning difficulties in self-advocacy groups and models of disability. *Health and Social Care in the Community*, 6(5): 438–46.

Halfpenny, P. (1984) *Principles of Method*. York: Longman.

Hanna, J. (1978) Advisor's role in self-advocacy groups. *American Rehabilitation*, 4(2): 31–2.

Hoffman, L. (1993) *Exchanging Voices: A Collaborative Approach to Family Therapy*. London: Karnac.

Howe, D. (1994) Modernity, postmodernity and social work. *British Journal of Social Work*, 24: 513–32.

Lincoln, Y. S. and Guba, E. G. (1985) *Naturalistic Inquiry*. Beverly Hills, CA: Sage.

Malinowski, B. (1922) *Argonauts of the Western Pacific*. London: Routledge.

Oliver, M. (1990) *The Politics of Disablement*. Basingstoke: Macmillan.

Oliver, M. (1996) *Understanding Disability: From Theory to Practice*. London: Macmillan.

Peberdy, A. (1993) Observing. In P. Shakespeare, D. Atkinson and S. French (eds) *Reflecting on Research Practice: Issues in Health and Social Welfare*. Buckingham: Open University Press.

Plummer, K. (1983) *Documents of Life: An Introduction to the Problems and Literature of a Humanistic Method*. London: George Allen and Unwin.

Potts, M. and Fido, R. (1991) *A Fit Person to Be Removed: Personal Accounts of Life in a Mental Deficiency Institution*. Plymouth: Northcote House.

Sarbin, T. R. (ed.) (1986) *Narrative Psychology: The Storied Nature of Human Conduct*. New York: Praeger.

Schatzman, L. and Strauss, A. L. (1973) *Field Research: Strategies for a Natural Sociology*. Englewood Cliffs, NJ: Prentice Hall.

Sidell, M. (1993) Interpreting. In P. Shakespeare, D. Atkinson and S. French (eds) *Reflecting on Research Practice: Issues in Health and Social Welfare*. Buckingham: Open University Press.

Stanley, L. and Wise, S. (1993) *Breaking Out Again: Feminist Ontology and Epistemology*. London: Routledge.

Walmsley, J. (1993) Explaining. In P. Shakespeare, D. Atkinson and S. French (eds) *Reflecting on Research Practice: Issues in Health and Social Welfare*. Buckingham: Open University Press.

Worrell, B. (1988) *People First: Advice for Advisors*. Ontario: National People First Project.

Index